Most people don't know—I certainly hadn't a clue—how different *recipe testing* is from *cooking*. In a way, these are opposite activities.

Cooking is for me a leisurely pursuit, an opportunity to give my busy mind a rest and engage in the physicality of ingredients. My instinctive understanding of the products and processes doesn't require much thought or concentration. I don't need to apply myself to anything, really, when I cook. I can listen to music or chat mindlessly to Karl.

Back in 2007, when Sami Tamimi and I were working on this book, I got my first taste of going through the very familiar motions of producing a dish, but with a new aim in mind: creating a trustworthy recipe, something one can casually follow and *cook* from. The clear irony, which now doesn't seem ironical at all to me anymore—that I need to engage in something so unlike cooking in order to allow others to cook—had become blatantly apparent.

I clearly remember the many many lots of chopped parsley that were wasted when I willy-nilly threw them into the bowl without passing via the now indispensible set of metal measuring spoons or my precious weighing scales. Seriously, it probably took about fifty recipes before I stopped forgetting to record quantity, time, temperature, weight—you name it.

Six years on and a thousand recipes later, recipe testing is second nature to me. Sorry, first nature. I now find it difficult *not* to measure the number of teaspoons of cumin that go into the sprout salad I prepare for dinner; so instead of fighting my new instinct I succumb to it and measure anyway, for the heck of it.

Working on *Ottolenghi: The Cookbook* was very much a virginal experience for both Sami and me. Recipe testing was one thing. Recipe curating was another: deciding what to include and where; how to divide the book into chapters; how to make it all make perfect sense. We also had to learn how to create a context and to write an introduction, how to tell a story and how to convey our thoughts. We needed to understand how to prepare food for the camera and how to decide what to shoot and when. There was a lot to take in.

But as this was *THE* book, our one and only chance to properly show our food to the world—the food we had been serving for a few years in our restaurants—we were both extremely eager to get it right, in somewhat an obsessive way. Quite honestly, we never thought there would be another book for us. We were chefs engaged in cooking for people, who just happened to take a little break from our day job and write a one-off cookbook.

Our weekly efforts culminated in regular Friday night dinners at Sami and Jeremy's, where friends and eager guinea pigs would gather to be fed generously and encouraged to freely express their demonstrative, hopefully very critical opinions. Dishes were served over and over again until we finally managed to please our crowd, unreservedly.

The "good practice" habits that we established when working on this book—putting infinite thought into the recipe selection, applying endless love and meticulous testing into every single recipe, telling a good story whenever we can—have made this, I have no doubt, into a very popular book the world over.

More importantly, what Sami and I learned, often the hard way, back in 2007—that good *recipe testing* leads to good *cooking*—is a valuable lesson that we applied to our later books, *Plenty* and *Jerusalem*, and still stands us in very good stead.

—Yotam Ottolenghi, April 2013

Our feast is, literally, a feast of bold colors and generous gestures. It is driven by an unapologetic desire to celebrate food and its virtues, to display abundance in the same way that a market stallholder does: show everything you've got and shout its praise wholeheartedly.

We got started in July 2002, not really sure what was ahead of us, when we opened Ottolenghi—food shop, patisserie, deli, restaurant, bakery. A place with no single description but at the same time a crystal-clear reflection of our obsessive relationship with food. In a small shop in Notting Hill, we began to cook and bake.

We did it while the white paint on the walls was still drying. Together with a small group of friends, and alongside some newly acquired staff (quickly turned friends), we began our experiment with food.

Our partner and designer, Alex Meitlis, supplied us with a blank canvas: "A white space with white shiny surfaces is what's going to make your concoctions stand out," he said. We argued a little but were soon persuaded. The white background turned out to be the perfect setting for our party. And we did not intend to be shy about it.

Our food impulse

We wanted to start this book with the quip, "If you don't like lemon or garlic ... skip to the last page." This might not be the funniest of jokes, but, considering lemon and garlic's prevalence in our recipes, it is as good a place as any to start looking for a portrait of our food. Regional descriptions just don't seem to work; there are too many influences and our food histories are long and diverse. True, we both come from a very particular part of the world—Israel/Palestine—with a unique culinary tradition. We adore the foods of our childhood: oranges from Jericho, used only to make the sweetest fresh juice; crunchy little cucumbers, full of the soil's flavors; heavy pomegranates tumbling from trees that can no longer support their weight; figs, walnuts, wild herbs.... The list is endless.

We both ate a lot of street food—literally, what the name suggests. Vendors selling their produce on pavements were not restricted to "farmers' markets." There was nothing embarrassing or uncouth about eating on the way to somewhere. Sami remembers frequently sitting bored in front of his dinner plate, having downed a few grilled ears of corn and a couple of *busbusa* (coconut and semolina) cakes bought at street stalls while out with friends.

However, what makes lemon and garlic such a great metaphor for our cooking is the boldness, the zest, the strong, sometimes controversial flavors of our childhood. The flavors and colors that shout at you, that grip you, that make everything else taste bland, pale, ordinary, and insipid. Cakes drenched with rose-water-scented sugar syrup; piles of raw green almonds on ice in the market; punchy tea in a small glass with handfuls of mint and sugar; the intense smell of charred mutton cooked on an open fire; a little shop selling twenty types of crumbly sheep and goat's milk cheeses, kept fresh in water; apricot season, when there is enough of the fruit lying around each tree to gorge yourself, the jam pot, and the neighborhood birds.

These are the sources of our impulse. It is this profusion of overwhelming sensations that inspires our desire to stun with our food, to make you say "wow!" even if you're not the expressive type. The colors, the textures, and finally the flavors that are unapologetically striking.

Our food philosophy

Like the market vendor, we make the best of what we have and don't interfere with it too much. We keep food as natural as possible, deliberately avoiding complicated cooking methods. Take our broccoli, the king of the Ottolenghi jungle. It is mightily popular, but it can't get any simpler. If you don't know it, you must try it (recipe on page 41); if you do, you will no doubt try it anyway.

Unfussiness and simplicity in food preparation are, for us, the only way to maintain the freshness of a dish. Each individual ingredient has a clear voice, plain characteristics that are lucid and powerful—images, tastes, and aromas you remember and yearn for.

This is where we differ deeply from both complicated haute cuisine and industrial food: the fact that you can clearly taste and sense cumin or basil in our salad, that there is no room for guessing. Etti Mordo, an ex-colleague and a chef of passion, always used to say that she hated dishes that you just knew had been touched a lot in the preparation.

We love real food, unadulterated and unadorned. A chocolate cake should, first and foremost, taste of chocolate. It doesn't have to involve praline, raspberries, layers of sponge, sticky liqueur, and hours in the freezer. Give us a clean chocolate flavor, a muddy, fudgy texture, and a plain appearance. Good solid food is a source of ageless pleasure and fun.

This ability to have fun, to really enjoy food, to engage with it lightheartedly and wholeheartedly is the key for us. After centuries of being told how bad their cuisine was, the British have started taking pride in their food in recent years, joining the European set of confident, passionate, and knowledgeable devourers. Then, suddenly, they were made to feel guilty for having fun. All of a sudden it is all about diets, health, provenance, morals, and food miles. Forget the food itself.

How boring, and what a mistake! This shift of focus sets us back two decades, to a time when food in the United Kingdom was just foodstuff, when it was practical instead of sensual, and so we risk once more losing our genuine pleasure in food. People will not care much about the origins of their food and how it's been grown and produced unless they first love it and are immersed in it. It is, yet again, about having fun. Don't get us wrong: supporting small farmers around the globe, treating animals humanely, making sure we don't pollute our bodies and our environment, resisting the total industrialization of agriculture—these are all precious causes. Our wealth and the cheapness of our food give us an added responsibility to eat sensibly and ethically.

But it isn't a black-and-white choice of good versus evil when it comes to food; you can be well informed and make wise decisions about what to buy and where without turning into a fanatic. Most people's lifestyles don't allow them to grow their own vegetables or source all their meat from a local free-range farm. They must compromise without feeling guilty. So they go shopping in a supermarket during the week and visit a farmers' market on the weekend. They might choose an organic egg alongside a frozen vegetable.

This carefree but realistic approach to cooking and eating is what we try to convey with our food: the idea that cooking can be enjoyable, simple, and fulfilling, yet look and taste amazing; that it mustn't be a chore or a bore, with lots of complicated ingredients to source and painstakingly prepare, but can be accessible, straightforward, and frank. For us, cooking and eating are not hazy, far-off ideals but part of real life, and should be left there.

Ottolenghi

The interaction

One thing immediately evident at Ottolenghi is that you often see the chefs bringing up trays and plates heavily piled with their creations. It is a source of pride for them and for us to see a customer smile, look closely, and then gasp and give them a huge compliment. So many chefs miss out on this kind of immediate response from the diner—the reaction that leads to a leisurely chat about food.

This communication is essential to our efforts to knock down the dividing walls that characterize so many food experiences today. When was the last time you went shopping for food and actually talked to the person who made it? In a restaurant? In a supermarket? It doesn't happen. And, since cooking at home has become less common, we are deprived of this dialogue. So at Ottolenghi we are simulating a domestic food conversation in a public, urban surrounding.

The space

When you sit down to eat, it is as close as it gets to a domestic experience. The communal dining reinforces a cozy, sharing family atmosphere. What you get is a taste of entering your mother's or grandmother's mythical kitchen, whether real or fictitious. Chefs and waiters participate, with the customer, in an intimate moment revolving around food—like a big table in the center of a busy kitchen.

But it's not only the way you sit; it is also what surrounds you. In Ottolenghi you will always find fresh produce, the ingredients that have gone into your food, stored somewhere where you can see them. The shelves are stacked high with fruit and vegetables from the market. A half-empty box of rutabagas might sit next to a mother with a baby in a buggy, until one of us comes upstairs and takes the vegetable down to the kitchen to cook.

The display

Once the food is on the counter, we try to limit the distance between it and the diner. We keep refrigeration to a minimum. Of course, chilling what we eat is sometimes necessary, but chilled food isn't something we'd naturally want to eat (barring ice cream and a few other exceptions). Most dishes come into their own only at room temperature or warm. It is a chemical fact. This is especially true with cakes and pastries. Their textures and flavors are destroyed beyond salvation through refrigeration.

It is a chilling experience to eat a cold sandwich, yet so many of us routinely do and are almost oblivious to it because it is considered a necessary evil. With most things prepared fresh, really fresh, there is no need to chill. Every customer who comes to Ottolenghi and doesn't hear the soul-destroying hum of a brigade of stainless-steel fridges is another convert to minimal refrigeration. None of us feels much confidence in a refrigerated deli counter full of mayonnaise-based salads that might have been sitting there (in the temperature "safe zone") for days. Conversely, it is reassuring to know that if there isn't a fridge, the salads must be fresh.

Our customers

Not many traditional hierarchies or clear-cut divisions exist in the Ottolenghi experience. You find sweet alongside savory, hot with cold; a tray of freshly baked breads might sit next to a scrumptious array of salads, a bowl of giant meringues, or a crate of tomatoes from the market. It is an air of generosity, mild chaos, and lots of culinary activity that greets customers as they come in: food being presented, replaced, sold; dishes changed, trays wiped clean, the counter rearranged; lots of other people chattering and queuing.

It is this relaxed atmosphere that we strive to maintain. Casual chats with customers allow us to cater to our clients' needs. We listen and know what they like. They bring their empty dishes in for us to make them "the best lasagna ever" (and if it's not, we will definitely hear about it). This is what encapsulates the spirit of Ottolenghi: a unique combination of quality and familiarity.

We guess that this is what drew in our first customers. So many of them have become regulars over the years, meaning not only that they come to Ottolenghi frequently but also that we recognize them, know their names and something about their lives. And vice versa. They have a favorite sales assistant who always gets their coffee just right (probably an Italian or an Aussie), their pastry of choice (Lou's rhubarb tart), their preferred seat at the table. Our close relationship with our customers extends to all of them, whether it's the bustling city stars forever on their way somewhere; the early riser eagerly tapping his watch at five-to-opening; the chilled and chatty sales assistant from next door; the eternal party organizer with a last-minute rushed order; or a mother on the lookout for something healthy to feed her and the children.

The Ottolenghi cookbook

The Ottolenghi cookbook came into existence through popular demand. So many customers asked for it that we simply had to do it. And we enjoyed every minute of it. We also loved devising recipes for our cooking classes at Leiths School of Food and Wine, some of which appear in this book. The idea of sharing our recipes with fans, as well as with a new audience, is hugely appealing. Revealing our "secrets" is another way of interacting, of knocking down barriers, of communicating about food.

The recipes we chose for the book are a nonrepresentative collection of old favorites, current hits, and a few specials. Some of them have appeared in different guises in "The New Vegetarian" column in the Guardian's *Weekend* magazine. They all represent different aspects of Ottolenghi's food—bread, the famous salads, hot dishes, patisserie, cakes, cold meat, and fish—and they are all typical Ottolenghi: vibrant, bold, and honest.

We have decided not to include dishes incorporating long processes that have been described in detail in other, more specialized books—croissants, sourdough bread, stock. We want to stick to what is achievable at home (good croissants rarely are) and what our customers want from the cookbook. We would much rather give a couple of extra salad recipes than spend the same number of pages on chicken stock.

Our histories *Yotam Ottolenghi*

My mother clearly remembers my first word, *ma*, short for *marak* ("soup" in Hebrew). Actually, I was referring to little industrial soup croutons, tiny yellowish pillows that she used to scatter over the tray of my highchair. I would say *ma* when I finished them all, and point toward the cupboard.

As a small child, I loved eating. My dad, always full of expressive Italian terms, used to call me *goloso*, which means something like "greedy glutton," or at least that's what I figured. I adored seafood: prawns, squid, oysters—not typical for a young Jewish lad from Jerusalem in the 1970s. A birthday treat would be to go to Sea Dolphin, a restaurant in the Arab part of the city and the only place that served nonkosher sea beasts. Their shrimp with butter and garlic was a building block of my childhood dreams.

Another vivid memory: me, aged five, my brother, Yiftach, aged three. We are out on our patio, stark naked, squatting like two monkeys. We are holding pomegranates! Whenever my mom brought us pomegranates from the market, we were stripped and banished outside so we didn't stain the rug or our clothes. Trying to pick the sweet seeds clean, we still always ended up with plenty of the bitter white skin in our mouths, covered head to toe with juice.

My passion for food sometimes backfired. My German grandmother, Charlotte, once heard me say how much I loved one of her signature dishes. The result: boiled cauliflower, with a lovely coating of buttered bread crumbs, served to me at 2:00 p.m. every Saturday for the next fifteen years.

My other *nonna*, Luciana, never quite got over her forced exile from the family villa in Tuscany. When I think of it, she never really left. She and my *nonno*, Mario, created a Little Italy in a small suburb of Tel Aviv, where they built a house with Italian furniture; they spoke Italian to the maid and a group of relatives, and ate Italian food from crockery passed down the family. Walking into their house felt like being teleported to a distant planet. There they were, sipping Italian coffee, nibbling the little savory *ciambelline* biscuits. And then there was an unforgettable dish, unquestionably my desert-island food: *gnocchi alla romana*, flat semolina dumplings grilled with butter and Parmesan.

But I started my professional life far away from the world of prawns, pomegranates, and Parmesan. In my early twenties, I was a student of philosophy and literature at Tel Aviv University, a part-time teaching assistant, and a budding journalist editing stories at the news desk of a national daily. My future with words and ideas was laid out for me in the chillingly clear colors of the inevitable—that is, a PhD.

I decided to take a little break first, an overdue gap year that was later extended into one of the longest "years" in living memory. I came to London and, much to my poor parents' alarm, embarked on a cookery course at Le Cordon Bleu. "Come on," I told them, "I just need to check this out, to make sure it's not the right thing for me."

And I wasn't so sure that it was. At thirty, you are ancient in the world of catering. Being a commis chef is plain weird. So I suffered a bit of abuse and had a few moments of teary doubt, but it became clear to me that this was the sort of creativity that suited me. I realized this when I was a pastry chef at Launceston Place, my first long-standing position in a restaurant, and one of the waiters shouted to me down the dumbwaiter shaft, "That was the best chocolate brownie I've ever had!" I've heard this many times since.

Sami Tamimi

I was born to Palestinian parents in the old city of Jerusalem. It was a small and intimate closed society, literally existing within the ancient city walls. People could have lived their entire lives within these confines, where Muslims shared a minute space with Arab Christians and Armenians, where food was always plentiful on the street.

In a place where religion is central to so many, ours was a nonreligious household. Although Arab culture and traditions were important at home, and are still very much part of my psyche, I did not have the identity that comes with a strong belief. I found it hard to know where I belonged, and this was something I could not talk about at home.

From an early age, I was interested in cooking and would spend many hours in the kitchen with my mother and grandmother. Cooking formed the main part of most women's lives. Men did not cook, at least not like women did. My father, however, loved cooking for pleasure alone. My mother cooked to share the experience with her friends and the food with her family. I believe I have inherited both my father's love of food and my mother's love of feeding people.

Some of my earliest memories are of my father squatting on the floor, preparing food in the traditional Arab way. He took endless trouble over preparation, as did my mother. She would spend ages rolling vine leaves, stuffed with lamb and rice, so thin and uniform they looked like green cigarettes. I remember my mother's kitchen before a wedding, when friends and relatives gathered to prepare. It seemed as if there was enough food to feed the whole world!

My father was the food buyer. I only had to mention his name at the shop selling freshly roasted coffee beans and I got a bag of "Hassan's mix." Dad used to come home with boxes piled high with fresh fruit and vegetables. Once, when I was about seven, he arrived with a few watermelons. Being the youngest, I insisted on carrying one of them into the house, just like my brothers and sisters. On the doorstep, I couldn't hold it any longer and the massive fruit fell on the floor and exploded, covering us all with wet, red flesh.

I was fifteen when I got my first job, as a kitchen porter at the Mount Zion Hotel. This is the lowliest and hardest job in any kitchen. You run around after everybody. I was lucky that the head chef saw my potential and encouraged me to cook. By then I was cooking at home all the time. I knew that this was what I wanted to do in life. It meant making the break from the Arab old city and entering Israeli life on the other side of the walls. I wanted to cook and explore the world outside, and Israeli culture allowed me to do this.

I made the significant move to Tel Aviv in 1989 and worked in various catering jobs before becoming assistant head chef at Lilith, one of the best restaurants in the city at the time. We served fresh produce, lightly cooked on a massive grill. I was entranced by this mix of Californian and Mediterranean cuisines, and it was there that I truly discovered my culinary identity and confidence. I moved to London in 1997 and was offered a job at Baker and Spice. During my six years there, I reshaped the *traiteur* section, introducing a variety of dishes with a strong Middle Eastern edge. This became my style. Recently I was in the kitchen looking at a box of cauliflower when my mother's cauliflower fritters came to mind, so that was what I cooked. Only then did I realize how much of my cooking is about recreating the dishes of my childhood.

Our shared history

It was definitely some sort of providence that led us to meet for the first time in London in 1999. Our paths might have crossed plenty of times—we had had many more obvious opportunities to meet before—and yet it was only then, thousands of miles away from where we started, that we got to know each other.

We were both born in Jerusalem in 1968, Sami on the Arab east side and Yotam in the Jewish west. We grew up a few kilometers away from each other in two separate societies, forced together by a fateful war just a year earlier. Looking back now, we realize how extremely different our childhood experiences were and yet how often they converged—physically, when venturing out to the "other side," and spiritually, sharing sensations of a place and a time.

As young gay adults, we both moved to Tel Aviv at the same time, looking for personal freedom and a sense of hope and normality that Jerusalem couldn't offer. There, we first formed meaningful relationships and took our first steps in our careers. Then, in 1997, we both arrived in London with an aspiration to expand our horizons even further, possibly to escape again from a place we had grown out of.

So finally, on the doorstep of Baker and Spice in west London, we chatted for thirty minutes before realizing that we shared a language and a history. And it was there, over the next two years, that we formed our bond of friendship and creativity.

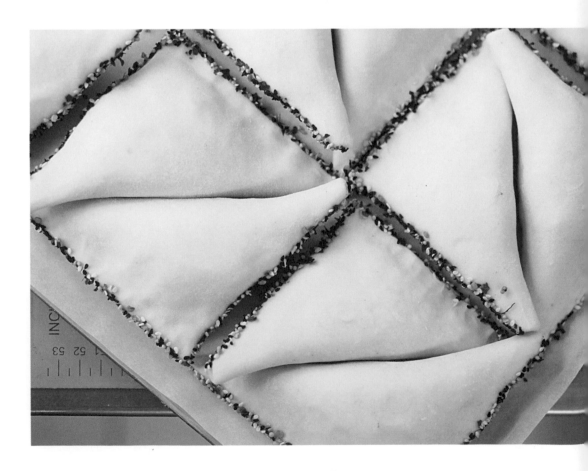

Just a few of our favorite things

We are not the type of systematically thorough chefs who are incredibly well versed in all kinds of exotic ingredients (you could easily embarrass us by naming some French cheese that we haven't got a clue about). Rather, we have some star ingredients that we feature over and over again, components that we love and feel at home with. These are the building blocks of our recipes.

Salt

We like salt, and we are not embarrassed to admit it. It is vital in any dish (cakes as well) and is often underused, meaning much of your culinary effort goes to waste. We recommend salting lightly at the beginning of the cooking process and then once again, after tasting, at the end.

We use ordinary sea salt when the texture is not an issue but recommend using coarse sea salt (our favorite is Maldon) for recipes in which the salt doesn't totally dissolve during the cooking process, particularly when roasting.

Garlic

In our mind, you can't go wrong with garlic, but we are aware that some find it overwhelming, or just plain stinky. We seriously advise that you try to get hooked like us. You won't look back. Good garlic is fresh, hard, and pale. Cloves that have started growing a shoot and are yellowish do not usually taste of much.

Lemon

This is another substance prone to foster addiction. Lemon juice can transform boring to exciting in a squirt.

Lemon prevents some ingredients, such as apple and avocado, from discoloring, but others, such as green beans and some fresh herbs, lose their color soon after coming into contact with lemon juice. We often use the zest instead, which gives a wonderful aroma. Unsprayed Italian lemons with their leaves still attached are great (you can tell by the leaves how fresh they are), but they don't always have much juice.

Olive oil

We use olive oil almost everywhere, even in some cakes, where it adds moisture and a rich depth of flavor. For most things, we use extra virgin oil. We like the Greek Iliada. It is semi-robust, with a light, grassy background aroma. For frying we use light olive oil or a good vegetable oil.

Fresh cilantro

Although it is often associated with pastes and curries, we like to use fresh cilantro in salads and light sauces. If you like the flavor, stir the leaves into roasted vegetables and wet-roasted meats and fish. It is easy and highly effective.

Mint

Alongside lemon, mint epitomizes freshness. A few leaves added to a leafy salad will give it a cleansing vibrancy. Some types of mint, though, can be a little tough and bitter, so you need to chop them finely. Dried mint goes very well with yogurt, and doesn't discolor as fresh mint does.

Yogurt

Any Ottolenghi fan knows how obsessed we are with yogurt. It has countless magical qualities for us. It adds an appealing lightness that counters the warmth of spicy or slow-cooked dishes. It balances and bridges contrasting flavors and textures. It lends freshness and moisture to dry ingredients. It goes well with almost anything you can think of: fresh vegetables, roasted meat and fish, hearty legumes, meringue, and berries.

For most purposes we use Greek yogurt, with up to 10 percent fat. Because some of the liquid has been drained out, it is creamy and intense. Ordinary plain yogurt, typically with 4 percent fat, produces a less flavorful sauce and you would need to use more of it to get the same result. Using low-fat yogurt doesn't make sense at all—it is watery in texture and taste. Pure sheep and goat's milk yogurts are fantastically powerful.

Pomegranate and pomegranate molasses

We are not sure that we can take credit for it, but Ottolenghi started using pomegranates well before Marks & Spencer began selling little baskets of the crunchy seeds, and before they won the (ever-fleeting) title of "superfood."

Pomegranates are easy to deseed (see Fennel and feta with pomegranate seeds and sumac on page 17) and make a fantastically attractive garnish for vegetable dishes, some roasted meat and fish, and when scattered over creamy desserts. Pomegranate molasses is cooked-down pomegranate juice. It is intense, a bit like balsamic vinegar, and should be used sparingly in sauces. You can buy it from Middle Eastern grocers and some supermarkets.

Tahini

Another invaluable item in our kitchen, tahini is a thick paste made from sesame seeds. We make it into a sauce (see page 272), which we add to vegetables, legumes, meat, or fish, giving them sharpness and a certain richness. We don't recommend the health-store variety of tahini, where the sesame seeds are left unhulled. It is heavy and overpowering. Use a Greek variety or a Lebanese brand, such as Al-Yaman, available from Middle Eastern groceries.

Sumac and za'atar

Sumac is a spice made from the crushed berries of a small Mediterranean tree. A dark red powder, it gives a sharp, acidic kick to salads and roasted meat.

Za'atar is a Middle Eastern blend of dried thyme, toasted sesame, and salt. It is earthy, slightly tangy, and used like sumac. Often the two are mixed together. Both make great garnishes for a plate of hummus or labneh (see page 272). Many supermarkets now stock sumac and za'atar with the herbs and spices.

Orange blossom water and rose water

These two syrups made of blossom infusions are basic building blocks in many Mediterranean and Middle Eastern cuisines. They are used to flavor the ubiquitous baklava, as well as other cakes and desserts, and make an unusual addition to savory dishes, mainly poultry. Use an original Lebanese brand like Cortas.

Maple syrup

We use maple syrup to sweeten many savory dishes. It has a substantial enough basic depth but isn't as dominant as honey. It doesn't need to dissolve, like brown sugar, so can be easily mixed into cold sauces and dressings. Use pure maple syrup, nothing else.

Stock

Ideally, you'd make your own stock. Nothing beats it. You can find reliable recipes in most comprehensive cookery books. Make a large amount and freeze in small portions. Our second choice would be purchased house-made stock. Butcher's shops, delis, and many supermarkets carry them. A third option is to use powder. The only one we can recommend is the Swiss Marigold brand. It isn't the real thing, but it does (part of) the job.

Feta cheese

Moist Greek feta and similar Turkish varieties are invaluable. They enhance any vegetable, some fruits, and all savory baked products. Always look at the cheese counter before going for the vacuum-packed varieties, preferably in a Balkan or Middle Eastern deli. The unbranded chunks, swimming in murky water, are best. Ask to taste!

Sweet potatoes

This is our comfort food of choice. The astonishing thing about sweet potatoes is how easy they are to cook. Throw one in the oven for up to an hour and you can scoop out the tasty, moist, and (obviously) sweet flesh, ready to be scoffed on its own with a little butter, mashed, turned into a pie, added to salads, gratinéed lightly, or served on the side with meat. Select potatoes with the ubiquitous orange flesh. The pale-fleshed ones don't do the trick.

Passion fruit

Not many ingredients taste as great as they look. Passion fruit are luscious and sensual in appearance and also have a sublime flavor. Despite their majestic qualities, they are very simple to use. Passion fruit pulp makes a most convincing sweet garnish (see the jam recipe on page 276) and the juice makes a curd almost as good as lemon curd.

Pink peppercorns

You don't need many of these little red jewels to transform the appearance of a dish and give it a sweet, perfumed, and yet not very peppery taste. We grind them in a pepper mill or with a mortar and pestle.

The fear of baking

We are aware of the angst the idea of baking or making desserts evokes in some. Sorry, we are not going to try to convince you that this phobia has no grounds. Cakes and pastries can sometimes go horribly wrong, they are almost impossible to resurrect, and they do take time to prepare.

Still, the gratification of good baking is unbeatable. A great tart or a bowl of homemade biscuits is a clear mark of a mature cook, and we desperately encourage any person who loves breads, cakes, and sweets to try to make them at home.

Most of the recipes we selected for this book should be feasible for beginners. A few require modest baking experience. We suggest that you read through a recipe and embark on it only if you feel relatively confident. Still, we wouldn't venture into most baking recipes without some basic equipment, some of it not found in every kitchen.

Mixer

The minimum, really, is a handheld electric mixer. This will allow you to cream butter and sugar, whisk eggs, and whip up cream. A much better option is a proper stand mixer, one with a whisk, a paddle (or beater) attachment, and a dough hook. A solid brand, like Kenwood or KitchenAid, will permit you to try your hand at making brioche, breads, serious meringues, and much more.

Blender

Although not essential, a blender is a very handy tool when making fruit purées and puréeing sauces and soups. The handheld immersion blender is exceptionally practical, cheap, and hassle free (saves you lots of washing up).

Pans and molds

Having the right baking pans and molds is essential. You can make some allowances with the shape of a cake pan or a tart pan or some of their ornamental features, but essentially you need them to have certain proportions. The risks of using a shallow pan for a recipe requiring a deep one or vice versa are endless. If you have a modest collection of baking pans, you should be fine.

Icing spatula and pastry brush

Small tools but absolutely essential if you want to get anywhere. Both straight-blade and offset-blade icing spatulas are handy.

And then there are a few ingredients and techniques that are specific to the patisserie or bakery and need to be understood a little.

Flour

All-purpose flour is what we use in most of the recipes. It is relatively soft, or low in gluten, which means it will make products with a short, crumbly consistency like most cakes and cookies. Bread flour is used to make breads and some pastries. It gives the characteristic elastic or chewy consistency. Don't substitute one type for the other when baking.

Chocolate

Unless we state otherwise, the chocolate used in our recipes should contain 52 to 64 percent cacao solids to yield the right result.

Commercial yeast

There are three main types of commercial yeast available. Fresh compressed yeast is what professional bakers use. You can find it in some health-food shops and a few supermarkets, or if you happen to have a friendly baker in the vicinity. The best option for a home baker is active dry yeast. It gives perfectly good results, is available in most supermarkets, and is easy to use. Active dry yeast, weight for weight, is twice as strong as fresh yeast.

The third type is quick-acting dry yeast (also known as fast-rising, instant, or quick-rise yeast). It comes as a powder that can be added directly to the flour and does not need hydrating. It is even stronger than ordinary dry yeast. Check the instructions on the packet for the required quantity.

Creaming

This is the starting process of many cakes and cookies, where you aerate a paste of butter and sugar before adding eggs and flour to it. It is important to incorporate as much air as the recipe specifies. The mix will go whiter and puffier the more you cream it. The eggs should be added a little at a time, proceeding only when the previous addition has been thoroughly incorporated into the butter and sugar. Once this is done, the dry ingredients must be added all at once and you should work the mix just until everything is incorporated, no longer. You can cream with a whisk—or, better, with an electric mixer.

Greasing and lining

Brush your pans and molds thoroughly with vegetable oil or melted butter and then line with parchment paper that has been cut to the right size. It pays off. The last thing you want is for a cake to stick obstinately to the pan.

Baking times

The issue of baking times could easily turn into a sore point after a colossal disappointment. People tend to underbake cookies, tarts, and breads and to overbake chocolate cakes and brownies. Keep in mind that baking times can vary a lot depending on your oven, the pan used, how full the pan is, and also on specific ingredients and techniques. Follow the instructions in the recipes but also try to develop an ability to observe and judge. Check often at different stages of the baking process (but don't open the oven unless absolutely necessary).

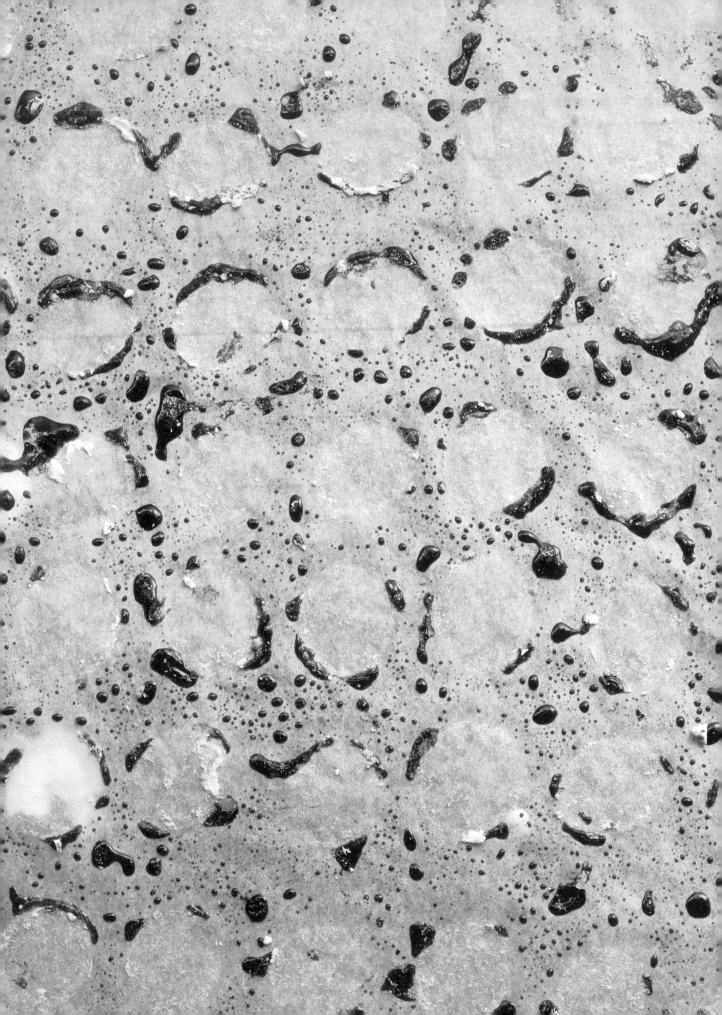

OTTOLENGHI

Yotam Ottolenghi and Sami Tamimi

To Ruth, Michael, and Karl —Yotam
To Na'ama, Hassan, and Jeremy —Sami

Photography by Richard Learoyd

OTTOLENGHI

THE COOKBOOK

Ten Speed Press
Berkeley

Published in the United States by Ten Speed
Press, an imprint of the Crown Publishing Group,
a division of Random House, Inc., New York.
www.crownpublishing.com
www.tenspeed.com

Originally published in slightly different form in
hardcover in Great Britain by Ebury Press, an
imprint of Ebury Publishing, a division of the
Random House Group Limited, London, in 2008.

Ten Speed Press and the Ten Speed Press
colophon are registered trademarks of
Random House, Inc.

Library of Congress Cataloging-in-Publication
Data is on file with the publisher.

Hardcover ISBN: 978-1-60774-418-4
eBook ISBN: 978-1-60774-419-1

Printed in China

Cover design by Sarah Adelman
Interior design by BLOK and objectif
Cover photograph by Jonathan Lovekin
Interior photography by Richard Learoyd

10 9 8 7 6 5 4 3 2 1

First United States Edition

Contents

Vegetables, legumes, and grains

　　　　Chapter 1　　Vegetables, legumes, and grains

A substantial starter, this salad is summer bliss, offering contrasting textures and aromas. Use the best ingredients you can get your hands on—it is crucial here. Taste the peaches; they mustn't be floury, just sweet and juicy.

Yellow-fleshed peaches are normally less watery than the white variety, so they will grill more readily. Grilling, though, is not essential. It will add to the presentation and give a slight smokiness, but you can choose to skip this step.

Peaches and speck with orange blossom

1 Cut the peaches in half and remove the pits. Slice each half into 3 wedges, place in a bowl, and add the olive oil and some salt and pepper. Toss well to coat them.
2 Place a ridged grill pan over high heat and leave for a few minutes so it heats up well. Place the peach wedges on the pan and grill for a minute on each side. You want to get nice charcoal lines on all sides. Remove the peaches from the pan and leave to cool.
3 To make the dressing, place the orange blossom water, vinegar, and maple syrup in a bowl and whisk to combine. Drizzle the oil in slowly while you whisk to get a thick dressing. Season to taste.
4 On a serving platter, arrange layers of peach, endive, watercress, chard, and speck. Spoon over enough dressing to coat all the ingredients but not to drench them. Serve straight away.

serves 4 to 6

5 ripe peaches
1 tbsp olive oil
2 rod or white endives,
  leaves separated
1¾ oz / 50 g watercress
1¾ oz / 50 g baby chard leaves
  or other small leaves
3½ oz / 100 g speck, thinly sliced
  (10 to 12 slices)
coarse sea salt and freshly
  ground black pepper

Dressing
3 tbsp orange blossom water
  ↗ page xii
1 tbsp good-quality balsamic
  vinegar
1 tbsp maple syrup
3 tbsp olive oil

Chapter 1   Vegetables, legumes, and grains

This is a recipe that is not worth making without the perfect components. Use black or green figs, or a mixture, just as long as they are ripe, sweet, and heavy. Remember, figs are very illusive. Somehow, the better they look, the more tasteless they are. So see if you can sneak a taste before you buy.

The cheese we use is *pecorino caciotta etrusca fresca*, from Patricia Michelson of La Fromagerie. It is subtle and delicate but still has an unmistakable "sheepy" flavor. Its soft texture complements that of the figs. Prosciutto will also work here, either instead of the cheese or in addition to it.

Figs with young pecorino and honey

serves 4 as a starter

2 tbsp good quality honey
3 tbsp olive oil
1⅓ lb / 600 g ripe green or black figs
10½ oz / 300 g young pecorino or a similar cheese
3 oz / 80 g arugula, preferably wild
⅓ oz / 10 g basil leaves
coarse sea salt and freshly ground black pepper

1 Whisk together the honey and olive oil and season with salt and pepper to taste. Cut the figs into quarters. Use your hands to tear the cheese into large chunks.
2 Arrange the arugula, basil, figs, and pecorino in layers on individual serving plates or a large platter. Drizzle over the honey dressing as you go along, and finish with some freshly ground black pepper.

This is an ideal brunch dish for a warm spring day. With the tahini sauce and bread, it makes a modest meal in itself; without them, a colorful salad—light, refreshing, and wholesome.

Here we come to the thorny issue of shelling fava beans. Many Arab recipes call for cooking and eating fava beans with their pods. This is recommended for young beans, early in the season, but wouldn't work for a fresh salad like this one. Going to the next level—skinning the beans—depends on how large the beans are, how thick their skin, and how hard you want to work. Most beans, especially the ones sold frozen, are perfectly fine eaten with the skin on. So if you prefer to skip the skinning stage, cook them for a minute longer. You'll lose a bit of the light, "bouncy" texture but save yourself a lot of time.

Radish and fava bean salad

serves 4

1 Place the fava beans in a pan of boiling water and simmer for 1 to 2 minutes, depending on size. Drain through a large colander and rinse in plenty of cold water to refresh them. Remove the beans from their skins by gently squeezing each one with your fingertips.
2 Cut the radishes into 6 wedges each and mix with the fava beans, onion, cilantro, preserved lemon, lemon juice, parsley, olive oil, and cumin. Season with salt and pepper to taste.
3 To serve, pile a mound of salad in one corner of each serving plate, pour the tahini sauce into a small bowl, and stand it next to the salad. Set a pita bread next to them.

1 lb / 500 g shelled fava beans, fresh or frozen
12 oz / 350 g small radishes
½ red onion, very thinly sliced
2 tbsp finely chopped cilantro
1 oz / 30 g preserved lemon, finely chopped ↗ page 273
juice of 2 lemons
2 tbsp chopped flat-leaf parsley
3 tbsp olive oil
1 tsp ground cumin
scant 1 cup / 200 ml Green tahini sauce ↗ page 272
4 thick pita breads
salt and freshly ground black pepper

This salad is a little festival in itself. The fennel and tarragon, with their echoing flavors, form a solid base on which stronger colors and flavors—pomegranate, feta, sumac—manifest themselves without overwhelming the whole salad. It is distinctly fresh and goes well with roast meats and grilled fish. Crusty bread is almost obligatory to soak up the juices from the plate.

Try substituting dried cranberries or sour cherries for the pomegranate. The fennel for this salad should be the round and bulky variety. It is crispier and sweeter than the long one.

Fennel and feta with pomegranate seeds and sumac

serves 4

1 Start by releasing the pomegranate seeds. The best way to do it is to halve the pomegranate along its "belly" (you only need half a pomegranate here), then hold the half firmly in your hand with the seeds facing your palm. Over a large bowl, start bashing the back of the fruit with a wooden spoon. Don't hit too hard or you'll bruise the seeds and break the skin. Magically, the seeds will just fall out. Pick out any white skin that falls in.

2 Remove the leaves of the fennel, keeping a few for garnish later, and trim the base, making sure you leave enough of it still attached to hold the slices together. Slice very thinly lengthwise (a mandoline would come in handy here).

3 In a bowl, mix the olive oil, sumac, lemon juice, herbs, and some salt and pepper. Add the fennel and toss well. Taste for seasoning but remember, the feta will add saltiness.

4 Layer the fennel, then the feta, and then the pomegranate seeds in individual serving dishes. Garnish with the reserved fennel leaves, sprinkle over some sumac, and serve immediately.

½ pomegranate
2 medium fennel heads
1½ tbsp olive oil
2 tsp sumac, plus extra
   to garnish ↗ page xii
juice of 1 lemon
4 tbsp tarragon leaves
2 tbsp coarsely chopped
   flat-leaf parsley
2½ oz / 70 g Greek feta cheese,
   sliced
salt and freshly ground black
   pepper

Our friend Ossi Burger says that Sami is a genius for having managed to turn something as dull as a cucumber into a delicacy in this salad. She is right about the genius thing, but that's beside the point. What Ossi has in mind is the typical mammoth cucumber that you find in supermarkets—a cucumber with no texture, no flavor, and no character.

Before coming to this country, neither of us had ever come across a fresh cucumber much bigger than the typical pickled variety. Normal cucumbers, or mini cucumbers as they are sometimes called, the ones eaten in the Middle East, have a distinctive taste and are much less watery. They are earthy and crunchy throughout and can carry a whole salad without getting lost in it. The Arab bread salad, *fattoush*, does not work without a gutsy cucumber.

Fortunately, some organic shops and Asian and Arab produce markets stock these cucumbers, so always choose them if you can. If you are using a large cucumber in this salad, halve it along its center and use a teaspoon to scoop out the seedy core, which is full of water.

Quartered radishes make a good colorful addition. Serve with other salads on a meze plate, take with you on a picnic, or eat with roast lamb or pork.

Cucumber and poppy seed salad

serves 4

1. Chop off and discard the ends of the cucumbers. Slice the cucumbers at an angle, so you end up with pieces ⅜ inch / 1 cm thick and 1¼ to 1½ inches / 3 to 4 cm long.
2. Mix together all the ingredients in a large bowl. Use your hands to massage the flavors gently into the cucumbers. Taste and adjust the amount of sugar and salt according to the quality of the cucumbers. The salad should be sharp and sweet, almost like a pickle.
3. If not serving immediately, you might need to drain some liquid off later. Adjust the seasoning again afterward.

6 small cucumbers (about 1 lb / 500 g)
2 mild red chiles, thinly sliced
3 tbsp coarsely chopped cilantro
4 tbsp / 60 ml white wine vinegar or rice vinegar
½ cup / 120 ml sunflower oil
2 tbsp poppy seeds
2 tbsp superfine sugar
salt and freshly ground black pepper

If we are totally honest, this salad is hard work. You must meticulously pick the leaves of six types of herbs, wash them carefully, and then dry well. You also have to fry almonds watchfully without burning them. And you should dress it no more than a minute, literally, before serving. Quite a headache.

If you are not put off by this, however, you will find this salad one of the most gratifying dishes you can possibly make. It is astonishingly fresh and actually makes you feel as if you are doing yourself a giant favor by eating it. Serve at the end of a substantial meal, before or instead of dessert. Otherwise, offer it alongside a hefty nonvegetarian main course. A small portion would suffice to clean the palate and make you feel a ton lighter.

This salad is the creation of Etti Mordo, the mega-talented chef who deserves lots of the credit for the creation of our Islington restaurant. A passionate perfectionist, she is one of those cooks who agonizes relentlessly over a dish until she gets it just right, regardless of time and effort. Etti's food always amazes you.

Etti's herb salad

serves 6

1 Gently immerse the herb leaves in plenty of cold water, being careful not to bruise them. Drain in a colander and then dry in a salad spinner or by spreading them over a clean kitchen towel. (Once dry, the herbs will keep in the fridge for up to 1 day. Store them in a sealed container lined with a few layers of paper towels.)

2 Heat the butter in a frying pan and add the almonds, salt, and pepper. Sauté for 5 to 6 minutes over low to medium heat, until the almonds are golden. Transfer to a colander to drain. Make sure you keep the butter that's left in the pan. Leave it somewhere warm so it doesn't set. Once the almonds are cool enough to handle, coarsely chop them with a large knife.

3 To assemble the salad, place the herbs in a large bowl. Add the almonds, cooking butter, lemon juice, and olive oil. Toss gently and season to taste, then serve immediately.

2 cups / 35 g cilantro leaves
1¼ cups / 40 g flat-leaf parsley leaves
2 cups / 20 g dill leaves
1 cup / 35 g tarragon leaves
1¼ cups / 30 g basil leaves
2 cups / 40 g arugula leaves
3½ tbsp / 50 g unsalted butter
heaping 1 cup / 150 g whole unskinned almonds
½ tsp coarse sea salt
½ tsp freshly ground black pepper
2 tbsp lemon juice
1 tbsp olive oil

As kids we used to sprinkle dried oregano over a piece of white bread covered with tomato purée and a cheap cheese, toast it, and call it pizza. Fresh oregano is one of the most underused and undervalued herbs. It is potent, like rosemary or sage, so must be applied with care, but it is very versatile. It works well when added to a marinade for roasted vegetables or substantial salads. It flavors gratins and bakes and makes a great addition to green salsas for pasta, potatoes, or grilled oily fish.

Marinated eggplant with tahini and oregano

1 Preheat the oven to 425°F / 220°C. Trim the stalk end off the eggplants, then cut each eggplant in half widthwise. Cut the fat lower piece lengthwise in half and then cut each half into 3 wedges. Do the same with the thinner piece, but cut each half into 2 wedges. You should end up with 10 similar-size pieces with skin on their curved side.
2 Place the eggplant pieces on a large baking sheet. Brush on all sides with plenty of olive oil and season with salt and pepper (if you want to get nice grill marks on the eggplants, place them on a very hot ridged grill pan at this stage and grill for 3 minutes on each side; return them to the baking sheet and continue with the next step). Place the sheet pan in the hot oven and roast the eggplants for 15 to 18 minutes, until they are golden brown and totally soft inside.
3 While the eggplants are roasting, make the marinade. Simply put all the ingredients in a bowl and mix well.
4 As soon as the eggplants come out of the oven, spoon the marinade over them and leave at room temperature for up to 2 hours before serving. You can store them in the fridge for up to 2 days at this stage. Make sure you don't serve them cold, though; leave them out of the fridge for an hour at least.
5 To serve, arrange the eggplant wedges on a plate. Now, you can either spoon the tahini sauce on top and garnish with a few oregano leaves, or serve the tahini in a bowl on the side, topped with oregano leaves.

serves 6 as a starter

3 small eggplants
olive oil for brushing
1 recipe Green tahini sauce
  ↗ page 272 **made without the parsley**
coarse sea salt and freshly ground black pepper

Marinade
1 mild red chile, seeded and finely chopped
2 tbsp finely chopped cilantro
2 tbsp finely chopped oregano, plus a few whole leaves for garnish
1 clove garlic, crushed
3 tbsp lemon juice
4 tbsp olive oil
1 tsp coarse sea salt
¼ tsp freshly ground black pepper

To get a sublimely deep, smoky flavor from an eggplant you need to burn it. Literally. All other cooking methods pale in comparison. The messy but most effective way to do this is to burn it on a gas burner on your stove top. Otherwise, you can place the eggplant under a very hot broiler and allow it to cook well, until it is totally shriveled and the skin starts to crack and flake dry.

If you go for the first choice, you will need to protect your stove top from staining. So before starting, remove the grates from two burners, cover the base with aluminum foil, and then place the grates back on.

This salad is Sami's mother's recipe, a variation on a Tunisian salad. Serve alongside other meze salads, with large chunks of bread.

Burnt eggplant with yellow pepper and red onion

serves 4

1 Place the eggplants directly on 2 separate moderate flames on the stove top and roast for 12 to 15 minutes, turning them occasionally with metal tongs, until the flesh is soft and the skin is burnt and flaky. By this stage your kitchen will have the most magnificent charred smell. (Alternatively, place the eggplants under a hot broiler for about an hour, turning them occasionally and continuing to cook even if they burst.) Leave to cool slightly.
2 Make a long cut through each warm eggplant. Using a spoon, scoop out the soft flesh while avoiding most of the burnt skin on the outside. If you don't like the seeds, try to remove them as well. Leave the eggplant flesh to drain in a colander for at least 1 hour or overnight.
3 Coarsely chop the eggplant flesh. Mix all the remaining ingredients together, then taste and adjust the seasoning. It should be robust and pungent. Serve within 24 hours.

2 medium eggplants
2 yellow or green peppers, cored and cut into ⅔-inch / 1.5-cm dice
1 medium red onion, coarsely chopped
24 cherry tomatoes, halved
1½ oz / 40 g flat-leaf parsley, coarsely chopped
4½ tbsp / 70 ml sunflower or nut oil
6 tbsp / 90 ml cider vinegar
1 tbsp ground cumin
coarse sea salt and freshly ground black pepper

This dish, one of Ramael Scully's, makes a superb warm vegetarian starter or main course. Scully, as he is known to everyone, is our evening chef in Islington, and serves complex dishes of outstanding quality without ever losing his cool.

You need to start this recipe at least four hours in advance, preferably the night before, for the gnocchi mix to rest properly. The quality of the ricotta is paramount.

Eggplant-wrapped ricotta gnocchi with sage butter

1 To make the gnocchi, place the pine nuts in a small frying pan and dry-roast over medium heat for 3 to 4 minutes, stirring them occasionally so they color evenly. Transfer to a large bowl and add the ricotta, egg yolks, flour, Parmesan, herbs, nutmeg, salt, and pepper. Stir well, then cover and refrigerate for 4 hours or up to overnight.

2 Preheat the oven to 350°F / 180°C. Trim the top and bottom off the eggplant and cut it lengthwise into ¼-inch / 5-mm thick slices; you will need 8 to 12 slices, depending on how many gnocchi you make. Lay the slices on a baking sheet lined with parchment paper and brush liberally with the olive oil. Place in the oven and roast for 10 to 15 minutes, until tender and golden (alternatively, you could grill the eggplant slices over a medium fire for 2 to 3 minutes on each side).

3 To shape the gnocchi, wet your hands and scoop out 1½ to 1¾-oz / 40- to 50-g portions (about 3 tablespoons). Roll into 8 or 12 elongated barrel shapes. Meanwhile, bring plenty of salted water to a boil in a large saucepan.

4 Carefully add a few dumplings to the simmering water; don't cook them all at once or they will stick to one other. After about 2 minutes, they should rise to the surface. Using a slotted spoon, transfer them to a kitchen towel to drain. Pat dry with paper towels and brush them with the melted butter.

5 Once the gnocchi have cooled down, take a strip of eggplant and wrap it around the center of each one, like a belt. Trim the eggplant so that the seam is at the bottom. Place the gnocchi in a greased baking dish and set aside. You can cover them with plastic wrap and keep them in the fridge for a day at this stage.

6 When ready to serve, sprinkle the gnocchi with the Parmesan and bake in the oven at 350°F / 180°C for 8 to 10 minutes, until they are heated through.

7 Meanwhile, quickly make the sage butter sauce, as it needs to be ready at the same time as the gnocchi. Place a small saucepan over medium heat. Add the butter and allow it to simmer for a few minutes until it turns a light golden brown and has a nutty smell. Remove from the heat and carefully add the sage, salt, and lemon juice, if using. Return to the heat for a few seconds to cook the sage lightly.

8 Divide the gnocchi among serving plates, pour the hot butter along with some sage leaves on top of each serving, and serve immediately.

serves 4 as a starter, 2 as a main course

Ricotta gnocchi
3½ tbsp / 30 g pine nuts
1 cup / 250 g ricotta cheese
2 free-range egg yolks
4½ tbsp / 35 g all-purpose flour
1½ oz / 40 g Parmesan cheese, freshly grated
1 tbsp chopped flat-leaf parsley
1 tbsp chopped basil
¼ tsp grated nutmeg
½ tsp salt
a good grinding of black pepper

1 small to medium eggplant
4 tbsp olive oil
4 tsp / 15 g unsalted butter, melted
3 tbsp / 15 g freshly grated Parmesan cheese

Sage butter
6½ tbsp / 90 g unsalted butter
20 sage leaves
a pinch of salt
1½ tsp lemon juice (optional)

This is probably the archetypal Ottolenghi salad: robust contrasting flavors, vibrant and vivacious colors, fresh herbs, and nuts. To create the most impact, we recommend that you serve it from a comunal plate brought out to the dining table. It makes an exciting starter and doesn't need much else alongside it.

Roasted eggplant with saffron yogurt

1   To make the sauce, infuse the saffron in the hot water in a small bowl for 5 minutes. Pour the infusion into a bowl containing the yogurt, garlic, lemon juice, olive oil, and some salt. Whisk well to get a smooth, golden sauce. Taste and adjust the salt, if necessary, then chill. This sauce will keep well in the fridge for up to 3 days.

2   Preheat the oven to 425°F / 220°C. Place the eggplant slices on a baking sheet, brush both sides with plenty of olive oil, and sprinkle with salt and pepper. Roast for 20 to 35 minutes, until the slices take on a beautiful light brown color. Let them cool down. The eggplants will keep in the fridge for 3 days; just let them come to room temperature before serving.

3   To serve, arrange the eggplant slices on a large plate, slightly overlapping. Drizzle the saffron yogurt over them, sprinkle with the pine nuts and pomegranate seeds, and lay the basil on top.

serves 4

Saffron yogurt
a small pinch of saffron threads
3 tbsp hot water
¾ cup / 180 g Greek yogurt
1 clove garlic, crushed
2½ tbsp lemon juice
3 tbsp olive oil
coarse sea salt

**3 medium eggplants, cut into
  slices ¾ inch / 2 cm thick, or
  into wedges** ↗ page 26
olive oil for brushing
2 tbsp toasted pine nuts
a handful of pomegranate seeds
20 basil leaves
**coarse sea salt and freshly
  ground black pepper**

• section of s...

small box

large box

• many sold

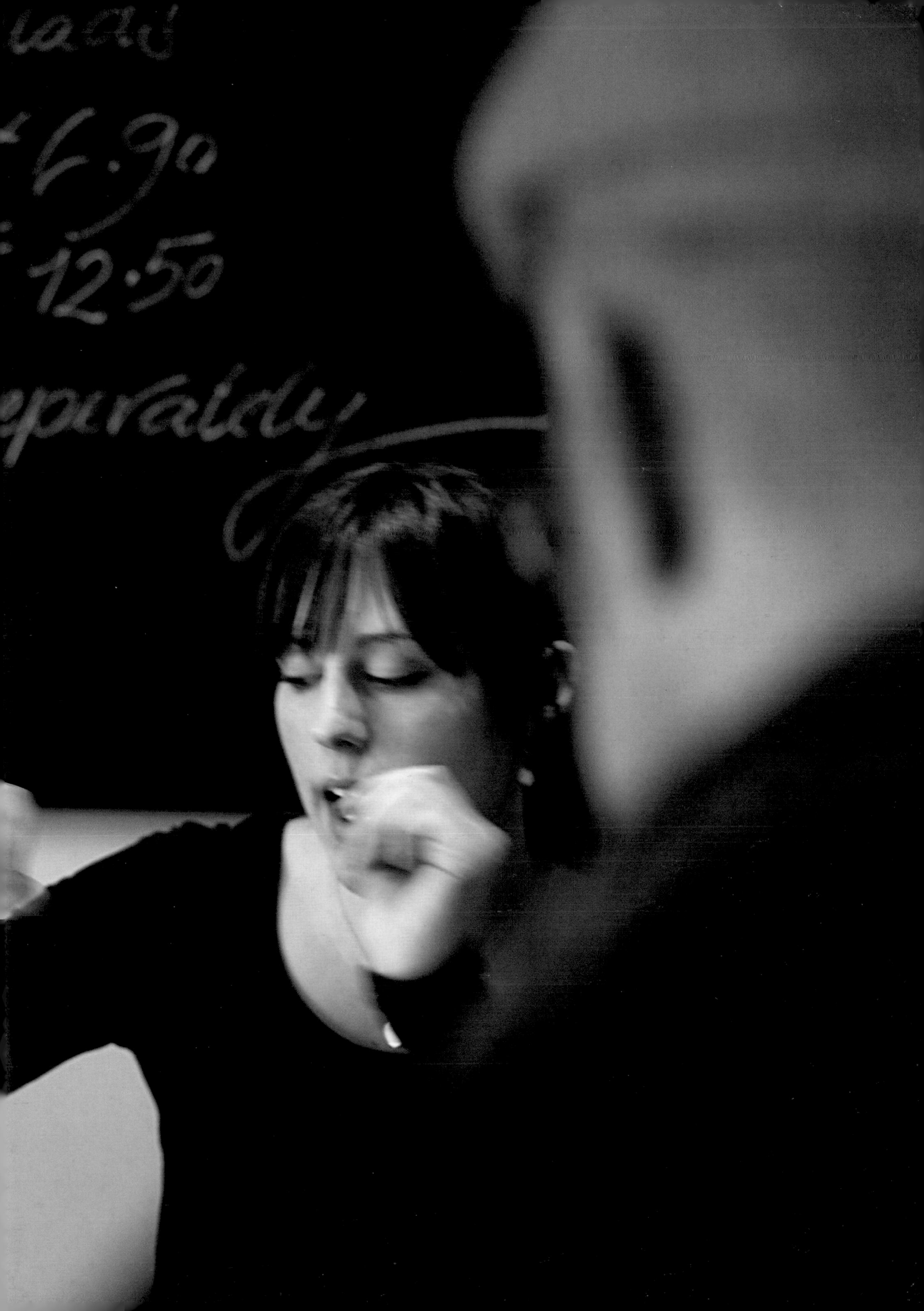
6.90
12.50

This generous salad is almost a meal in itself. It is laden with enough colors, textures, and aromas to be the center of a light spring supper. Its generous creator is Helen Goh, with whom we have had the pleasure of working for the past two years. Since arriving from Australia, Helen has been a continuous source of inspiration and insight for everybody at Ottolenghi, both as a chef and as a sensitive friend.

Manouri is a Greek semisoft fresh cheese produced from the drained whey left over after making feta. It is light and creamy and we love using it for its subtlety and the fact that it fries well and keeps its shape. If you can't get hold of it, use a fresh goat cheese but skip the frying, as it will disintegrate. If you like haloumi, it fries and grills very well and will also work here.

Grilled asparagus, zucchini, and manouri

serves 4 to 6

1 There is a fair amount of vegetable preparation here before making the basil oil and assembling the salad. Start with the tomatoes. Preheat the oven to 325°F / 170°C. Mix the tomatoes with 3 table-spoons of the olive oil and season with some salt and pepper. Spread them out on a baking sheet lined with parchment paper, skin side down. Roast in the oven for 50 minutes, until semidried. You can leave them there a bit more or a bit less, depending on how dry you like them. They will be delicious anyway. Remove from the oven and leave to cool.

2 Trim the woody bases of the asparagus and blanch for 4 minutes in plenty of boiling water. Drain and refresh under cold water, making sure the spears are completely cold. Drain well again, then transfer to a mixing bowl and toss with 2 tablespoons of the olive oil and some salt and pepper.

3 Slice the zucchini very thinly lengthwise, using a mandoline (this inexpensive tool will make your kitchen life dramatically easier) or a vegetable peeler. Mix with 1 tablespoon of the olive oil and some salt and pepper.

4 Place a ridged grill pan over high heat and leave there for a few minutes. It should be very hot. Grill the zucchini and asparagus, turning them over after about a minute. You want to get nice char marks on all sides. Remove and leave to cool.

5 Heat the remaining 3 tablespoons olive oil in a pan. Fry the manouri cheese for 3 minutes on each side, until it is golden. Place on paper towels to soak up the excess oil. Alternatively, grill the cheese on the hot grill pan for about 2 minutes on each side.

6 To make the basil oil, blitz all the ingredients in a blender until smooth. You might need to double the quantity for some blender blades to be effective. Keep any extra oil for future salads.

7 To assemble, arrange the arugula, vegetables, and cheese in layers on a flat serving plate. Try to build the salad up while showing all the individual components. Drizzle with as much basil oil as you like and serve.

12 oz / 350 g cherry tomatoes, halved
9 tbsp / 140 ml olive oil
24 asparagus spears
2 zucchini
7 oz / 200 g manouri cheese, sliced ¾ inch / 2 cm thick
1¼ cups / 25 g arugula
coarse sea salt and freshly ground black pepper

Basil oil
5 tbsp / 75 ml olive oil
1 clove garlic, chopped
1 cup / 25 g basil leaves
pinch of salt
¼ tsp freshly ground black pepper

Salty, tender, and juicy, samphire grows on tidal stretches of the British coast from June to September. It can be a challenge to get your hands on, especially at both ends of the season, but we highly recommend nagging your fishmonger for some. There's also a type of samphire that grows along both coasts in the United States. It adds the flavor of the sea to fish and salads in the same way that seaweed does, but has a unique, succulent texture. Here we combine "poor man's asparagus," as it is sometimes referred to, with its rich counterpart to create an attractive salad, full of flavors and many shades of green. Serve as an accompaniment to fried fish or on its own as a starter.

Asparagus and samphire

serves 4

1 tbsp black sesame seeds (if not available, use white ones)
24 medium-thick asparagus spears
3½ oz / 100 g samphire, washed
2 tbsp olive oil
1 tbsp sesame oil
1 clove garlic, crushed
2 tbsp tarragon leaves
coarse sea salt and freshly ground black pepper

1 Put the sesame seeds in a nonstick pan and place over medium heat for 2 to 3 minutes, just to toast them gently. Remove from the heat and set aside.

2 To cook the greens, fill a large saucepan with plenty of cold water and bring to a boil. You don't need to add salt; samphire is salty enough. Trim the woody bases of the asparagus and put the spears in the boiling water. Blanch for 2 to 3 minutes, then add the samphire. Cook for another minute, until the asparagus is tender but still firm.

3 Drain the greens in a large colander and run lots of cold water over them. It's very important to get them completely cold. Leave in the colander to drain and then dry with a kitchen towel.

4 To finish the salad, put the asparagus and samphire in a bowl and mix with the rest of the ingredients. Toss well, then taste and adjust the seasoning. You might not need any extra salt. Serve straightaway, or chill and serve within 24 hours.

Green beans are so popular at Ottolenghi that we seem to be constantly on the lookout for new combinations. Orange and hazelnut go wonderfully well together. They offer a good balance of freshness and earthiness, and the flavors are subtle enough to complement the beans without overpowering them.

 The beans can be cooked and chilled a day in advance and then dressed before serving. Sugar snaps, green peas, and fava beans can be substituted for the French beans or snow peas or can be added to the salad.

Haricots verts and snow peas with hazelnut and orange

serves 6

14 oz / 400 g haricots verts
14 oz / 400 g snow peas
½ cup / 70 g unskinned hazelnuts
1 orange
¾ oz / 20 g chives, coarsely
 chopped
1 clove garlic, crushed
3 tbsp olive oil
2 tbsp hazelnut oil
 (or another nut oil, if unavailable)
coarse sea salt and freshly ground
 black pepper

1 Preheat the oven to 350°F / 180°C. Using a small, sharp knife, trim the stalk ends off the beans and the snow peas, keeping the two separate. Bring plenty of unsalted water to a boil in a large saucepan. You need lots of space for the beans, as this is crucial for preserving their color. Blanch the beans in the water for 4 minutes, then drain into a colander and run them under plenty of tap water until cold. Leave to drain and dry. Repeat with the snow peas, but blanch for only 1 minute.

2 While the beans are cooking, scatter the hazelnuts over a baking sheet and toast in the oven for 10 minutes. Leave until cool enough to handle, then rub them in a clean kitchen towel to get rid of most of the skin. Chop the nuts with a large, sharp knife. They should be quite rough; some can even stay whole.

3 Using a vegetable peeler, remove the zest from the orange in strips, being careful to avoid the bitter white pith. Slice each piece of zest into very thin strips (if you have a citrus zester, you could do the whole job with that).

4 To assemble the dish, mix all the ingredients together in a bowl, toss gently, then taste and adjust the seasoning. Serve at room temperature.

This combination is a manifestation of spring. The pink peppercorns add a sweet, scented aroma to the freshness of the vegetables.

Claudia Roden, the godmother of Middle Eastern cookery and a venerable inspiration for us, has a similar recipe. She suggests using frozen artichoke bottoms and fava beans as alternatives to fresh. It she can do it, so can you. This will definitely save you lots of time without paying a huge price in terms of flavor.

Serve this dish at room temperature. You can chill it and keep in the fridge for up to one day.

Baked artichokes and fava beans

serves 2 to 4

1 Preheat the oven to 400°F / 200°C. Juice the lemons and discard all but 2 of the empty lemon halves.

2 To clean the artichokes, cut off most of the stalk and start removing the tough outer leaves by hand. Once you reach the softer leaves, take a sharp serrated knife and trim off ⅜ to ¾ inch / 1 to 2 cm from the top of the artichoke. Cut the artichoke in half lengthwise so you can reach the heart and scrape it clean. Use a small, sharp knife to remove all the "hairs." Immediately rub the heart with a little lemon juice to prevent discoloring. Cut each artichoke half into slices ¼ inch / 5 mm thick. Place in cold water and stir in half the remaining lemon juice.

3 Drain the artichoke slices and spread them on a baking sheet. Add the remaining lemon juice, the 2 reserved lemon halves, bay leaves, thyme, garlic, peppercorns, wine, and oil. Cover with aluminum foil and bake for 45 to 60 minutes, or until the artichokes are tender. Remove from the oven, take off the foil, and let the artichokes cool.

4 Fill a large saucepan with plenty of cold water and bring to a boil. Add the fava beans and peas and blanch for 2 minutes, then drain in a colander and run under cold water to refresh. Leave in the colander to dry. If the fava beans are large and have tough skins, you may want to remove them. Simply press each one gently with your fingertips until the bean pops out.

5 Remove the lemon halves from the artichokes. Mix the artichokes with the beans, peas, and parsley and stir in the lemon slices. Taste for salt and pepper, sprinkle with peppercorns, and serve.

4 lemons, plus a few thin lemon slices to finish
2 large globe artichokes
2 bay leaves
2 sprigs thyme
2 cloves garlic, thinly sliced
1 tbsp pink peppercorns, plus extra to garnish ↗ page xiv
½ cup / 125 ml white wine
4 tbsp / 60 ml olive oil
1⅔ cups / 250 g shelled fava beans
1⅔ cups / 250 g shelled peas
1 bunch flat-leaf parsley, coarsely chopped
salt and freshly ground black pepper

This is another of Helen's contributions, bringing an Asian brushstroke to the generally Mediterranean Ottolenghi canvas. Served at room temperature, it is soothingly sweet and goes well with roast chicken or beef.

Broccolini, or tender-stem broccoli, is a hybrid between broccoli and Chinese kale (*gai lan*). Cooked very lightly, it has a great tender bite.

Use *kecap manis* (sweet soy sauce), if you can get hold of it. Otherwise, use a standard variety. For the chile sauce, choose one that is not too sweet. Reduce the quantity if it is very hot.

Sweet broccolini with tofu, sesame, and cilantro

serves 4

3 tbsp kecap manis (sweet soy sauce)
4 tbsp chile sauce or paste
2 tbsp sesame oil
9 oz / 250 g firm tofu (tau kwa)
1 lb / 450 g broccolini
1 tbsp sesame seeds
1 tbsp peanut oil
3 tbsp cilantro leaves
salt

1 First, marinate the tofu. In a bowl, whisk the soy sauce, chile sauce, and sesame oil together. Cut the tofu into strips about ³⁄₈ inch / 1 cm thick, mix gently (so it doesn't break) with the marinade, and leave in the fridge for half an hour.

2 Trim any hard leaves off the broccolini and discard. Place the broccolini in a large saucepan full of boiling water and blanch for 2 minutes. Drain in a colander and run at once under a cold tap to stop further cooking. Leave to dry.

3 Scatter the sesame seeds in a nonstick pan and place it over medium heat for about 5 minutes. Jiggle them around so they toast evenly, and then remove from the heat.

4 Place a wok or a cast-iron pan over high heat and allow it to heat up well. Add the peanut oil. Lower the heat to medium to prevent the oil from spitting (it may spit a little), then carefully add the tofu strips and leave for 2 to 3 minutes, until they color underneath. Using tongs, gently turn them over to color the other side. (If you are making a large quantity, you may need to fry the tofu in 2 or 3 batches, otherwise it will "stew" rather than fry.)

5 Add any remaining marinade to the pan, plus the cooked broccolini. Add the cilantro and half the sesame seeds and stir together gently. Remove from the heat and let everything come to room temperature in the pan. Taste and add more sesame oil, soy sauce, or salt if necessary. Divide among serving plates and sprinkle with the remaining sesame seeds.

Chapter 1 Vegetables, legumes, and grains

If there's a dish that's become synonymous with Ottolenghi, second only to our meringues, it is this one. Customers come especially for it and always complain that their broccoli is never as exciting as ours. In all honesty, broccoli is a boring vegetable and you do need a magic touch to bring it to life.

If followed carefully, this recipe does the trick. It has a bit of a history in itself. Sami started cooking it at Baker and Spice after having brought it over from Lilith, a restaurant in Tel Aviv. It is still a winner at Baker and Spice and at Ottolenghi, even though standard broccoli is losing popularity to the tender purple sprouting broccoli.

For even more oomph, add four chopped anchovy fillets to the chile and garlic when cooking them in the oil.

Grilled broccoli with chile and garlic

1 Prepare the broccoli by separating it into florets (leave on the individual small stems that the florets grow on). Fill a large saucepan with plenty of water and bring to a boil. It should be big enough to accommodate the broccoli easily. Throw in the broccoli and blanch for 2 minutes only. Don't be tempted to cook it any longer! Using a large slotted spoon, quickly transfer the broccoli to a bowl full of ice-cold water. You need to stop the cooking at once. Drain in a colander and allow to dry completely. It is important that the broccoli isn't wet at all. In a mixing bowl, toss the broccoli with 3 tablespoons / 45 ml of the olive oil and a generous amount of salt and pepper.

2 Place a ridged grill pan over high heat and leave it there for at least 5 minutes, until it is extremely hot. Depending on the size of your pan, grill the broccoli in several batches. The florets mustn't be cramped. Turn them around as they grill so they get char marks all over. Transfer to a heatproof bowl and continue with another batch.

3 While grilling the broccoli, place the remaining scant 5 tablespoons / 70 ml oil in a small saucepan with the garlic and chiles. Cook them over medium heat until the garlic just begins to turn golden brown. Be careful not to let the garlic and chile burn—remember, they will keep on cooking even when off the heat. Pour the oil, garlic, and chile over the hot broccoli and toss together well. Taste and adjust the seasoning.

4 Serve warm or at room temperature. You can garnish the broccoli with almonds or lemon just before serving, if you like.

serves 2 to 4

2 heads broccoli (about 1 lb / 500 g)
scant ½ cup / 115 ml olive oil
4 cloves garlic, thinly sliced
2 mild red chiles, thinly sliced
coarse sea salt and freshly ground black pepper
toasted almonds or very thin lemon slices (with skin), for garnish (optional)

This hearty combination of flavors makes an impressive vegetarian starter. It is assembled at the last minute and served warm.

Salsify is a long root that can be hard to find but is worth the effort for its delicate, earthy flavor. Good substitutes would be celery root or Jerusalem artichokes. Purple sprouting broccoli is available in late winter and early spring. The stems can be quite woody and will need trimming down from the excess leaves (Helen uses the leaves in a delicious dish of shiitake mushrooms and oyster sauce). If the stems are thick, cut them lengthwise into two or four pieces so they are the same thickness as an asparagus spear. Broccolini (↗ page 39) can be substituted for the purple sprouts.

Purple sprouting broccoli and salsify with caper butter

serves 4 as a starter

juice of 2½ lemons
4 salsify (or scorzonera) roots
14 oz / 400 g trimmed purple sprouting broccoli (about 1⅓ lb / 600 g before trimming)
7 tbsp / 100 g cold unsalted butter
2 tbsp baby capers, drained
2 tbsp finely chopped chives
2 tbsp finely chopped flat-leaf parsley
2 tbsp finely chopped tarragon
2 tbsp coarsely chopped dill
salt and freshly ground black pepper

1 Bring a pan of salted water to a boil with 2 tablespoons of the lemon juice. Peel the salsify and cut each one into 3 batons. Add to the boiling water and simmer for 10 minutes, until al dente. Remove from the water with a slotted spoon and allow to cool a little. Cut each baton in half lengthwise and then the same way again.

2 Simmer the broccoli in the same water for 3 minutes, until slightly tenderized, then drain and keep warm. (You can stop at this stage and do the rest just before serving; if you choose to do this, you will need to refresh the broccoli under cold water after draining and then reheat it before serving by quickly tossing it with a little oil in a small pan.)

3 Heat half the butter in a frying pan over medium heat. When it is foaming, add the salsify and fry until golden brown. Season with salt and pepper, then remove from the pan and arrange on serving plates with the broccoli. Give it height by shaping it like a pyramid. Keep in a warm place.

4 To make the caper butter sauce, reheat the frying pan until nearly smoking. Throw in the remaining butter and cook it from gold to a nut brown. Be brave! When you reach the right color, take the pan off the heat and gently pour in the remaining lemon juice. Be careful; it will spit. Throw in the capers and herbs and season well.

5 Immediately pour the caper butter over the arranged vegetables and serve.

You either love it or hate it? Not totally so. This okra dish should convert some stubborn okra haters. Okra can be slimy but here that is minimized by removing the stalks carefully, without exposing the gloopy seeds, and by baking the okra whole rather than stewing it. The gingery sauce is light and clean.

Baked okra with tomato and ginger

serves 2 to 4

1 Preheat the oven to 400°F / 200°C. To prepare the okra, take a small, sharp knife and carefully remove the stalk end. Try not to cut very low; leave the end of the stalk to seal the main body of the fruit, so the seeds are not exposed.
2 Mix the okra with 3 tablespoons of the olive oil and some salt and pepper. Scatter on a baking sheet in a single layer, then place in the oven and bake for 15 to 20 minutes, until just tender.
3 Meanwhile, prepare the sauce. Heat the remaining 2 tablespoons oil in a large saucepan, add the garlic, ginger, and red pepper flakes, and fry for about a minute. Add the tomatoes, sugar, and some salt and pepper and cook, uncovered, over medium heat for 10 minutes, until the mixture thickens slightly.
4 When the okra is ready, stir it gently into the sauce and cook for 2 minutes. To serve warm, spoon the okra onto serving plates and scatter the cilantro on top. If serving at room temperature, adjust the seasoning again before serving and garnish with the cilantro.

1 lb / 500 g okra
5 tbsp olive oil
2 cloves garlic, crushed
1 knob fresh ginger
(scant ½ oz / 12 g),
fincly choppod
¼ tsp red pepper flakes
3 large ripe tomatoes, finely
chopped
2 tsp superfine sugar
1½ tbsp cilantro leaves
salt and freshly ground black
pepper

Butternut squash has softer skin than other winter squashes and is therefore easier to prepare. For us it is almost a staple.

Butternut's mild sweetness and firm flesh make it suitable to go alongside most main courses, but also to serve on its own as a vegetarian centerpiece.

Roasted butternut squash with burnt eggplant and pomegranate molasses

serves 2 to 4

1. Preheat the oven to 425°F / 220°C. Trim the top and bottom off the butternut squash and cut it in half lengthwise. Remove the seeds using a small knife or a spoon. Cut each half into wedges ¾ to 1¼ inches / 2 to 3 cm thick. Arrange the wedges on a baking sheet, standing them up with the skin underneath if possible. Brush with half the olive oil and season generously with salt and pepper. Place in the oven for 25 to 30 minutes, by which time the wedges should be tender and slightly browned. Leave to cool.
2. Reduce the oven temperature to 350°F / 180°C. Scatter the seeds and almonds on a baking sheet and toast for 8 to 10 minutes, until lightly browned. Leave to cool.
3. For the sauce, place the eggplant directly on a medium flame on a gas burner or your stove top (you might want to cover the base of the burner with aluminum foil before you begin ↗ page 27). Burn the eggplant for 12 to 15 minutes, until the skin dries and cracks and smoky aromas are released. Turn it around occasionally, using metal tongs. Remove from the heat and leave to cool slightly. (Alternatively, you can place the eggplant under a very hot broiler for about an hour, turning it around occasionally; continue until well shriveled on the outside, even if it bursts.)
4. Make a long cut through the eggplant. Using a spoon, scoop out the soft flesh while avoiding most of the burnt skin. Drain in a colander for 10 minutes, then transfer to a board and chop coarsely.
5. In a mixing bowl, stir together the eggplant flesh, yogurt, oil, pomegranate molasses, lemon juice, parsley, and garlic. Taste and season with salt and pepper. It should be sweetly sharp and highly flavorful.
6. Arrange the squash wedges on a serving platter, piling them up on top of one another. Drizzle with the remaining olive oil, sprinkle the nuts and seeds over the top, and garnish with the basil. Serve the sauce on the side.

1 large butternut squash
4 tbsp olive oil
1 tbsp pumpkin seeds
1 tbsp sunflower seeds
**1 tbsp black sesame seeds
(if unavailable, use white ones)**
1 tsp nigella seeds
3 tbsp / 10 g sliced almonds
scant ½ cup / 10 g basil leaves
**coarse sea salt and freshly
ground black pepper**

Sauce
1 medium eggplant
**⅔ cup / 150 g Greek yogurt,
at room temperature**
2 tbsp olive oil
1½ tsp pomegranate molasses
↗ page xii
3 tbsp lemon juice
**1 tbsp coarsely chopped
flat-leaf parsley**
1 clove garlic, crushed
**coarse sea salt and freshly
ground black pepper**

Nir Feller, who's got the most infectious zeal for food, helped develop this dish when running our kitchen in Notting Hill. It is ideal for preparing ahead of time. Have it ready in the baking dish and put it in the oven just when you need it. It makes an impressive starter for a cold winter night.

Caramelized endive with serrano ham

serves 6

1   Preheat the oven to 400°F / 200°C. Begin by caramelizing the endives. You will probably have to do it in 2 or 3 batches, depending on the size of your largest frying pan; the endive halves need to fit lying flat without overlapping. If working in 2 batches, put half the butter and half the sugar in the pan and place over high heat. Stir to mix. As soon as the butter starts to bubble, place 6 endive halves cut side down in the pan and fry for 2 to 3 minutes, until golden. You might need to press them down slightly. Don't worry if the butter goes slightly brown. Remove and repeat the process with the remaining butter, sugar, and 6 endive halves.

2   Line a baking sheet with parchment paper, and arrange the endives on it, caramelized side up. Sprinkle with a little salt and pepper.

3   Mix the bread crumbs, Parmesan, thyme, cream, 1/4 teaspoon salt, and a good grind of black pepper. Spoon this mixture over the endives and top each one with a slice of ham. Roast in the oven for 15 to 20 minutes, until the endives feel soft when poked with a knife. Serve hot or warm, drizzled with some olive oil and sprinkled with the chopped parsley, if using.

6 Belgian endives, cut in half lengthwise
3 tbsp / 40 g unsalted butter
4 tsp superfine sugar
1 cup / 50 g fresh sourdough bread crumbs
2½ oz / 70 g Parmesan cheese, freshly grated
2 tbsp thyme leaves
½ cup / 120 ml heavy cream
12 thin slices serrano ham
olive oil for drizzling
2 tsp chopped flat-leaf parsley (optional)
coarse sea salt and freshly ground black pepper

These addictive fritters are Sami's mother's recipe. She used to make them once a week and give them to the kids in a pita to take to school for lunch. They are not dissimilar to Indian *pakoras*. Best eaten hot or warm or taken on a picnic—in a pita, of course, with some hummus and tomato.

Cauliflower and cumin fritters with lime yogurt

1 To make the sauce, put all the sauce ingredients in a bowl and whisk well. Taste—looking for a vibrant, tart, citrusy flavor—and adjust the seasoning. Chill or leave out for up to an hour.
2 To prepare the cauliflower, trim off any leaves and use a small knife to divide the cauliflower into little florets. Add them to a large pan of boiling salted water and simmer for 15 minutes, until very soft. Drain into a colander.
3 While the cauliflower is cooking, put the flour, chopped parsley, garlic, shallots, eggs, spices, salt, and pepper in a bowl and whisk together well to make a batter. When the mixture is smooth and homogenous, add the warm cauliflower. Mix to break down the cauliflower into the batter.
4 Pour the sunflower oil into a wide pan to a depth of ⅔ inch / 1.5 cm and place over high heat. When it is very hot, carefully spoon in generous portions of the cauliflower mixture, 3 tablespoons per fritter. Take care with the hot oil! Space the fritters apart with a fish slicer, making sure they are not overcrowded. Fry in small batches, controlling the oil temperature so the fritters cook but don't burn. They should take 3 to 4 minutes on each side.
5 Remove from the pan and drain well on a few layers of paper towels. Serve with the sauce on the side.

serves 4

Lime sauce
1⅓ cups / 300 g Greek yogurt
2 tbsp finely chopped cilantro
grated zest of 1 lime
2 tbsp lime juice
2 tbsp olive oil
salt and freshly ground black pepper

1 small cauliflower (about 11 oz / 320 g)
scant 1 cup / 120 g all-purpose flour
3 tbsp chopped flat-leaf parsley, plus a few extra leaves for garnish
1 clove garlic, crushed
2 shallots, finely chopped
4 free-range eggs
1½ tsp ground cumin
1 tsp ground cinnamon
½ tsp ground turmeric
1½ tsp salt
1 tsp freshly ground black pepper
2 cups / 500 ml sunflower oil for frying

Like broccoli, cauliflower can be rather dull. So here we give it the classic Ottolenghi treatment of grilling and then drenching with vigorous flavors while still hot. The combination of ingredients in this recipe might sound unusual but it works wonderfully well. Try it with a plain roast chicken.

Grilled cauliflower with tomato, dill, and capers

serves 2 to 4

1 First make the dressing, either by hand or in a food processor. Mix together the capers, mustard, garlic, vinegar, and some salt and pepper. Whisk vigorously or run the machine while adding half the oil in a slow trickle. You should get a thick, creamy dressing. Taste and adjust the seasoning.
2 Add the cauliflower florets to a large pan of boiling salted water and simmer for 3 minutes only. Drain in a colander and run under a cold tap to stop the cooking immediately. Leave in the colander to dry well. Once dry, place in a mixing bowl with the remaining olive oil and some salt and pepper. Toss well.
3 Place a ridged grill pan over the highest possible heat and leave it for 5 minutes, until very hot. Grill the cauliflower in a few batches—make sure the florets are not cramped. Turn them around as they grill, then once nicely charred, transfer to a bowl. While the cauliflower is still hot, add the dressing, dill, spinach, and tomatoes. Stir together well, then taste and adjust the seasoning.
4 Serve warm or at room temperature, adjusting the seasoning again at the last minute.

2 tbsp capers, drained and coarsely chopped
1 tbsp French whole-grain mustard
2 cloves garlic, crushed
2 tbsp cider vinegar
½ cup / 120 ml olive oil
1 small cauliflower, divided into florets
1 tbsp chopped dill
1⅔ cups / 50 g baby spinach leaves
20 cherry tomatoes, halved
coarse sea salt and freshly ground black pepper

Considering the colossal amounts of food coming out of our kitchen in Notting Hill, visitors are always astonished to see how small it is. Sharing such small quarters can lead to extraordinary kinds of personal interaction, with the occasional tense moment between the savory chefs and the pastry department.

On a culinary level, this yields some unusual hybrids. Using the pastry department's crumble mix for this gratin was originally Sami's revenge for some freshly squeezed lemon juice that was "stolen" by a pastry chef to make curd. It turned out that the creamy sweetness of the crumble offsets the dominant savory tones of the fennel and the acidity of the tomato to create a most comforting experience.

You can have this ready well in advance and put it in the oven at the last minute.

Fennel, cherry tomato, and crumble gratin

serves 6 to 8

1 Preheat the oven to 400°F / 200°C. Trim off the fennel stalks and cut each bulb in half lengthwise. Cut each half into slices ⅔ inch / 1.5 cm thick. Place in a large bowl with the olive oil, thyme leaves, garlic, salt, and pepper and toss together. Transfer to an ovenproof dish and pour the cream over the fennel. Mix the crumble with the grated Parmesan and scatter evenly on top.
2 Cover the dish with aluminum foil and bake for 45 minutes. Remove the aluminum foil and arrange the tomatoes on top. You can leave some on the vine and scatter some loose. Scatter a few thyme sprigs on top. Return to the oven and bake for another 15 minutes. By now the fennel should feel soft when poked with a knife and the gratin should have a nice golden color. Remove from the oven and allow to rest for a few minutes. Sprinkle the chopped parsley over and serve hot or warm.

2¼ lb / 1 kg fennel bulbs
3 tbsp olive oil
1 tbsp thyme leaves, plus a few
  whole sprigs
3 cloves garlic, crushed
1 tbsp coarse sea salt
1 tsp freshly ground black
  pepper
scant 1 cup / 200 ml heavy
  cream
⅓ recipe Crumble ↗ page 279
3½ oz / 100 g Parmesan cheese,
  freshly grated
10½ oz / 300 g cherry tomatoes,
  on the vine
1 tsp chopped flat-leaf parsley

Romano (or romero) peppers are vibrant red and have an appealing long, pointy shape. To maintain their shape and visual impact, we roast them briefly and don't peel them. This means you get a bit of skin and seeds on the plate. If you mind this, roast the peppers for another 10 minutes, place in a sealed container until cool, and then peel and remove the seeds. The peppers will disintegrate slightly.

It is vital that you use good-quality buffalo mozzarella for this recipe. Ordinary mozzarella will just get lost with all the intense flavors. Instead of mozzarella you could use feta or small pieces of broken Parmesan. The peppers can be marinated well ahead of time and assembled just before serving.

Marinated romano peppers with buffalo mozzarella

serves 6 as a starter

1 Preheat the oven to 400°F / 200°C. Spread the peppers out on a baking sheet, drizzle with 2 tablespoons of the olive oil, and sprinkle with salt and pepper. Mix well and roast for 12 to 15 minutes, until the peppers become tender and their skin begins to color.
2 Meanwhile, mix together the cilantro, parsley, garlic, vinegar, and 5½ tablespoons / 80 ml of the olive oil. Season liberally and taste to make sure the flavors are robust. Put the warm peppers in a bowl, pour the marinade over them, then cover and leave at room temperature for at least 2 hours.
3 To serve, lay out the peppers and arugula on a serving plate and spoon the marinade over them. Break the mozzarella into large chunks with your hands and dot it over the peppers. Drizzle with the remaining oil and garnish with parsley.

6 romano peppers
½ cup / 120 ml olive oil
2½ tbsp finely chopped cilantro
2½ tbsp finely chopped flat-leaf parsley, plus extra for garnish
1 clove garlic, crushed
3 tbsp cider vinegar
5 cups / 100 g arugula
7 oz / 200 g buffalo mozzarella
coarse sea salt and freshly ground black pepper

This bold treatment for mushrooms, with a sharp intensity of flavor, makes a refreshing starter. Don't necessarily restrict yourself to the types of mushrooms specified. You can mix and match to suit your taste. In any case, provide some substantial chunks of bread to soak up the juices.

Mixed mushrooms with cinnamon and lemon

serves 6 to 8

1 First you will need to pick through the mushrooms, paring away dirt from the feet of the mushrooms and using a stiff pastry brush to clear any dirt from the caps and gills (don't be tempted to clean them in a bucket of water, as they will absorb the water and go soggy).

2 Put a large sauté pan over medium heat and add the olive oil to heat it slightly. Sprinkle in the thyme, garlic, parsley, cinnamon sticks, salt, and pepper. Lay the button, poplar, and shiitake mushrooms on top. Do not stir. Turn the heat up to high and cook for 5 minutes. Only then give the pan a good shake and add the oyster mushrooms. Give a little stir and leave to cook for another 3 minutes. Turn off the heat and add the enoki mushrooms, followed by the lemon juice. Give the pan another good shake around, taste, and add more salt and pepper if necessary. Serve warm or at room temperature.

14 oz / 400 g button mushrooms
14 oz / 400 g black poplar mushrooms
10½ oz / 300 g shiitake mushrooms
14 oz / 400 g oyster mushrooms
7 oz / 200 g enoki mushrooms
⅔ cup / 160 ml olive oil
½ cup / 30 g chopped thyme
10 cloves garlic, crushed
3½ oz / 100 g flat-leaf parsley, chopped
6 cinnamon sticks
1½ tbsp / 25 g coarse sea salt
1 tbsp coarsely ground black pepper
4 tbsp / 60 ml lemon juice

This is another of Scully's creations. The mushrooms are cooked with lots of butter and herbs and then served warm with the most soothing topping. You can prepare the mushrooms and barley ahead of time, then heat them up and add the lemon, feta, and herbs at the last minute.

Try your hand at preserving lemons if you have the patience (⊅ page 273). Otherwise, seek them out at a shop or online site specializing in North African food.

Portobello mushrooms with pearled barley and preserved lemon

serves 6 as a starter

1. First cook the barley. Heat the sunflower oil in a heavy-based saucepan and sauté the onion and garlic until translucent. Add the stock and bring to a boil. Stir in the barley, lower the heat, then cover and simmer for 1 hour, until all the liquid has been absorbed and the barley is tender.

2. Meanwhile, preheat the oven to 350°F / 180°C. Take a large baking sheet and grease it heavily with two-thirds of the butter. Scatter the thyme sprigs over it. Stem the mushrooms and place the mushroom caps, stem side up, on top of the thyme. Pour over the wine and stock and scatter the sliced garlic over. Dot each mushroom with a couple of knobs of the remaining butter, then season with salt and pepper. Cover the pan with aluminum foil and place in the oven for 15 to 20 minutes, until the mushrooms are tender. Leave them in their cooking juices until you are ready to serve.

3. When the barley is done, remove the pan from the heat and stir in the preserved lemon, feta, parsley, and thyme. Taste and add salt and pepper. To serve, reheat the mushrooms in the oven for a few minutes, if necessary. Place each mushroom, stem side up, on a serving plate. Scoop the barley on top and spoon some of the mushroom cooking juices over. Garnish with the basil sprouts and drizzle over the olive oil.

Pearled barley
1 tbsp sunflower oil
1 medium onion, finely chopped
1 clove garlic, finely chopped
3 cups / 750 ml vegetable or chicken stock
heaping ½ cup / 110 g pearled barley
¼ preserved lemon, flesh removed and skin finely chopped
1¾ oz / 50 g feta cheese, crumbled
1 tbsp chopped flat-leaf parsley
2 tsp thyme leaves
2 tbsp purple basil sprouts, radish sprouts, or purple basil leaves, shredded
1 tbsp olive oil
salt and freshly ground black pepper

7 tbsp / 100 g unsalted butter
15 sprigs thyme
6 large portobello mushrooms
¾ cup / 180 ml dry white wine
1 cup / 250 ml vegetable stock
2 cloves garlic, finely sliced
coarse sea salt and freshly ground black pepper

The appeal here is the complementary flavors of earth (artichokes and potatoes) and acid (lemon and tomato), with the dominant background note of the oily black olives. It goes well with most light, simply cooked main courses—fish, meat, or vegetarian—served warm or at room temperature.

Jerusalem artichokes are a bit of a con—neither artichokes nor (unlike us) from Jerusalem. Still, they have a superb deep flavor that spreads throughout a whole dish. Some varieties, the tough-skinned ones resembling fresh ginger, require peeling. Others are fine unpeeled, as long as you slice them thinly.

Roast potatoes and Jerusalem artichokes with lemon and sage

serves 4 to 6

1 Preheat the oven to 400°F / 200°C. Wash the potatoes well, put them in a large saucepan, and cover with plenty of salted water. Bring to a boil and simmer for 20 minutes, until half cooked. Drain, cool slightly, and then cut each potato in half lengthwise. Put them on a large baking sheet.

2 Wash the Jerusalem artichokes, cut them into slices ¼ inch / 5 mm thick, and add to the potatoes. Add the garlic, olive oil, sage, salt, and pepper. Mix everything well with your hands and put in the oven.

3 Meanwhile, thinly slice the lemon and remove the seeds. After the vegetables have been roasting for about 30 minutes, add the sliced lemon, stir with a wooden spoon, and return to the oven for 20 minutes. Now add the cherry tomatoes and olives, stir well again, and cook for a further 15 minutes.

4 Remove from the oven and stir in some of the chopped parsley. Transfer to a serving dish and garnish with the remaining parsley.

1 lb / 500 g new potatoes or other small boiling potatoes
1 lb / 500 g Jerusalem artichokes
4 cloves garlic, crushed
3½ tbsp / 50 ml olive oil
2 tbsp coarsely chopped sage
1 tsp salt
½ tsp freshly ground black pepper
1 lemon
9 oz / 250 g cherry tomatoes
heaping 1 cup / 170 g kalamata olives, pitted
2 tbsp coarsely chopped flat-leaf parsley

Chapter 1   Vegetables, legumes, and grains

Golden beets, popular in Victorian Britain, have recently made a comeback and are now widely available from the early autumn throughout the winter. Here we mix them with the red variety to create a multicolored salad. If you can't get both, use only one type.

Beets go well with most soft herbs and are complemented by subtle young cheeses. Their mild sweetness always benefits from acidity, so try mixing beets with fruits such as apples or citrus.

This salad will keep well in the fridge for two days.

Roasted red and golden beets

serves 4

1. Preheat the oven to 400°F / 200°C. Wash the beets well and wrap them in aluminum foil individually. Bake in the oven for anything from 40 to 90 minutes, depending on their size (baby beets might take even less). Check each one, as cooking times can vary a lot: the beets should be tender when pierced with a sharp knife.
2. Spread the sunflower seeds out in an ovenproof dish and toast in the oven alongside the beets for 8 minutes, just until lightly colored.
3. Once the beets are ready, unwrap them and peel with a small knife while still warm. Cut each into halves, quarters, or ¾- to 1¼-inch / 2- to 3-cm dice. Mix the beets with the rest of the ingredients in a bowl. Toss well and then taste: there should be a clear sweetness balanced by enough salt. Adjust the seasoning if necessary, sprinkle with more chervil, and serve.

1 lb / 500 g golden beets
1 lb / 500 g red beets
scant ⅓ cup / 80 g sunflower seeds
6 tbsp / 90 ml maple syrup
4 tbsp sherry vinegar
4 tbsp olive oil
2 cloves garlic, crushed
1¼ cups / 20 g chervil leaves, plus more for garnish
2 oz / 60 g baby chard leaves, baby spinach, or arugula
coarse sea salt and freshly ground black pepper

Somewhere between a mash and a potato salad, this dish is very satisfying both warm and at room temperature. Adjust the seasoning and the horseradish to suit your taste (recheck once it has cooled down).

Sorrel is not always available. If necessary, substitute arugula, or any soft herb, and a little lemon juice. Horseradish sauce or wasabi paste (beware, it's strong) makes a good alternative to fresh horseradish. Again, taste and judge how much you need.

Crushed new potatoes with horseradish and sorrel

serves 6

1. Wash the potatoes well but don't peel them. Put them in a pan with plenty of salted water, bring to a boil, and simmer for 25 to 30 minutes, until tender. Drain well, transfer to a large mixing bowl, and crush while still hot with a fork or a potato masher. Make sure most of the hard lumps are crushed.
2. In another bowl, mix together the yogurt, olive oil, garlic, horseradish, and salt and pepper to taste. Pour this dressing over the hot potatoes, add the sorrel, and mix well. Taste and adjust the seasoning.
3. Just before serving, garnish with the cress, green onions, and a drizzle of olive oil.

2¼ lb / 1 kg new potatoes
1⅓ cups / 300 g Greek yogurt
7 tbsp / 100 ml olive oil, plus some for drizzling
2 cloves garlic, crushed
scant 1 oz / 25 g fresh horseradish root, grated
4 tbsp coarsely chopped sorrel leaves
½ cup / 25 g garden cress (or another small sprouting leaf)
2 green onions, sliced
coarse sea salt and freshly ground black pepper

This winter dish demonstrates how seasonal roots can be used playfully to create the opposite of the usual weighty casseroles. It is a bit like a rémoulade in its tang, but also has multilayered sweet (dried cherries) and savory (capers) flavors to create a magnificently intense accompaniment to fish or lamb. It also makes a great addition to a vegetarian meze selection. A small amount will go a long way.

Variations on this dish are endless. Try using kohlrabi, beets, turnip, carrot, or cabbage, or a combination of them. Most soft herbs would suit, and don't forget acidity from citrus juice or vinegar to lighten it up.

This particular salad will look more professional if you have a mandoline or a shredding attachment for shredding the celery root and rutabaga. Coarsely grating them is also perfectly fine. The flavors will not be affected.

Sweet-and-sour celery root and rutabaga

serves 4 to 6

1 Place the celery root and rutabaga in a mixing bowl. Add all the rest of the ingredients and use your hands to mix everything together thoroughly. "Massaging" the vegetables a little will help them absorb the flavors. Taste and add salt and pepper to your liking. You might also want to add some extra sugar and vinegar.
2 Allow the salad to sit for an hour so the flavors can evolve. It will keep for up to 2 days in the fridge. For a fresher look, add more herbs just before serving.

9 oz / 250 g celery root, peeled and thinly shredded
9 oz / 250 g rutabaga, peeled and thinly shredded
4 tbsp coarsely chopped flat-leaf parsley
4 tbsp coarsely chopped dill
6 tbsp / 50 g capers, drained and coarsely chopped
4 tbsp lemon juice (about 1 large lemon)
1 tsp cider vinegar
4 tbsp olive oil
4 tbsp sunflower oil
1 tbsp Dijon mustard
2 cloves garlic, crushed
2 tsp superfine sugar
2/3 cup / 100 g dried sour cherries
salt and freshly ground black pepper

The slightly burnt onion and sweet, creamy mash create an appealing mixture of textures and soothing flavors. You could substitute turnip, celery root, potato, carrot, or sweet potato for the parsnip or pumpkin. Just keep the colors in mind.

Parsnip and pumpkin mash

serves 4 to 6

1 Preheat the oven to 400°F / 200°C. Toss the pumpkin or squash with the olive oil and a little salt and pepper and spread out on a baking sheet. Roast for 30 to 45 minutes, until soft and mashable. Once out of the oven, keep somewhere warm. Meanwhile, using a good serrated knife, cut about ⅜ inch / 1 cm off the top of the garlic head and place the bottom part in the oven next to the roasting pumpkin. Bake it for approximately 30 minutes, until the cloves are completely tender.

2 While the pumpkin is roasting, cook the parsnips in boiling salted water for 30 minutes, until they are completely soft. Drain and keep warm. Pour the sunflower oil into a medium saucepan, heat well, and fry the onion rings in it in 2 or 3 batches. They should turn brown, almost burned. Transfer to a colander and sprinkle with salt.

3 Take a large bowl that can accommodate the whole mixture. Hold the bottom of the head of garlic and gently press upward to release the cooked flesh into the bowl. Add the butter, nutmeg, some seasoning, and then the parsnips. Crush well, using a potato masher. Add the cooked pumpkin and mash very lightly (use a fork). Don't overmix; the mash should remain chunky and the pumpkin and parsnip distinct.

4 Gently fold in the crème fraîche and chives to form a ripple in the mash. Spoon a mound onto each serving plate, garnish with the fried onions and a drizzle of olive oil, and serve at once.

1⅓ lb / 600 g (peeled weight) pumpkin or butternut squash, cut into ¾- to 1¼-inch / 2- to 3-cm dice
3 tbsp olive oil, plus extra for drizzling
1 head garlic
5 medium parsnips, peeled and cut into large chunks
scant 1 cup / 200 ml sunflower oil
2 onions, sliced into rings
5½ tbsp / 80 g unsalted butter
1 tsp ground nutmeg
1⅓ cups / 300 g crème fraîche, at room temperature
½ oz / 15 g chives, coarsely chopped
salt and freshly ground black pepper

This recipe is the exact opposite of what's typically associated with its name: crunchy carrots, fresh peas, and lots of robust flavors of sweet and spice. It's excellent served hot for Christmas dinner (omitting the pea shoots), or as a light spring salad.

Carrot and peas

serves 6

1 Start by making the sweet sauce for roasting the carrots. Pour the orange juice, wine, and honey into a saucepan, add the cinnamon and star anise, and bring to a simmer. Cook gently, uncovered, for 20 to 40 minutes (depending on the size of your pan and the heat level), until reduced to about one-third. Set aside.

2 Preheat the oven to 450°F / 230°C. Heat a small frying pan, add the coriander seeds, and dry toast them over high heat for about 3 minutes. Put the seeds in a bowl and mix with the carrots, olive oil, garlic, and some salt and pepper. Spread the mixture out on a large baking sheet and put in the oven. After about 15 minutes (the carrots should have taken on some serious color by now), remove the pan carefully, add the sweet sauce (including the cinnamon and star anise), stir well, and return to the oven for about 7 minutes, until the carrots are cooked through but still have a bit of bite. Remove from the oven and let cool.

3 Throw the peas into a pot containing plenty of boiling salted water and simmer for a minute. Drain at once into a colander, run under a cold tap to stop the cooking, and then leave to drain thoroughly.

4 Before serving, gently stir together the carrots and peas. Taste and add more salt and pepper if you like. Dot with the pea shoots as you pile the vegetables onto a serving plate.

½ cup plus 1 tbsp / 130 ml orange juice
4 tbsp / 60 ml red wine
scant 2½ tbsp / 50 g honey
2 cinnamon sticks
4 star anise
1½ tbsp coriander seeds
2¼ lb / 1 kg carrots, peeled and cut at an angle into slices ⅜ inch / 1 cm thick
6 tbsp / 90 ml olive oil
3 cloves garlic, crushed
3 cups / 450 g shelled peas, fresh or frozen
2½ oz / 75 g pea shoots (use mâche, if unavailable)
salt and freshly ground black pepper

You might think this recipe doesn't sound right. It didn't sound quite right to us either when we came across it on the highly useful recipe site www.epicurious.com. The idea of adding maple syrup and golden raisins to an (already) sweet potato and then mixing in lots of herbs and spices just couldn't be right . . . unless you are an American. But we were somehow tempted to try it and it did work, creating a vivid and intense mix of tastes and textures.

This version boasts additional old favorites of ours: chile and cilantro. Try it as a side dish at your Christmas table or as an original picnic salad.

Roasted sweet potato with pecan and maple

serves 4

1 Preheat the oven to 375°F / 190°C. Start with the sweet potatoes. Don't peel them! Cut them into ¾-inch / 2-cm cubes, spread them out on a baking sheet, and drizzle with the olive oil. Sprinkle with some salt and pepper, mix well with your hands, and then roast in the oven for about 30 minutes, until just tender. Turn them over gently halfway through cooking.

2 On a separate baking sheet, toast the pecans for 5 minutes. Remove from the oven and chop coarsely.

3 To make the dressing, whisk together all the ingredients in a small bowl with some salt and pepper. Taste and adjust the seasoning, if necessary.

4 When the potatoes are ready, transfer them to a large bowl while still hot. Add the green onions, parsley, cilantro, pepper flakes, pecans, and raisins. Pour the dressing over and toss gently to blend, then season to taste. Serve at once or at room temperature.

2 sweet potatoes (about scant 2 lb / 850 g in total)
3 tbsp olive oil
4 tbsp / 35 g pecans
4 green onions, coarsely chopped
4 tbsp coarsely chopped flat-leaf parsley
2 tbsp coarsely chopped cilantro
¼ tsp red pepper flakes
4 tbsp / 35 g golden raisins
salt and freshly ground black pepper

Dressing
4 tbsp olive oil
2 tbsp maple syrup
1 tbsp sherry vinegar
1 tbsp lemon juice
2 tbsp orange juice
2 tsp grated fresh ginger
½ tsp ground cinnamon
salt and freshly ground black pepper

This comforting dish was created by Danielle Postma, who is now back home in South Africa running her own blossoming food business, Moema's. We would have loved to take some credit for Danielle's success, but she actually had it all before coming to Ottolenghi. Danielle's big personality and warmth make everybody fall in love with her in an instant. She has a natural gift for presentation and, like herself, her food constantly smiles.

This dish is simple but effective due to the way the potatoes are arranged in the baking dish. You can prepare everything a day in advance and have it ready in the fridge to just pop in the oven. The sage can be replaced with thyme, or you could use both. Make sure you choose orange-fleshed sweet potatoes (as opposed to the paler variety).

Danielle's sweet potato gratin

serves 4 to 6

1 Preheat the oven to 400°F / 200°C. Wash the sweet potatoes (do not peel them) and cut them into disks ¼ inch / 5 mm thick. A mandoline is best for this job but you could use a sharp knife.

2 In a bowl, mix together the sweet potatoes, sage, garlic, salt, and pepper. Arrange the slices of sweet potato in a deep, medium-size ovenproof dish by taking tight packs of them and standing them up next to one another. They should fit together quite tightly so you get parallel lines of sweet potato slices (skins showing) along the length or width of the dish. Throw any remaining bits of garlic or sage from the bowl over the potatoes. Cover the dish with aluminum foil, place in the oven, and roast for 45 minutes. Remove the aluminum foil and pour the cream evenly over the potatoes. Roast, uncovered, for a further 25 minutes. The cream should have thickened by now. Stick a sharp knife in different places in the dish to make sure the potatoes are cooked. They should be totally soft.

3 Serve immediately, garnished with sage, or leave to cool down. In any case, bringing the potatoes to the table in the baking dish, after scraping the outside clean, will make a strong impact.

**6 medium sweet potatoes
(about 3¼ lb / 1.5 kg in total)**
**5 tbsp coarsely chopped sage,
plus extra for garnish**
6 cloves garlic, crushed
2 tsp coarse sea salt
½ tsp freshly ground black pepper
1 cup / 250 ml heavy cream

A colorful salad, both in appearance and in flavor. It is well worth planning ahead and soaking the butterbeans overnight. Freshly cooked, they have a silky, rich texture, just as the name implies. Serve at a weekend brunch, with grilled lamb for example.

Lima beans with sweet chile sauce and fresh herbs

serves 6

1 Put the lima beans in a large bowl and fill with enough water to cover them by twice their volume. Leave to soak overnight at room temperature.

2 The next day, drain the beans and place in a large saucepan. Cover with plenty of cold water and bring to a simmer. Cook for 35 to 55 minutes, skimming froth from the surface and topping up with boiling water if necessary, until tender. The cooking time will vary according to the bean size and freshness, so try them a few times during cooking to make sure they don't turn to a mush. In case they begin to overcook, remove from the heat and add plenty of cold water to the pan to stop the cooking. When they are done, drain in a colander and set aside.

3 While the beans are cooking, make the sauce. Place the crushed garlic in a bowl large enough to hold the beans. Add the sweet chile sauce, sesame oil, soy sauce, and lemon juice and mix well with a small whisk. Add the red peppers, season the mixture with salt and pepper, and set aside.

4 Once the beans have cooled down slightly but are still warm, add them to the sauce, together with the green onions, herbs, and plenty of seasoning. Mix gently with your hands. Taste and adjust the seasoning. Eat warm or cold—just remember to readjust the seasoning before serving.

14 oz / 400 g dried lima beans
6 cloves garlic, crushed
4½ tbsp / 70 ml sweet chile sauce
2 tbsp sesame oil
3 tbsp soy sauce
3 tbsp lemon juice
2 red peppers, halved, seeded, and cut into ¾-inch / 2-cm squares
4 green onions, white and green parts, chopped
2 cups / 35 g cilantro, chopped
scant 6 tbsp / 30 g mint leaves, chopped
coarse sea salt and freshly ground black pepper

Don't be put off by the health-food-store connotations wheat berries may have. This is a highly refreshing salad. Its biting astringency and light sweetness make it a perfect companion to plainly grilled meat or fish. On its own, it makes a modest vegetarian main course.

Wheat berries need soaking for a good 14 to 18 hours. If you didn't plan ahead, substitute pearled barley for the wheat berries, following the cooking instructions on the packet. Thanks to Helen for the inspiration.

Wheat berries and mushrooms with celery and shallots

serves 4

1 Wash the wheat berries in plenty of cold water, then transfer to a large bowl and cover with fresh water. Leave to soak overnight.
2 The next day, drain the wheat berries, put them in a large pan with plenty of fresh water to cover, and simmer for 45 to 60 minutes. They should have now softened up but still have a bite. Drain in a colander and leave to cool.
3 You need to make the dressing at least an hour before serving the salad. Whisk together the sugar and vinegar until the sugar has completely dissolved. Add the shallots and celery and leave to marinate.
4 To assemble the salad, put the mushrooms in a mixing bowl and toss with the dressing. Add the wheat berries and then tear in the parsley leaves. Add the whole tarragon leaves, plus the olive oil and some salt and pepper. Taste, adjust the seasoning accordingly, and serve.

2 cups / 200 g wheat berries
3 tbsp light brown sugar
3½ tbsp / 50 ml good-quality sherry vinegar
2 or 3 shallots, finely chopped
3 celery stalks, finely chopped
7 oz / 200 g button mushrooms, sliced ¼ inch / 5 mm thick
⅔ cup / 40 g flat-leaf parsley leaves
¾ cup / 10 g tarragon leaves
3½ tbsp / 50 ml olive oil
coarse sea salt and freshly ground black pepper

Camargue red rice and quinoa with orange and pistachios (↗ page 76)

Chapter 1   Vegetables, legumes, and grains

Couscous and mograbiah with oven-dried tomatoes (↗ page 77)

Tricia Jadoonanan, for a long period the head chef at our Islington branch, brought Camargue red rice to Ottolenghi and does wonders with it, including this recipe. This French rice has an outstanding nutty flavor, a good dry consistency, and a color much more appealing than other whole-grain varieties.

Quinoa, a native of South America, has a satisfying "bouncy" texture and is probably one of the healthiest foodstuffs available. It has more protein than any other grain and the perfect set of amino acids (not that this would make us eat it if it didn't taste great).

Camargue red rice and quinoa with orange and pistachios

serves 4

1 Preheat the oven to 325°F / 170°C. Spread the pistachios out on a baking sheet and toast for 8 minutes, until lightly colored. Remove from the oven, allow to cool slightly, and then chop coarsely. Set aside.
2 Fill 2 saucepans with salted water and bring to a boil. Simmer the quinoa in one for 12 to 14 minutes and the rice in the other for 20 minutes. Both should be tender but still have a bite. Drain in a sieve and spread out the 2 grains separately on flat trays to hasten the cooling.
3 While the grains are cooking, sauté the white onion in 4 tablespoons of the olive oil, stirring occasionally, for 10 to 12 minutes, until golden brown. Leave to cool completely.
4 In a large mixing bowl, combine the rice, quinoa, cooked onion, and the remaining oil. Add all the rest of the ingredients, then taste and adjust the seasoning. Serve at room temperature.

⅓ cup / 60 g shelled pistachio nuts
1 heaping cup / 200 g quinoa
1 cup / 200 g Camargue red rice
1 medium onion, sliced
⅔ cup / 150 ml olive oil
grated zest and juice of 1 orange
2 tsp lemon juice
1 clove garlic, crushed
4 green onions, thinly sliced
¾ cup / 100 g dried apricots, coarsely chopped
2 cups / 40 g arugula
salt and freshly ground black pepper

Mograbiah, a large variety of couscous made from semolina, is common throughout the Arab world. It is also known as pearl or giant couscous and, in North Africa, as *berkukis.* It is more difficult to find than ordinary couscous. We buy it from Green Valley, the luscious Middle Eastern supermarket just off London's Edgware Road. If you can't get hold of it, try to find the Sardinian equivalent, *fregola,* which is stocked by some Italian delis. If all this leads you nowhere, use couscous only (increasing the quantity below up to 1 pound / 500 g). You will lose out a little on the interesting combination of textures but still enjoy the explosive mix of flavors.

The dried tomatoes are a great pantry ingredient. Keep them immersed in oil if you want them to last a long time. The caramelized onion is also handy to have in the fridge. It will keep there for at least five days and makes a great addition to omelets, quiches, bruschetta, pasta—anything, really.

Couscous and mograbiah with oven-dried tomatoes

serves 6 to 8

1 Preheat the oven to 300°F / 150°C. Arrange the tomato halves, skin side down, on a baking sheet and sprinkle with the sugar, 2 tablespoons of the olive oil, the balsamic vinegar, and some salt and pepper. Place in the oven and bake for 2 hours, until the tomatoes have lost most of their moisture.

2 Meanwhile, put the onions in a large pan with 4 tablespoons of the olive oil and sauté over high heat for 10 to 12 minutes, stirring occasionally, until they are a dark golden color.

3 Throw the mograbiah into a large pan of boiling salted water (as for cooking pasta). Simmer for 15 minutes, until it is soft but still retains a bite; some varieties might take less time, so check the instructions on the packet. Drain well and rinse under cold water.

4 In a separate pot, bring the stock to a boil with the saffron and a little salt. Place the couscous in a large bowl and add 3 tablespoons of the olive oil and the boiling stock. Cover with plastic wrap and leave for 10 minutes.

5 Once ready, mix the couscous with a fork or a whisk to get rid of any lumps and to fluff it up. Add the cooked mograbiah, the tomatoes and their juices, the onions and their oil, the tarragon, and half the nigella seeds. Taste and adjust the seasoning and oil. It is likely that it will need a fair amount of salt. Allow the dish to come to room temperature. To serve, arrange it gently on a serving plate, place the labneh on top (in balls or spoonfuls), drizzle with the remaining oil, and finish with the rest of the nigella seeds.

16 large, ripe plum tomatoes, cut in half lengthwise
2 tbsp muscovado sugar
⅔ cup / 150 ml olive oil
2 tbsp balsamic vinegar
2 onions, thinly sliced
1½ cups / 250 g mograbiah
1⅔ cups / 400 ml chicken or vegetable stock
a pinch of saffron threads
1½ cups / 250 g couscous
1 tbsp tarragon leaves
1 tbsp nigella seeds
3½ oz / 100 g Labneh ↗ page 272
coarse sea salt and freshly ground black pepper

Adding lots of "wet" elements, as we do here, prevents cold couscous from turning into a dry mouthful. You can keep on piling on the herbs (chervil, cilantro, chives—they all work); the more the merrier.

Couscous with dried apricots and butternut squash

serves 4

1 Preheat the oven to 350°F / 180°C. Place the onion in a large frying pan with 2 tablespoons of the oil and a pinch of salt. Sauté over high heat, stirring frequently, for about 10 minutes, until golden brown. Set aside.

2 Meanwhile, pour enough hot water from the tap over the apricots just to cover them. Soak for 5 minutes, then drain and cut into ¼-inch / 5-mm dice.

3 Mix the diced squash with 1 tablespoon of the olive oil and some salt and pepper. Spread the squash out on a baking sheet, place in the oven, and bake for about 25 minutes, until lightly colored and quite soft.

4 While waiting for the butternut squash, cook the couscous. Bring the stock to a boil with the saffron. Place the couscous in a large heatproof bowl and pour the boiling stock over it, plus the remaining 3 tablespoons olive oil. Cover with plastic wrap and leave for about 10 minutes; all the liquid should have been absorbed.

5 Use a fork or a whisk to fluff up the couscous, then add the onion, butternut squash, apricots, herbs, cinnamon, and lemon zest. Mix well with your hands, trying not mash the butternut squash. Taste and add salt and pepper if necessary. Serve warmish or cold.

1 large onion, thinly sliced
6 tbsp olive oil
scant ½ cup / 50 g dried apricots
1 small butternut squash (about 1 lb / 450 g), peeled, seeded, and cut into ¾-inch / 2-cm dice
1½ cups / 250 g couscous
1⅔ cups / 400 ml chicken or vegetable stock
pinch of saffron threads
3 tbsp coarsely chopped tarragon
3 tbsp coarsely chopped mint
3 tbsp coarsely chopped flat-leaf parsley
1½ tsp ground cinnamon
grated zest of ½ lemon
coarse sea salt and freshly ground black pepper

Sweet, sour, and musky-salty, this dish has many contrasting flavors, yet it still ends up harmoniously synchronized—the sweet and acid hitting first, followed by a mellowing savory taste. It makes a heady starter.

Puy lentils with sour cherries, bacon, and Gorgonzola

serves 2 to 4 as a starter

1   Wash the lentils under cold running water and then drain. Transfer to a saucepan and add enough water to cover them by 3 times their height. Add the bay leaves, bring to a boil, and then simmer for about 20 minutes, until the lentils are al dente.

2   Meanwhile, make the sauce. Place the shallots in a pan with 2 tablespoons of the olive oil and sauté over medium heat for about 10 minutes, until golden. Add the water, sugar, cherries, and vinegar and continue simmering over low heat for 8 to 10 minutes, until you get a thick sauce. Taste and season with salt and pepper.

3   Drain the lentils well and immediately add them to the sauce so they can soak up all the flavors. Stir together, taste, and adjust the salt again. It will need quite a lot, but remember you are adding bacon and Gorgonzola later, which are salty. Set aside to cool down.

4   Heat the remaining 1 tablespoon olive oil in a saucepan and fry the bacon in it for 3 minutes on each side, until it turns quite crisp. Transfer to a paper towel to cool. Tear the bacon into large pieces and add to the lentils, then add the spinach and stir well. Taste and see if the salad needs any more oil, salt, or pepper.

5   Transfer to serving plates and dot with broken chunks of Gorgonzola.

⅔ cup / 125 g Puy lentils
2 bay leaves
2 or 3 shallots, finely chopped
3 tbsp olive oil
3 tbsp water
1 tsp superfine sugar
scant ½ cup / 60 g dried sour cherries
4½ tbsp / 70 ml red wine vinegar
8 slices bacon
scant 3 cups / 80 g baby spinach
4 oz / 120 g creamy Gorgonzola cheese
salt and freshly ground black pepper

Don't be put off by what may seem like a carbohydrate overkill. The soft, warm sweet potato almost melts over the chickpeas, while the yogurt sauce lightens them with its velvety smoothness. The result is an extremely satisfying vegetarian main course.

In her book, *Amaretto, Apple Cake and Artichokes* (Vintage, 2006), Anna Del Conte suggests adding a paste of baking soda, flour, and salt to chickpeas when soaking them, in order to soften very hard skins. (We can't recommend this book enough for the most thorough introduction to Italian ingredients and methods.) In most cases, baking soda alone does the trick. No matter what you do, you will need to soak chickpeas for at least 12 hours and up to 24 before cooking them.

Chickpeas and spinach with honeyed sweet potato

1 Start the night before by putting the chickpeas in a large bowl. Fill with enough cold water to cover the chickpeas by twice their height. Add the baking soda and leave to soak overnight at room temperature.

2 The next day, drain and rinse the chickpeas, place them in a large saucepan, and cover with plenty of fresh water. Bring to a boil, then lower the heat and simmer for 1 to 1½ hours (they could take much longer in extreme cases). They should be totally tender but retain their shape. Occasionally you will need to skim the froth off the surface. You might also need to top up the pan with boiling water so the chickpeas remain submerged. When they are ready, drain them in a colander and set aside.

3 To make the sweet potatoes, put the sweet potatoes in a wide saucepan with the water, butter, honey, and salt. Bring to a boil, then lower the heat and simmer for 35 to 40 minutes, until the potatoes are tender and most of the liquid has been absorbed. Turn them over halfway through the cooking to color evenly. Remove from the heat and keep warm.

4 While the sweet potatoes are cooking, prepare the sauce for the chickpeas. Heat the olive oil in a large frying pan and add the onion, cumin seeds, and coriander seeds. Fry for 8 minutes, while stirring, until golden brown. Add the tomato paste, cook for a minute while you stir, and then add the tomatoes, sugar, and ground cumin. Continue cooking for about 5 minutes over medium heat. Taste and season with salt and pepper.

5 Stir the spinach into the tomato sauce, then add the cooked chickpeas. Mix together and cook for another 5 minutes. Taste again and adjust the seasoning.

6 To make the yogurt sauce, whisk together all the ingredients. Season with salt and pepper to taste.

7 To serve, spoon the warm chickpeas into a serving dish, arrange the sweet potato slices on top, and garnish with the cilantro leaves. Spoon the yogurt sauce on top or serve on the side.

serves 6 to 8

1 cup / 200 g dried chickpeas
1 tsp baking soda
2 tbsp olive oil
1 onion, finely chopped
1 tsp cumin seeds
1 tsp coriander seeds
1 tbsp tomato paste
14 oz / 400 g canned tomatoes, chopped
1 tsp superfine sugar
1½ tsp ground cumin
3 cups / 100 g baby spinach leaves
⅔ cup / 10 g cilantro leaves, for garnish
salt and freshly ground black pepper

Honeyed sweet potato
1 lb / 500 g sweet potatoes, peeled and cut into slices 1 inch / 2.5 cm thick
scant 3 cups / 700 ml water
3½ tbsp / 50 g unsalted butter
4 tbsp honey
½ tsp salt

Yogurt sauce
scant ½ cup / 100 g Greek yogurt
1 clove garlic, crushed
grated zest and juice of 1 lemon
3 tbsp olive oil
1 tsp dried mint
salt and freshly ground black pepper

This lentil and rice dish is one of the most popular in Egypt, sold hot by street vendors and specialty restaurants. It is not too far removed from the Indian *kitchari,* ancestor to the British *kedgeree.* In Egypt it is usually served with a spicy tomato sauce, but it's also delicious with a cucumber, tomato, and yogurt salad.

Kosheri

serves 4

1 To make the sauce, heat the olive oil in a saucepan, add the garlic and chiles, and fry for 2 minutes. Add the chopped tomatoes, water, vinegar, salt, and cumin. Bring to a boil, then lower the heat and simmer for 20 minutes, until slightly thickened. Remove the sauce from the heat, stir in the cilantro, and then taste. See if you want to add any salt, pepper, or extra cilantro. Keep hot or leave to cool; both ways will work with the hot kosheri. Just remember to adjust the seasoning again when cold.

2 Place the lentils in a large sieve and wash them under a cold running tap. Transfer to a large saucepan, cover with plenty of cold water, and bring to a boil. Lower the heat and simmer for 25 minutes. The lentils should be tender but far from mushy. Drain in a colander and set aside.

3 In a large bowl, cover the rice with cold water, wash, and then drain well. Melt the butter in a large saucepan over medium heat. Add the raw vermicelli, stir, and continue frying and stirring until the vermicelli turns golden brown. Add the drained rice and mix well until it is coated in the butter. Now add the stock, nutmeg, cinnamon, salt, and pepper. Bring to a boil, cover, and then lower the heat to a minimum and simmer for 12 minutes. Turn off the heat, remove the lid, cover the pan with a clean kitchen towel, and put the lid back on. Leave like that for about 5 minutes; this helps make the rice light and fluffy.

4 Heat the olive oil in a large frying pan, add the onions, and sauté over medium heat for about 20 minutes, until dark brown. Transfer to paper towels to drain.

5 To serve, lightly break up the rice with a fork and then add the lentils and most of the onions, reserving a few for garnish. Taste for seasoning and adjust accordingly. Pile the rice high on a serving platter and top with the remaining onions. Serve hot, with the tomato sauce.

Spicy tomato sauce
4 tbsp olive oil
2 cloves garlic, crushed
2 hot red chiles, seeded and finely diced
8 ripe tomatoes, chopped (canned are fine)
1½ cups / 370 ml water
4 tbsp cider vinegar
1 tbsp salt
2 tsp ground cumin
⅔ oz / 20 g cilantro leaves, chopped
salt and freshly ground black pepper

1½ cups / 300 g green lentils
1 cup / 200 g basmati rice
3 tbsp / 40 g unsalted butter
1¾ oz / 50 g vermicelli noodles, broken into 1½-inch / 4-cm pieces
1⅔ cups / 400 ml chicken stock or water
½ tsp grated nutmeg
1½ tsp ground cinnamon
1½ tsp salt
½ tsp freshly ground black pepper
4 tbsp olive oil
2 white onions, halved and thinly sliced

Stuffing vegetables is a rare culinary experience in these busy days. It is time-consuming and provides pleasure that we don't often experience anymore—the kind of bliss that results from communal cooking, when time is not an object and the purpose is the process as well as the end result.

Luckily, we were fortunate enough to experience this when Tamara Meitlis, mother of our designer-partner Alex, visited us recently and taught us some old secrets of Turkish cookery . . . and patience. This is one of them.

These grape leaves are so delicious that you might want to double the recipe.

Tamara's stuffed grape leaves

makes about 20 small rolls

1 To make the filling, heat the olive oil in a medium saucepan, add the onion, and sauté over medium heat for 8 minutes, until softened but not colored. Add the rice and cook for 2 minutes, stirring to coat it in the oil. Add all the remaining filling ingredients and cook over medium heat for 10 minutes, stirring from time to time (the mixture should be sweet and sour, the rice still hard). Remove from the heat and leave to cool.

2 Pour boiling water over the grape leaves and leave to soak for 10 minutes. Remove the leaves from the water and pat dry. Using a pair of kitchen scissors, cut the stalks from the leaves. Put any torn or unusable leaves in the bottom of a heavy-bottomed medium saucepan, making sure it is covered with a layer of leaves 1/8 to 1/4 inch / 3 to 5 mm thick. This will prevent the stuffed leaves from burning later.

3 To fill and roll the grape leaves, choose medium leaves, about 5½ inches / 14 cm wide (you can cut them to this size with scissors, if necessary). If possible, use fine, pale leaves, not dark, thick ones. Place a leaf on a work surface, the beautiful veiny side down, and spoon about ¾ teaspoon of the filling onto the center bottom of the leaf, steering clear of the edges. Take the two sides and fold them tightly over the rice. Now roll neatly toward the top of the leaf, ending with a tight, short cigar. They should be small—roughly 1¼ by ⅜ inch / 3 by 1 cm.

4 Repeat with all the leaves and arrange inside the lined saucepan in neat layers. They should fit quite tightly. Pour in enough water just to cover, then add the olive oil, lemon juice, and salt. Place a small plate or saucer on top to prevent the leaves from moving during cooking. Bring to a gentle boil, cover, and cook on the lowest possible heat for 50 to 60 minutes, until the leaves are tender and almost no cooking liquid is left. You may need to add a little more boiling water during cooking.

5 Transfer the stuffed grape leaves to a serving platter and set aside to cool. Serve cold, with the yogurt, if you like.

Filling
1 tbsp olive oil
1 onion, finely chopped
½ cup / 110 g short-grain rice
1½ tbsp lemon juice
2½ tbsp dried currants
2 tbsp pine nuts
2 tbsp chopped flat-leaf parsley
½ tsp ground allspice
¼ tsp ground cinnamon
¼ tsp ground cloves
½ tsp dried mint
½ tsp salt
**a generous grinding
of black pepper**

**20 to 25 pickled grape leaves,
plus extra for lining the pan**
1½ tsp olive oil
1 tbsp lemon juice
¼ tsp salt
**⅔ cup / 150 g full-fat yogurt or
goat's milk yogurt (optional)**

We love chard and hope more people will learn to enjoy its earthy, lemony flavor, which surpasses that of spinach. Here it is mixed with lentils and spices to create a highly aromatic soup that will instantly win you many admirers. The lemon at the end is essential.

Red lentil and chard soup

serves 6

1 Wash the lentils in plenty of cold water. Place in a large saucepan with the water, bring to a boil, and simmer for 35 minutes, until soft. Skim off any scum that rises to the surface during cooking.
2 Using a slotted spoon, remove about half the lentils from the cooking liquid and set aside in a bowl. Add a generous pinch of salt to the lentils and water in the pan and process with an immersion blender (or in a food processor). Return the reserved lentils to the soup.
3 Now comes the arduous chopping part of the recipe. Peel the red onions, halve, and thinly slice them. Place a frying pan over medium heat, add the olive oil and onions, and cook, stirring occasionally, for 4 to 5 minutes, until the onions soften and become translucent. Meanwhile, remove and discard the large stems from the Swiss chard. Wash and rinse the leaves thoroughly, then chop them coarsely. Do the same with the cilantro, leaving a few whole leaves for garnish later, and that's all the chopping done.
4 Mix the cooked onions, chard leaves, and chopped cilantro into the lentil soup and season with the cumin, cinnamon, and some salt and pepper to taste. Reheat the soup and simmer gently for 5 minutes.
5 With a mortar and pestle, or using the flat blade of a large knife, crush the cilantro seeds and garlic together. Melt the butter gently in a small saucepan over medium heat, add the garlic and coriander seeds, and fry for 2 minutes, until the garlic starts to color slightly. Stir this into the soup, remove the pot from the stove, and cover with a lid. Leave the soup to infuse for 5 minutes before serving.
6 Serve garnished with lemon zest and cilantro leaves and pass around some sourdough bread and lemon wedges. Make sure everybody squeezes the lemon into their soup.

2½ cups / 500 g split red lentils
2½ quarts / 2.5 liters cold water
2 medium red onions
2 tbsp olive oil
7 oz / 200 g Swiss chard
3 cups / 50 g cilantro leaves
2 tsp ground cumin
1 tsp ground cinnamon
1 tbsp cilantro seeds
3 cloves garlic, crushed
3½ tbsp / 50 g unsalted butter
grated zest of ½ lemon
sourdough bread
4 lemons, cut into wedges
salt and freshly ground black pepper

Creamy, lemony, and comforting, this is something you can easily get hooked on. The recipe is based, again, on burning an eggplant to get a deep, smoky flavor (↗ Burnt eggplant with yellow pepper and red onion, page 27), which enhances and yet balances the sharper notes.

Grilled eggplant and lemon soup

serves 4 to 6

3 large eggplants
   (about 3 lb / 1.4 kg in total)
½ cup / 120 ml sunflower oil
4½ cups / 1 liter chicken
   or vegetable stock
2 tbsp lemon juice
4½ tbsp / 70 ml heavy cream
10 basil leaves
salt and freshly ground black
   pepper

1   First you need to grill 2 of the eggplants to impart the smoky flavor necessary for this soup. If you have a gas stove, cover your stove top with aluminum foil and place the whole eggplants directly on 2 separate open flames. Using a pair of metal tongs, turn the eggplants regularly until the skin becomes crisp and the eggplants are very soft—about 15 minutes. Remove to a bowl and leave to cool. (If you don't have a gas stove, place the eggplants under a hot broiler for roughly an hour, turning them occasionally. Don't worry if they burst slightly during the cooking.)
2   Cut the remaining eggplant into ¾-inch / 2-cm cubes. Put a large frying pan over medium heat and pour in half the oil. When it is hot, add half the eggplant cubes and fry, turning with a wooden spoon, until brown on all sides. Drain on paper towels and sprinkle with a little salt. Repeat the process with the rest of the eggplant cubes and the remaining oil.
3   When the grilled eggplants have cooled down a little, make an incision along each one and spoon out the cooked flesh, avoiding any black bits of skin. Chop the flesh coarsely with a large knife and place in a saucepan with the stock, lemon juice, 1½ teaspoons of salt, and 1 teaspoon of pepper. Bring to a boil, then lower the heat and simmer for 30 minutes. Add the fried eggplant cubes and cook for a further 5 minutes. Taste the soup and adjust the seasoning if needed.
4   To serve, mix the cream into the hot soup and ladle into warmed bowls. Tear the basil leaves and scatter them on top.

Clockwise from top left corner: Grilled eggplant and lemon soup (↗ page 91), Chilled red pepper soup with sour cream (↗ page 94), Jerusalem artichoke and arugula soup (↗ page 94), Harira (↗ page 95), Red lentil and chard soup (↗ page 90)

The yogurt gives this soup a light freshness. Adding it to the cooked soup requires tempering (which sounds much more complicated than it actually is) to prevent it from splitting. Make sure that once the yogurt is added, you don't bring the soup to a rapid boil.

Jerusalem artichoke and arugula soup

serves 4

1 Peel the artichokes with a potato peeler, wash them thoroughly, and cut into ⅜-inch / 1-cm dice, not too perfect. Put them in a large saucepan with the arugula, stock, garlic, and a couple of pinches of salt. Bring to a boil and then simmer lightly for 25 minutes, until the artichokes are tender; insert a small knife in one to make sure they are totally soft.
2 While the soup is cooking, cut the green onions in half lengthwise and then cut across these lengths into small dice. Set aside. Break the egg into a large mixing bowl and whisk well with the yogurt.
3 When you are ready to serve the soup, reheat it to the boiling point. Take a ladleful of hot soup and whisk it into the yogurt mix, stirring constantly. Repeat a few times, using about half the soup. You need to bring up the temperature of the yogurt. Now pour the warm yogurt into the soup pan, whisking constantly. Bring back to a very(!) gentle boil and leave there for a minute or two.
4 Taste the soup and season with plenty of salt and pepper. Stir in the green onions and serve garnished with arugula.

14 oz / 400 g Jerusalem artichokes
2¼ cups / 45 g arugula, coarsely chopped, plus extra for garnish
4½ cups / 1 liter chicken or vegetable stock
10 cloves garlic, crushed
6 green onions
1 free-range egg
1½ cups / 350 g Greek yogurt
salt and freshly ground black pepper

Chilled red pepper soup with sour cream

serves 4

1 Peel the onion and chop it coarsely. Heat the oil in a large saucepan. Add the onion and sage and sauté over medium heat for 5 minutes, until the onion is translucent.
2 While the onion is cooking, halve the peppers lengthwise. Take a pepper half, remove the seeds and white flesh, and cut it into ⅔-inch / 1.5-cm dice. Set aside.
3 Remove the seeds from the rest of the peppers, coarsely chop them, and stir into the saucepan with the onions. Add ¾ teaspoon salt, the bay leaves, ground cumin, sugar, and red pepper flakes.
4 Sauté for another 5 minutes. Add the stock and bring to a gentle simmer. Cover the pot and cook over very low heat for 15 minutes.
5 Once the peppers are soft, remove the bay leaves from the soup. While still hot, use a regular blender or an immersion blender to purée the soup until it is totally smooth. This may take a few minutes. Leave to cool down a little.
6 Once the soup is just warm, stir in the celery, diced red pepper, lemon zest, and garlic. Leave until it comes to room temperature and then refrigerate for a few hours or overnight.
7 Remove the soup from the fridge half an hour before serving. Stir well, taste, and adjust the seasoning. Divide among serving bowls, sprinkle over a generous amount of chopped basil and parsley, add a spoonful of sour cream per portion, and finish with a drizzle of olive oil.

1 large onion
3 tbsp olive oil, plus extra for drizzling
8 sage leaves, finely chopped
4 large red peppers
2 bay leaves
2 tsp ground cumin
1 tsp superfine sugar
pinch of red pepper flakes
2 cups / 500 ml chicken or vegetable stock
1 celery stalk, cut into ⅔-inch / 1.5-cm dice
grated zest of ½ lemon
1 clove garlic, crushed
1 cup / 25 g basil leaves, coarsely chopped
⅓ cup / 10 g flat-leaf parsley, coarsely chopped
scant ½ cup / 100 g sour cream
salt

This is a variation on the traditional Moroccan *harira* soup, flavored in the same way but without the extra carbs that are often added in the form of rice or pasta. Traditionally a meal for breaking the Ramadan fast, this hearty dish is perfect on a cold winter's evening. You can also use canned chickpeas here (roughly 3 cups / 500 g) instead of dried.

We dedicate the recipe to Khalid Assyb, our pastry genius, who has been tormented by our constant eating through many Ramadans.

Harira (lamb, chickpeas, and spinach)

serves 4 to 6

1 Start preparing the soup the night before by putting the dried chickpeas in a large bowl with the baking soda and covering them with plenty of cold water—it should cover the chickpeas by at least twice their height. Leave at room temperature to soak overnight.
2 The next day, drain the soaked chickpeas, place in a large saucepan, and cover with plenty of fresh water. Bring to a boil and simmer for about 1 to 1½ hours, until the chickpeas are tender. Drain in a colander and set aside.
3 Place a large saucepan over medium heat and add the olive oil. Add the onion and fry until soft and translucent. Increase the heat, add the diced lamb, and cook for 2 to 3 minutes, until the lamb is sealed on all sides and has taken on a bit of color. Add the tomato purée and sugar and mix well. Cook for 2 minutes, then add the chopped tomatoes, drained chickpeas, stock, and some salt and pepper.
4 Bring the soup to a boil and lower the heat to a simmer. Use a large spoon to skim off any scum that forms on the surface, then cook for about 35 minutes, until the meat is tender.
5 Squeeze the lemon juice into the soup. Season the soup with the cumin, ginger, and saffron. Taste and adjust the salt and pepper.
6 When ready to serve, bring the soup back to a boil. Wash and drain the spinach leaves and chop them coarsely. Add the spinach and cilantro to the soup just before you bring it to the table. Serve with a wedge of lemon.

1 cup / 200 g dried chickpeas
1 tsp baking soda
3 tbsp olive oil
1 large onion, cut into ⅜ inch / 1-cm dice
7 oz / 200 g boneless lamb rack or shoulder, cut into ⅜-inch / 1-cm dice
2 tbsp tomato purée
1 tbsp superfine sugar
2½ lb / 1 kg canned tomatoes, chopped
5 cups / 1.2 liters chicken stock or water
juice of 1 lemon
1 tsp ground cumin
1 tsp ground ginger
pinch of saffron threads
3 cups / 100 g baby spinach leaves
4 tbsp coarsely chopped cilantro
4 to 6 lemon wedges
salt and freshly ground black pepper

Meat and fish

Chapter 2   Meat and fish

Sweet and sour, hot or cold, this lamb will satisfy everybody and is dead easy to make if you plan a day ahead. It is also multifunctional: an impressive main course; served as individual chops on a picnic; grilled outdoors; a sandwich filling (try it with the Italian bread ↗ page 162 and mayonnaise ↗ page 273)—anything goes.

Marinated rack of lamb with cilantro and honey

serves 4

1 Make sure most of the fat is trimmed off the lamb, leaving a uniform thin layer that will keep the meat moist and add to the flavor. Use a very sharp knife to separate the rack into portions of 2 or 3 chops. Place in a nonmetal container.

2 Blitz together all the remaining ingredients in a blender or food processor. Pour them over the lamb and make sure it is well covered in the marinade. Refrigerate overnight.

3 Preheat the oven to 400°F / 200°C. Heat up a heavy cast-iron pan, preferably a ridged grill pan. Remove the meat from the marinade and shake off the excess. Sear well on all sides, about 5 minutes total. Transfer to a baking sheet and cook in the oven for about 15 minutes, depending on the size of the rack sections and how well you want them cooked.

4 Meanwhile, heat the marinade in a small saucepan and simmer for 5 minutes. Put the chops on serving plates and serve the sauce in a separate bowl. Both the chops and the sauce can be served hot or at room temperature.

2¼ lb / 1 kg rack of lamb, French trimmed (you can ask your butcher to do this)
⅔ oz / 20 g flat-leaf parsley, leaves and stalks
1 oz / 30 g mint, leaves and stalks
1 oz / 30 g cilantro, leaves and stalks
4 cloves garlic, peeled
½ oz / 15 g fresh ginger, peeled and sliced
3 chiles, seeded
½ tsp salt
3½ tbsp / 50 ml lemon juice
4 tbsp / 60 ml soy sauce
½ cup / 120 ml sunflower oil
3 tbsp honey
2 tbsp red wine vinegar
4 tbsp water

Every person who has ever worked with Ramael Scully, our evening chef in Islington, ended up adoring him for the rare combination of a seriously great talent—both in creation and in faultless execution—and a warm, modest, and peaceful personality. Scully was born in Malaysia and grew up and trained as a chef in Australia. His multifaceted ethnic background (Malay, Chinese, Indian, and even Scottish) comes out as a clear solid voice through his magical cooking.

Here is another one of Scully's brilliant flavor combinations, and a good option for a main course for a fancy dinner party. Everything except the meat can be prepared in advance ready to serve.

Choose a good soft fresh goat cheese. Delicious figs are also essential here. Copper-colored Brown Turkey figs are especially good. They are typically available from late summer into fall.

Lamb rib chops with walnut, fig, and goat cheese salad

1 First you need to marinate the lamb. Take the chops, throw the marinade ingredients on, and massage them lightly into the meat. Place in a sealed container and refrigerate for at least 4 hours or up to overnight.
2 To prepare the sauce, place all the ingredients in a heavy-bottomed saucepan, stir, and put over medium heat. Bring to a boil, lower the heat, and simmer for 30 to 40 minutes, until reduced by two-thirds. Remove from the heat and keep warm.
3 To make the salad, place the walnuts in a nonstick frying pan and toast over medium heat for 5 minutes, stirring occasionally. Set aside to cool.
4 To finish the dish, heat up grill or a ridged grill pan until piping hot. Season both sides of the lamb chops with salt and pepper. Place on the heat for 3 to 4 minutes on each side; this will give rare to medium meat. Cook longer if you prefer. Remove the lamb from the grill and leave to rest in a warm place for 2 minutes. While you wait, gently toss together the toasted walnuts, cheese, mint, parsley, and oil, seasoning with salt and pepper. Make sure the components stay separate and that the cheese doesn't smear the leaves.
5 To serve, put the chops on serving plates, pile the salad next to them, and place the figs alongside. Spoon a scant tablespoon of sauce over each portion of lamb and drizzle a small amount of it over the figs and salad. Serve at once.

serves 4

12 lamb rib chops, French trimmed (you can ask your butcher to do this)
coarse sea salt and freshly ground black pepper

Marinade
leaves from 6 thyme sprigs, coarsely chopped
leaves from 1 rosemary sprig, coarsely chopped
2 cloves garlic, crushed
6 tbsp olive oil

Sauce
½ cup / 125 ml freshly squeezed orange juice
4 tbsp / 60 ml red wine vinegar
scant 2½ tbsp / 50 g honey
1 star anise
1 cinnamon stick

Salad
½ cup / 50 g walnuts, broken
3½ oz / 100 g fresh goat cheese, crumbled
6 tbsp / 20 g mint leaves
scant ½ cup / 25 g flat-leaf parsley leaves
2 tbsp olive oil
4 fresh figs, halved or quartered lengthwise
salt and freshly ground black pepper

Kebabs or *koftas*—Middle Eastern meatballs made with ground meat and spices—offer endless possibilities for combining flavors and textures. The bread we use here can be replaced with potato, couscous, or bulgur. Many alternative herbs and spices also work. Try playing with your favorite ingredients.

Some of our favorite kebabs are served at Al-Waha restaurant in Bayswater and Abu Zaad in Shepherds Bush. They are simply made with ground lamb, grilled over a fire, and always delicious.

The kebabs here are turned fancy by the zucchini wrapping. This is more work, so if you prefer to keep it casual you could omit the zucchini. The kebabs can be made in advance up to the stage where you finish them off in the oven. You can then chill them and finish the cooking at the last minute. The sauce can also be chilled and then reheated.

Zucchini-wrapped lamb kebabs

serves 2 to 4

1 To make the sauce, place the olive oil and crushed garlic in a saucepan and stir over medium heat for 1 to 2 minutes, just until the garlic cooks lightly. Add the canned tomatoes and season with the pepper flakes and some salt. Bring to a boil, then lower to a gentle heat and simmer for 25 minutes, until slightly thickened. Remove from the heat, and taste and adjust the seasoning. Set aside.
2 Toast the pine nuts in a small, dry frying pan for 4 to 5 minutes, shaking the pan occasionally, just until they get a little color. Remove from the heat and leave to cool.
3 Soak the bread in cold water for 2 minutes, then drain and squeeze to remove most of the water. Crumble the bread into a large mixing bowl and add the lamb, feta, pine nuts, spices, garlic, egg, parsley, salt, and pepper. Time to roll up your sleeves and get your hands dirty. Mix all of the ingredients together with your hands until well combined; do not overwork the mixture. Shape it into fingers, roughly 4 by 2 inches / 10 by 5 cm. There should be 12.
4 Pour olive oil to a depth of ¼ inch / 5 mm into a large frying pan and shallow-fry the kebabs for 1 minute on each side, until they have taken on a nice brown color. Remove from the pan and set aside on a baking sheet.
5 Preheat the oven to 400°F / 200°C. To prepare the zucchini, use a small knife to slice off both ends and then cut long, thin slices down the length of each zucchini (a mandoline will make this job much easier). You will need 12 slices. Brush each slice with a little olive oil and season with salt and pepper. Place a ridged grill pan over high heat and leave it there for a few minutes to heat up well. Lay the zucchini slices on the hot pan and cook for 2 minutes on each side, so that they get distinctive char marks. Remove to a baking sheet and leave to cool.
6 Wrap each meat finger in a slice of zucchini and arrange them in a single layer in a baking dish, seam side down. Bake in the preheated oven for 8 to 10 minutes, until cooked through.
7 To serve, bring the sauce back to a boil, tear the basil leaves roughly, and stir them in. Arrange the kebabs on serving plates and spoon the sauce over. Drizzle with a little olive oil to finish.

Sauce
2 tbsp olive oil
2 cloves garlic, crushed
14 oz / 400 g canned plum tomatoes, chopped
pinch of red pepper flakes
10 basil leaves
salt

2 tbsp pine nuts
1¾ oz / 50 g stale white bread, crusts removed
10½ oz / 300 g ground lamb
2 oz / 55 g feta cheese, crumbled
1½ tsp ground allspice
1 tsp ground cinnamon
¼ tsp ground nutmeg
1 clove garlic, crushed
1 free-range egg
4 tbsp / 15 g flat-leaf parsley, finely chopped
½ tsp salt, plus more for seasoning
½ tsp freshly ground black pepper, plus more for seasoning
light olive oil for frying, plus a little extra for brushing and drizzling
2 medium zucchini

This dish and variations on it, common in Lebanon, Palestine, and Syria, make an unusual use of tahini (↗ page xii). Instead of being served cold, the sauce is cooked with the meatballs to give an added boldness and richness. It doesn't look pretty—a problem we solve with the colorful garnish—but the flavors are heavenly. It goes well with Kosheri (↗ page 85) or plain rice. This is one of Sami's favorites.

Beef and lamb meatballs baked in tahini

1   To make the tahini sauce, in a bowl, mix together the tahini paste, water, vinegar, garlic, and salt. Whisk well until it turns smooth and creamy, with a thick, saucelike consistency. You might need to add some more water. Set the sauce aside while you make the meatballs.

2   Preheat the oven to 400°F / 200°C. Soak the bread in cold water for 2 to 3 minutes, until it goes soft. Squeeze out most of the water and crumble the bread into a mixing bowl. Add the beef, lamb, garlic, ⅔ cup / 35 g parsley, salt, spices, and egg and mix well with your hands.

3   Shape the meat mixture into balls, about the size of golf balls. Pour olive oil to a depth of ¼ inch / 5 mm into a large frying pan. Heat it, being careful it doesn't get too hot or it will spit all over when frying. Shallow-fry the meatballs in small batches for about 2 minutes, turning them around as you go, until they are uniformly brown on the outside.

4   Put the meatballs on paper towels to soak up the oil and then arrange them in a single layer in an ovenproof serving dish. Place in the oven for 5 minutes. Carefully remove from the oven, pour the tahini sauce over and around the meatballs, and return to the oven for another 10 minutes. The tahini will take on just a little bit of color and thicken up; the meatballs should be just cooked through. Transfer to individual plates, garnish liberally with the 1 tbsp parsley and lemon zest, and serve at once.

serves 4 to 6

Tahini sauce
⅔ cup / 150 ml tahini paste
    ↗ page xii
⅔ cup / 150 ml water
4½ tbsp / 70 ml white wine vinegar
1 clove garlic, crushed
pinch of salt

1¼ oz / 35 g stale white bread, crusts removed
10½ oz / 300 g minced beef
10½ oz /300 g minced lamb
3 cloves garlic, crushed
⅔ cup / 35 g flat-leaf parsley, finely chopped, plus 1 tbsp for garnish
1 tsp salt
½ tsp freshly ground black pepper
2½ tsp ground allspice
1½ tsp ground cinnamon
1 free-range egg
light olive oil for frying
grated zest of ½ lemon, for garnish

Although there are more flavorful pieces, the fillet of beef remains a favorite with Ottolenghi customers. Whether it's due to its tenderness or the small amount of visible fat, the fact remains that beef fillet withstood the no-red-meat fad and other fleeting trends to remain one of our biggest sellers. The sauces we choose to accompany it are gutsy and powerful, yet not sweet or sour—flavors that can overshadow the fillet.

When buying fillet, you should look for some fat marbling through the meat and ask the butcher to trim off any sinewy bits on the outside. If you require less than a whole fillet, always ask for a piece cut from the center. This will ensure more even cooking.

Roasted beef fillet (plus three sauces)

serves 6 to 8

1 whole beef fillet, trimmed (around 3¼ lb / 1.5 kg)
3 tbsp olive oil
1½ tsp coarse sea salt
1 tsp freshly ground black pepper

1 Preheat the oven to 425°F / 220°C. To get the strong, meaty flavors from the fillet, start by grilling it. Depending on the size of your grill pan, divide the whole fillet into 2 or 3 pieces that will easily fit in the pan. The head-end piece will be the thickest and therefore will need to cook the longest when it is later put in the oven.

2 After dividing the fillet, place the pieces in a bowl with the oil, salt, and pepper and engage in a short massage, rubbing the seasoning into the meat. Place a heavy ridged grill pan over the highest possible heat and leave for a few minutes, until very hot. Now sear each piece individually, turning it around to get nice dark char marks on all sides; each piece should take 2 to 3 minutes total.

3 Transfer the seared pieces to a baking sheet and put them in the oven to roast. This should take 10 to 14 minutes for medium-rare, 15 to 18 minutes for medium, and longer for well done. Remember, these are just guidelines. Not all ovens are the same, and neither are fillets, so you should check the meat at different stages. Pressing it with your finger is one option. The more the meat tends to bounce back, the clearer the indication that it is cooked through. If it doesn't, it is still rare. Another option is to stick a sharp knife into the fillet and try to look inside. This is safer but not as elegant. If the knife comes out cold, the meat is definitely not cooked. But keep in mind that the meat will carry on cooking in its own heat after it comes out of the oven.

4 When ready, remove from the oven and leave the fillet on the baking sheet to rest for 10 minutes, then cut it into slices ⅜ to ¾ inch / 1 to 2 cm thick. You can also leave it longer and serve at room temperature. Serve with sauce on the side (↗ opposite).

A Trinidadian recipe from Tricia (the former head chef at our Islington branch)—red, spicy, and full of smoky character. Some like it hot. If you don't, consider reducing the amount of chile or leaving it out altogether.

Choka (smoky tomato sauce)

serves 6 to 8 as an accompaniment

1   Place a large, heavy-bottomed frying pan over high heat and allow it to heat up well. Put the whole tomatoes in it and cook for about 15 minutes, turning them occasionally. The burnt skin will give the sauce its smoky flavor (beware, though; it will take a bit of scrubbing to clean the pan once you're done). Place the hot tomatoes in a bowl and crush them coarsely with a wooden spoon. Pick out most of the skin.

2   In a saucepan, heat the oil well. Remove the pan from the heat while you add the onion so it doesn't spit all over. Return to the heat and cook for 3 minutes over medium heat just to soften slightly. Add the onion and oil to the crushed tomatoes, together with the chile, garlic, cilantro, paprika, and pepper flakes. Taste and season liberally with salt and pepper. Serve warm or at room temperature.

1 lb / 450 g plum tomatoes
3 tbsp sunflower oil
1 small onion, thinly sliced
1 mild red chile, seeded and chopped
2 cloves garlic, crushed
2 tbsp chopped cilantro
1 tbsp paprika
pinch of red pepper flakes
salt and freshly ground black pepper

Arugula and horseradish sauce

serves 6 to 8 as an accompaniment

Put all the ingredients except the yogurt in a blender or food processor and pulse until smooth. Transfer to a bowl, add the yogurt, and mix well. This sauce will keep for a few days in a sealed container in the fridge.

2½ cups / 50 g arugula
2 tbsp freshly grated horseradish root
2 cloves garlic, crushed
2 tbsp olive oil
1 tbsp milk
½ tsp salt
½ tsp freshly ground black pepper
½ cup / 125 g Greek yogurt

Watercress and mustard sauce

serves 6 to 8 as an accompaniment

Put all the ingredients except the sour cream in a blender or food processor and pulse until smooth. Transfer to a bowl, add the sour cream, and mix well. This sauce will keep for a few days in a sealed container in the fridge.

1½ oz / 40 g watercress
4 tsp / 20 g whole-grain mustard
1 tbsp Dijon mustard
2 cloves garlic, crushed
2 tbsp olive oil
2 tbsp milk
½ tsp salt
½ tsp freshly ground black pepper
scant ½ cup / 110 ml sour cream

Roasted beef fillet (↗ page 110)

Roast pork belly (↗ page 114)

Scully, the undisputed king of evening service at Ottolenghi Islington, makes the crispiest and tastiest pork belly. You enjoy it in two stages: first, when the crackling breaks in your mouth with a crunch, like flaky pastry; second, when the perfectly tender layers of fat and meat melt on your tongue, imparting delectable smoky and herby flavors.

Scully also comes up with the perfect seasonal relishes to go with the pork. Here are two of his creations, but there are infinite other combinations of fruit and spice that we would encourage you to explore. The quantities suggested here will probably leave you with some leftover relish to use later. Serve with anything from mackerel to roast turkey. They should keep in the fridge for at least 10 days, probably longer.

When cooking the pork expect quite a lot of smoke in the kitchen due to the high initial oven temperature. Make sure you keep a window open.

Roast pork belly (plus two relishes)

serves 6 to 8

1 Preheat the oven to 500°F / 250°C or its highest setting. Place the herbs, garlic, and olive oil in a heavy-duty blender or food processor and purée them coarsely.
2 Lay the pork belly on a baking sheet, skin side down, and sprinkle lightly with salt and pepper. Use your hands to spread the herb mixture evenly all over the top, pressing it on so it sticks to the meat.
3 Turn the belly skin side up, wipe the skin dry with paper towels, and sprinkle sea salt evenly all over the skin (but don't put too much on, as it might create a crust and prevent the crackling from forming). Put the pan in the oven and roast for 1 hour, turning the pan around every 20 minutes. Once the skin has formed some crackling, turn the oven down to 325°F / 170°C, pour the white wine into the pan (avoiding the pork skin), and continue roasting for another hour. If the belly starts turning black, cover it with aluminum foil.
4 For the last cooking stage, turn the oven down to 225°F / 110°C and continue roasting for another hour, until the skin has crackled completely and thoroughly dried.
5 Remove the pork from the oven. Use a sharp knife to divide it into segments of a few ribs, cutting between the rib bones. Give as many ribs per portion as the appetite demands. Serve with relish on the side (↗ opposite).

1 bunch thyme,
  coarsely chopped
1 bunch rosemary,
  coarsely chopped
1 head garlic, cloves
  peeled and crushed
⅔ cup / 150 ml olive oil
1 piece pork belly,
  weighing 4½ to 6½ lb /
  2 to 3 kg
1 (750 ml) bottle white wine
coarse sea salt and freshly
  ground black pepper

Gooseberry, ginger, and elderflower relish

serves 6 to 8 as an accompaniment

**small knob fresh ginger,
peeled and thinly sliced**
1 tsp mustard seeds
**heaping 2 cups / 330 g
gooseberries, trimmed**
6½ tbsp / 80 g superfine sugar
**4½ tbsp / 70 ml elderflower
liqueur**

1 Put the ginger and mustard seeds into a square of cheesecloth,
   tie it up tightly, and put in a heavy-bottomed saucepan. Add the
   gooseberries, sugar, and liqueur, stir, and place over very low heat.
   Simmer gently for an hour, stirring occasionally. You might need to
   skim off the froth that accumulates on the surface.

2 When ready, the relish should have the consistency of a runny jam.
   To check this, chill a saucer, put a teaspoonful of the relish on it,
   then run your finger through it; it should stay separated but still be
   slightly runny.

3 Remove the cheesecloth bag, transfer the relish into a jar, and leave
   to cool. Either serve straightaway with the pork or store in the fridge.
   It will keep for a week or two.

Spiced red plum, ginger, and rhubarb relish

serves 6 to 8 as an accompaniment

**5 red plums (about scant 9 oz /
240 g), pitted and cut into
quarters**
1 red chile, halved and seeded
2 cinnamon sticks
1 star anise
7 tbsp / 100 ml red wine vinegar
1 cup / 200 g superfine sugar
**4 stalks champagne rhubarb
(about 7 oz / 200 g), cut into
1¼-inch / 3-cm lengths**
**small knob fresh ginger, peeled,
very thinly sliced, then cut into
very narrow strips**

1 Preheat the oven to 300°F / 150°C. Place the plums and chile in a
   heavy-bottomed saucepan and add the cinnamon, star anise, vinegar,
   and half the sugar. Stir well, bring to a light boil, and simmer for 20 to
   25 minutes, stirring occasionally and skimming any froth from the
   surface if necessary. The plums should have a jamlike consistency. To
   check this, chill a saucer, put a teaspoonful of the relish on it, then run
   your finger through it; it should stay separated. Remove from the heat
   and leave to cool.

2 While the plums are simmering away, place the rhubarb, ginger,
   and remaining sugar in a baking dish. Rub them together with your
   hands and place in the oven. Cook for 20 to 30 minutes, stirring from
   time to time, until the rhubarb is tender. Remove from the oven and
   leave to cool.

3 Remove the chile from the plums. Combine the plums and rhubarb
   and mix well, then transfer to a jar and leave to cool. Either serve the
   relish straightaway with the pork or store in the fridge, where it will
   keep for a week or two.

There may not be a lot of meat on an oxtail, but the long, slow cooking on the bone imparts a magical flavor to this dish. The warm, hearty flavors get a kick of freshness at the end from what the Italians call *gremolata*—a mixture of parsley, garlic, and citrus zest.

Thanks to Nir for the inspiration for this recipe.

Oxtail stew with pumpkin and cinnamon

1 Preheat the oven to 350°F / 180°C. Place a large, heavy-bottomed pan (large enough to accommodate the whole stew later; there will be a lot!) over high heat and add 2 tablespoons olive oil. When this is smoking hot, add some of the oxtail pieces and fry on all sides for about 4 minutes, browning the meat well. Make sure you don't sear too many pieces at once or they will boil in their own liquid rather than fry. Transfer the oxtail to a colander and leave to drain off excess fat while you brown the remaining pieces.

2 Remove most of the fat from the pan and add the shallots, carrots, and garlic. Return to medium-high heat and sauté, stirring occasionally, for about 10 minutes, until the vegetables are golden brown.

3 Add the wine to the pan and scrape the bottom with a wooden spoon to mix in any flavorful bits left there. Bring to a boil and simmer until it has almost evaporated. Now add the tomatoes. Tie together the thyme and rosemary sprigs with string and drop them in as well, then add the orange zest, bay leaves, cinnamon, star anise, black pepper, and some salt. Transfer the simmering mixture into a deep baking dish and lay the oxtail pieces on top of the sauce in one layer (keep the pan for later). Cover first with a sheet of parchment paper, placed directly on the oxtail, and then with a tight-fitting lid or a couple of layers of aluminium foil, then place in the oven and bake for 2 to 3 hours. The meat is ready when it comes easily away from the bone. Lift the oxtail from the sauce, place in a large bowl, and leave to cool slightly. If a lot of fat accumulates at the bottom of the bowl, drain some of it but keep the rest.

4 When the oxtail is cool enough to handle, pick all the meat from the bones and place back in the large pan. Add the sauce the meat was cooked in, along with the pumpkin cubes and the water. Bring to a boil, then lower the heat to a gentle simmer and cook for 30 minutes, until the pumpkin is soft. Taste and season the sauce with salt and more black pepper.

5 To make the gremolata garnish for the stew, simply mix the parsley, lemon zest, and garlic together. Transfer the stew to a serving bowl and sprinkle the gremolata on top. Serve at once.

serves 6

olive oil for frying
4½ lb / 2 kg oxtail pieces
7 oz / 200 g shallots, coarsely chopped
3 large carrots, coarsely chopped
2 cloves garlic, crushed
1⅔ cups / 400 ml red wine
3⅔ cups / 650 g chopped canned plum tomatoes
10 sprigs thyme
5 sprigs rosemary
zest of ½ orange, removed in long strips
2 bay leaves
2 cinnamon sticks
2 star anise
1 tsp freshly ground black pepper
1 lb / 500 g pumpkin or butternut squash, peeled, seeded, and cut into 1-inch / 2.5-cm cubes
1¼ cups / 300 ml water
salt

Gremolata
2 tbsp coarsely chopped flat-leaf parsley
grated zest of 1 large lemon
2 cloves garlic, crushed

Making your own *harissa*, a key component in Tunisian cooking, is extremely satisfying. The heady, potent paste can be used for flavoring meat and fish, finishing stews, mixing with grilled vegetables—go with it wherever your culinary imagination takes you.

In this recipe, Scully mixes it with yogurt to get a spicy, smooth marinade in which he leaves the chicken overnight. He normally uses chicken thighs, which are flavorful and rich. Some supermarkets now offer the thigh meat with bones and skin removed, or you can ask your butcher to bone them for you. If you prefer to use breast meat, skin four breasts and cut them in half crosswise, then slice each half horizontally so you get four thin fillets.

Harissa-marinated chicken with red grapefruit salad

1 To make the marinade, over the flame on a gas stove top or under a very hot broiler, roast the red pepper until blackened on the outside. This typically takes about 8 minutes on an open flame or 15 to 20 minutes under a very hot broiler. Place the pepper in a bowl, cover with plastic wrap, and leave to cool. Peel the pepper and discard the seeds.

2 Place the coriander, cumin, and caraway seeds in a dry frying pan over low heat and toast lightly for 2 minutes. You should be able to smell the aromas of the spices. Transfer them to a mortar and grind to a powder with a pestle.

3 Heat the olive oil in a frying pan, add the onion, garlic, and fresh and dried chiles, and fry over medium heat for 6 to 8 minutes, until they turn a dark, smoky color. Now blitz together all the marinade ingredients except the yogurt in a food processor or blender; you will have a pure harissa paste.

4 To marinate the chicken, mix the paste with the yogurt and use your hands to rub it all over the chicken thighs. Layer them in a plastic container, seal, and refrigerate overnight.

5 The next day, to make the grapefruit salad, take each grapefruit and use a small, sharp knife to slice off the top and tail. Now cut down its sides, following its natural lines, to remove the skin and white pith. Over a small bowl, cut in between the membranes to remove the individual segments. Squeeze any remaining juice into a bowl and keep it to make up the ⅔ cup / 150 ml juice required for the sauce.

6 Preheat the oven to 425°F / 220°C. Lay out the marinated chicken pieces, spaced well apart, on a large baking sheet and place in the hot oven. After 5 minutes, lower the oven temperature to 350°F / 180°C and cook for another 12 to 15 minutes, until the chicken is almost cooked through. Now place the chicken under a hot broiler for 2 to 3 minutes to give it extra color and cook it through completely.

7 Meanwhile, place all the sauce ingredients in a small pan and bring to a light simmer. Simmer for about 20 minutes, or until reduced to one-third.

8 To serve, toss the arugula and grapefruit segments with the olive oil, salt, and pepper. Pile in the center of 4 serving plates, put the warm chicken on top, and drizzle about 1 tablespoon of the sauce over each portion.

serves 4

Harissa marinade
1 red bell pepper
¼ tsp coriander seeds
¼ tsp cumin seeds
¼ tsp caraway seeds
½ tbsp olive oil
1 small red onion, coarsely chopped
3 cloves garlic, coarsely chopped
2 mild fresh red chiles, seeded and coarsely chopped
1 dried red chile, seeded and coarsely chopped
1½ tsp tomato paste
2 tbsp lemon juice
½ tsp salt
1 tbsp Greek yogurt

1¾ lb / 800 g organic or free-range chicken thigh meat (8 to 10 thighs)

Red grapefruit salad
2 red grapefruits
4 oz / 120 g peppery wild arugula
1 tsp olive oil
coarse sea salt and freshly ground black pepper

Sauce
⅔ cup / 150 ml pink grapefruit juice
generous ½ cup / 130 ml lemon juice
⅔ cup / 150 ml maple syrup
¼ tsp salt
pinch of ground cinnamon
1 star anise

Roast chicken with sumac, za'atar, and lemon (↗ page 122)

Roast chicken with saffron, hazelnuts, and honey (↗ page 123)

This is a simplified version of the traditional Palestinian dish *m'sakhan*, in which chicken is spiced with sumac and then roasted in the oven over bread. Sumac and *za'atar* (↗ page xii) that we love and use so much are combined here with fresh lemon to give the chicken a powerful sharp kick. It works fantastically well and is almost addictive. Try serving the chicken with warm pita bread and a garlicky yogurt sauce, made by mixing Greek yogurt with crushed garlic, olive oil, salt, and pepper.

Roast chicken with sumac, za'atar, and lemon

serves 4

1 In a large bowl, mix the chicken with the onions, garlic, olive oil, spices, lemon, stock, salt, and pepper. Leave in the fridge to marinate for a few hours or overnight.

2 Preheat the oven to 400°F / 200°C. Transfer the chicken and its marinade to a baking sheet large enough to accommodate all the chicken pieces lying flat and spaced well apart. They should be skin side up. Sprinkle the za'atar over the chicken and onions and put the pan in the oven. Roast for 30 to 40 minutes, until the chicken is colored and just cooked through.

3 Meanwhile, melt the butter in a small frying pan, add the pine nuts and a pinch of salt, and cook over medium heat, stirring constantly, until they turn golden. Transfer to a plate lined with paper towels to absorb the fat.

4 Transfer the hot chicken and onions to a serving plate and finish with the chopped parsley, pine nuts, and a drizzle of olive oil. You can sprinkle on more za'atar and sumac, if you like.

1 large organic or free-range chicken, divided into quarters: breast and wing, leg and thigh
2 red onions, thinly sliced
2 cloves garlic, crushed
4 tbsp olive oil, plus extra for drizzling
1½ tsp ground allspice
1 tsp ground cinnamon
1 tbsp sumac ↗ page xii
1 lemon, thinly sliced
scant 1 cup / 200 ml chicken stock or water
1½ tsp salt, plus extra
1 tsp freshly ground black pepper
2 tbsp za'atar ↗ page xii
4 tsp / 20 g unsalted butter
6 tbsp / 50 g pine nuts
4 tbsp chopped flat-leaf parsley

This dish is inspired by a recipe from Claudia Roden's classic book, *Tamarind and Saffron* (Viking, 1999). It is one of our favorites: it is easy to make, yet looks stunning, and has the most delicate and exotic combination of flavors (rose water, saffron, and cinnamon), which takes you straight to the famous Jemaa el Fna in Marrakech. Serve with rice or plain couscous.

Roast chicken with saffron, hazelnuts, and honey

serves 4

1 In a large bowl, mix the chicken pieces with the onions, olive oil, ginger, cinnamon, saffron, lemon juice, water, salt, and pepper. Leave to marinate for at least an hour, or overnight in the fridge.
2 Preheat the oven to 375°F / 190°C. Spread the hazelnuts out on a baking sheet and toast for 10 minutes, until lightly browned. Chop coarsely and set aside.
3 Transfer the chicken and marinade to a baking sheet large enough to accommodate everything comfortably. Arrange the chicken pieces skin side up and put the pan in the oven for about 35 minutes.
4 While the chicken is roasting, mix the honey, rose water, and nuts together to make a rough paste. Remove the chicken from the oven, spoon a generous amount of nut paste onto each piece, and spread it to cover. Return to the oven for 5 to 10 minutes, until the chicken is cooked through and the nuts are golden brown.
5 Transfer the chicken to a serving dish and garnish with the chopped green onions.

1 large organic or free-range chicken, divided into quarters: breast and wing, leg and thigh
2 onions, coarsely chopped
4 tbsp olive oil
1 tsp ground ginger
1 tsp ground cinnamon
a generous pinch of saffron threads
juice of 1 lemon
4 tbsp cold water
2 tsp coarse sea salt
1 tsp freshly ground black pepper
scant ¾ cup / 100 g unskinned hazelnuts
3½ tbsp / 70 g honey
2 tbsp rose water ↗ page xii
2 green onions, coarsely chopped

This dish is delicious and nutritious (for once the cliché is utterly true), and also a great way to use up leftover roast chicken. If you happen to have some, skip the roasting part and go straight on to the salad bit.

Shiso is grown in East Asia. We first came across shiso leaves first in one of our favorite Japanese restaurants, Tosa, in Hammersmith. They are from the mint family, taste mildly like cumin and cilantro, and look a little like nettles. They are available in some Asian markets, but if you can't get them, arugula makes a satisfactory substitute.

Roast chicken and three-rice salad

serves 8

1 Preheat the oven to 425°F / 220°C. Rub the chicken with a scant 3 tablespoons / 40 ml of the olive oil and season liberally with salt and pepper. Place in a roasting pan and put in the oven for 10 minutes. Lower the temperature to 375°F / 190°C and continue to roast for 50 to 60 minutes, basting with the juices occasionally, until the chicken is thoroughly cooked. Remove from the oven and leave to cool to room temperature. Reserve the cooking juices.

2 While the chicken is roasting, cook the rice. Place the basmati in a saucepan with 1⅔ cups / 400 ml water and a pinch of salt. Bring to a boil, then lower the heat to minimum, cover, and simmer for 20 minutes. Remove from the heat and leave, covered, for 10 minutes. Uncover and leave to cool completely.

3 Place the wild and brown rices in a saucepan and pour in enough cold water to cover the rice by at least 3 times its volume. Bring to a boil and simmer gently, uncovered, for 40 to 45 minutes, until the rice is tender but still retains a little firmness. If the water runs low, top up with extra boiling water. Drain through a sieve and run under plenty of cold water to stop the cooking. Leave there to drain.

4 Carve the meat from the chicken or simply tear it off in largish chunks. Put it in a bowl large enough to hold the whole salad.

5 To make the dressing, in a separate bowl, whisk all the dressing ingredients together with the cooking juices from the chicken. Pour the dressing over the chicken and set aside.

6 Heat the remaining 1½ tablespoons / 30 ml olive oil in a pan, add the onion and a pinch of salt, and fry over medium heat until golden. Remove from the heat and leave to cool.

7 Add the 3 rices, the fried onion and green onions, chiles, and chopped herbs to the chicken. Mix well, then taste and adjust the seasoning.

1 organic or free-range chicken, weighing about 3¼ lb / 1.5 kg
4½ tbsp / 70 ml olive oil
heaping 1 cup / 200 g basmati rice
⅓ cup / 50 g wild rice
scant ⅓ cup / 50 g brown rice
1 onion, thinly sliced
6 green onions, thinly sliced
4 mild red chiles, seeded and cut into thin strips
3 cups / 50 g cilantro, chopped
4 tbsp / 20 g mint leaves, chopped
20 shiso leaves, shredded (or arugula)
salt and freshly ground black pepper

Dressing
4 tbsp plus 1 tsp / 65 ml lemon juice
2 tbsp / 30 ml sesame oil
2 tbsp / 30 ml Thai fish sauce
2 tbsp plus 1 tsp / 35 ml olive oil

Now you see them, now you don't. That's the fate of these meatballs in our Ledbury Road branch. As soon as we bring them out to the shop they disappear, as if by command of a magician's wand.

Turkey and corn meatballs with roasted pepper sauce

serves 4

1 Preheat the oven to 400°F / 200°C. To make the sauce, quarter the peppers with a sharp knife and shave off the white parts and the seeds. Put them in a baking pan and toss with 2 tablespoons of the olive oil and ½ teaspoon of the salt, then roast in the oven for 35 minutes, until soft. Transfer the hot peppers to a bowl and cover it with plastic wrap. Once they have cooled down a little, you can peel them, although it isn't essential. Place them in a blender or food processor with their roasting juices and add the rest of the sauce ingredients. Process until smooth, then taste and adjust the salt if necessary. Set aside.

2 For the meatballs, place a heavy, nonstick frying pan over high heat and throw in the corn kernels. Toss them in the hot pan for 2 to 3 minutes, until lightly blackened. Remove and leave to cool.

3 Soak the bread in cold water for a minute, then squeeze well and crumble it into a large bowl. Add all the rest of the ingredients except the sunflower oil and mix well with your hands.

4 Pour the sunflower oil to a depth of ¼ inch / 5 mm into the same heavy frying pan. Allow it to heat up well and then fry about a teaspoonful of the meat mixture in it. Remove, let cool, and then taste. Adjust the amount of salt and pepper in the uncooked mixture.

5 With wet hands, shape the mixture into balls about the size of golf balls. Cook them in small batches in the hot oil, turning them in the pan until they are golden brown all over. Transfer to a baking sheet, place in the oven, and cook for about 5 minutes. When you press one with your finger, the meat should bounce back. Serve hot or warm, with the pepper sauce on the side.

Roasted pepper sauce
4 red bell peppers
3 tbsp olive oil
1 tsp salt
scant 1 oz / 25 g cilantro, leaves and stalks
1 clove garlic, peeled
1 small mild chile, seeded
2 tbsp sweet chile sauce
2 tbsp cider vinegar or white wine vinegar

⅔ cup / 100 g corn kernels (fresh or frozen)
3 slices stale white bread, crusts removed
1 lb / 500 g ground free-range or organic turkey breast
1 free-range egg
4 green onions, finely chopped
2 tbsp finely chopped flat-leaf parsley
2½ tsp ground cumin
1½ tsp salt
½ tsp freshly ground black pepper
1 clove garlic, crushed
sunflower oil for frying

Although turkey is more frequently associated with a sweet red relish, we serve it here with a lemony sauce of herbs and cumin. It is enormously popular around Christmas and Thanksgiving, as it is both traditional and original. The same sauce would work very well with lamb. You can serve this dish either warm or at room temperature.

Marinated turkey breast with cumin, coriander, and white wine

serves 4 to 6

1 Put all the ingredients except the turkey breast in a food processor or blender and process for 1 to 2 minutes to get a smooth marinade. Put the turkey in a nonmetallic container and pour the marinade over it. Massage the marinade into the meat, cover the container, and leave in the fridge for 24 hours. Make sure the turkey is immersed in the sauce.

2 Preheat the oven to 425°F / 220°C. Remove the turkey from the marinade (keep the marinade for later) and put it on a baking sheet. Place in the oven and roast for 15 minutes, then lower the temperature to 400°F / 200°C. Continue to cook for 15 minutes, then lower the temperature again to 350°F / 180°C. Cook until the turkey is done, another 30 to 45 minutes. To check, stick a small knife all the way into the center; it should come out hot. If the meat gets too dark before it is ready, cover it with aluminum foil.

3 To prepare the sauce, heat the turkey marinade in a small saucepan and simmer for 15 minutes, until reduced by about half. Taste and season with some more salt and pepper.

4 Remove the turkey from the oven and let it rest for 10 minutes. Slice it thinly and serve with the warm sauce.

5 To serve cold, leave the meat to cool completely and then slice. Adjust the seasoning of the sauce once it is cold and serve on the side.

4 tbsp mint leaves
4 tbsp flat-leaf parsley leaves
4 tbsp cilantro leaves
1 clove garlic, peeled
4 tbsp / 60 ml lemon juice
4 tbsp / 60 ml olive oil
½ cup / 125 ml white wine
½ tsp ground cumin
½ tsp salt
½ tsp freshly ground black pepper
½ small organic or free-range turkey breast (about 2¼ lb / 1 kg)

Here is a twist on that out-of-favor classic, duck à l'orange, yet quite far removed from the original. It is spicy and rich, full of intense, multilayered flavors, a recipe you'd always want to return to for some winter comfort.

The English Gressingham duck is the best choice here, as it is bred especially for its larger, more succulent breast. The French Muscovy would make a good alternative. Blood oranges are in season throughout the first part of the year, but you can easily substitute ordinary oranges.

This dish would go well with a rough mash of orange roots, such as sweet potato, pumpkin, or carrot.

Seared duck breast with blood orange and star anise

serves 4

1 Score the skin of each duck breast in 3 or 4 parallel incisions, without cutting into the meat. Repeat at a 90-degree angle to the other cuts to get square-shaped incisions. Mix the fennel seeds, pepper flakes, cumin, black pepper, and salt together, then rub them thoroughly all over the duck breasts with your hands. Place in a bowl, cover with plastic wrap, and leave to marinate for a few hours or in the fridge overnight.

2 Using a small, sharp knife, trim off ⅜ inch / 1 cm from the top and bottom of each orange. Standing them up, neatly follow the natural curves of each one with the knife to cut off the skin and white pith. Cut each orange horizontally into roughly 6 slices. Remove the seeds, place the slices in a small bowl, and set aside.

3 To sear the duck, thoroughly heat a large, heavy frying pan (one for which you have a lid). Place the duck breasts in it, skin side down, and cook for 3 minutes, until the skin is golden brown and crisp. Turn and cook the other side for 3 minutes, then remove the duck from the pan and keep in a warm place.

4 Discard most of the fat from the frying pan and add the orange juice, wine, vinegar, and star anise. Bring to a boil and simmer for 5 to 6 minutes, until reduced by about half. Taste and add salt and pepper if necessary. Return the duck breasts to the pan and stir to coat them in the sauce. Cover with a lid and simmer gently for 7 minutes.

5 Take the dried chiles and orange slices, plus any extra juice in their bowl, and place carefully next to the duck breasts. Cover again and simmer for another 3 minutes. By this time the meat should be medium-rare.

6 Remove the duck breasts from the sauce, place on a cutting board, and leave to rest for 3 to 4 minutes. While you wait, check the sauce. It may need to be simmered a little longer to thicken it slightly. Taste again and adjust the seasoning if necessary.

7 Slice each breast at an angle into pieces ⅜ inch / 1 cm thick, and place on serving plates. Pick the oranges from the sauce and arrange them on the plates with the duck. Pour some of the sauce on top and serve the rest on the side.

4 duck breasts,
  6½ to 7 oz / 180 to 200 g each
2 tbsp fennel seeds
pinch of red pepper flakes
2 tsp ground cumin
2 tsp coarsely ground
  black pepper
1 tsp coarse sea salt
4 whole blood oranges
1 cup / 240 ml blood orange
  juice (from about 4 oranges)
¾ cup / 180 ml red wine
2 tbsp sherry vinegar
16 star anise
6 dried chiles

Another one of Scully's original creations: a warm quail, sweet, piquant, and tender, served on a bed of fresh lemony salad spiked with a load of herbs. Perfect for an informal Sunday lunch, especially if the weather is nice and you can grill the quail outdoors.

There is a fair amount of preparation involved here, but if you start the day before, you'll get the bulk of the work done in advance and also give the birds a longer marinade and a deeper flavor. Make sure you don't get stuck with preparing the quail; it's a fiddly and unrewarding job. Instead, ask your butcher to remove the backbone and ribs and flatten, or butterfly, the birds for you.

For information on *mograbiah* and where to get it, ↗ page 77. Couscous makes an adequate alternative; just follow the cooking instructions on the packet. Dark chicken meat (leg or thigh) could be substituted for the quail.

Grilled quail with mograbiah salad

1 To make the marinade, put all the spices and the salt in a small food processor bowl or a spice grinder and pulse to get a fine, homogenous powder (you could use a mortar and pestle instead, although the mixture won't become as fine). Add the garlic and ginger and work into a paste. Transfer the mixture to a large bowl and whisk in the honey and oil until you get a light, uniform mixture. Add the prepared quail, fold back your sleeves, and massage the birds intensively with the marinade. Transfer the birds and marinade to a smaller container, then cover and chill for at least 4 hours, preferably overnight.

2 The next day, to make the salad, bring 4½ cups / 1 liter water to a boil with a pinch of salt and add the mograbiah. Simmer for 15 to 18 minutes, until tender but with quite a substantial bite (the cooking time will vary according to the brand, so check the instructions on the packet). Strain into a colander, leave to drain well, and then transfer to a bowl. Add the butter and oil, stir well, and season with plenty of salt and pepper. Set aside to cool. While you wait, cut the chile in half lengthwise, remove the seeds, and chop it finely. Finely slice the green onion. Add them to the cooling mograbiah.

3 To segment the lemon, use a small, sharp knife to trim off ⅜ inch / 1 cm from the top and bottom. Stand it up on a board and neatly follow its natural curves with the knife to take off the skin and all the white pith. Holding the lemon over the bowl of mograbiah, cut along the white membranes encasing the segments to release the segments into the bowl. Squeeze in any remaining juice.

4 To cook the quail, place a ridged grill pan over medium heat and leave for a few minutes so it heats up well. Lay the quail on it, spaced well apart, and grill for 10 to 14 minutes, turning them over halfway through. The birds should be just cooked through. Make sure the heat is not too fierce or the birds will darken before they cook through; if this does happen, you could finish them off in a hot oven.

5 When the quail are almost ready, stir the herbs into the mograbiah. Taste and see if you need any more salt, pepper, or olive oil.

6 Pile the salad onto serving dishes and place the quail on top, 2 per portion. Serve at once.

serves 4 generously,
or makes 8 tapas-size portions

Marinade
1 tbsp ground cinnamon
2 tbsp ground cumin
10 whole cardamom pods
4 allspice berries
1 tbsp ground turmeric
½ tbsp paprika
pinch of salt
4 cloves garlic, peeled
2 knobs fresh ginger
    (about 1 oz / 30 g), peeled
    and coarsely chopped
2 tbsp honey
¾ cup / 180 ml olive oil

8 large quail, butterflied
    (see above)

Salad
¾ cup / 125 g mograbiah
    or fregola
2 tsp / 10 g unsalted butter
1 tbsp olive oil
1 mild red chile
1 green onion
1 lemon
3 tbsp coarsely chopped
    flat-leaf parsley
3 tbsp coarsely chopped
    cilantro
3 tbsp coarsely chopped mint
coarse sea salt and freshly
    ground black pepper

You can almost smell the Mediterranean in this salad, with its fresh seafood, herbs, garlic, and sumac. The best way to serve it is as part of a meze selection, with rustic white bread to soak up the juices.

Seafood, fennel, and lime salad

serves 4

1 Trim the bases and tops of the fennel bulbs, then slice crosswise as thinly as you can. A mandoline would be useful here. In a large bowl, mix the fennel and red onion with the lime zest and juice, garlic, dill, parsley, chile, 2 tablespoons of the olive oil, and ½ teaspoon salt. Set aside.

2 To prepare the prawns, peel the shells away from the bodies, keeping the tail segment of the shell on. Cut a shallow slit along the back of each prawn and use the tip of a small knife to remove the dark vein.

3 Place a heavy cast-iron pan, preferably a ridged grill pan, over high heat and leave for a few minutes until piping hot. Meanwhile, mix the prawns and squid with the remaining 2 tablespoons oil and a pinch of salt. Grill them in small batches, turning them over after 1 minute and continuing until just done (about 1 more minute for the squid and 2 to 3 for the prawns). Transfer to a cutting board and slice the squid into thick rings. You can leave the prawns whole or cut them in half.

4 Add the seafood to the salad bowl and toss together. You can serve the salad immediately or leave it in the fridge for up to 1 day. To serve, stir in the sumac and cilantro, then taste and adjust the seasoning. When pomegranate seeds are available, they make a beautiful garnish.

2 small fennel bulbs
½ red onion, very thinly sliced
grated zest and juice of 1 lime
2 cloves garlic, crushed
2 tbsp chopped dill
2 tbsp chopped flat-leaf parsley
1 mild chile, seeded and
   finely chopped
4 tbsp olive oil
8 tiger prawns
12 oz / 350 g cleaned baby squid
1 tbsp sumac ↗ page xii
2 tbsp chopped cilantro
coarse sea salt
pomegranate seeds,
   for garnish (optional)

All the seemingly contradictory flavors come together here surprisingly well to create a harmonious and balanced delicacy. Mackerel, probably our favorite fish, takes the sweetness and the saltiness wonderfully well, producing a light, clean result.

This simple dish relies heavily on the freshness and quality of the ingredients. Mackerel, in particular, is incredible when fresh and inedible when not, so make sure you buy the best.

Broiled mackerel with green olive, celery, and raisin salsa

1   To make the salsa, stir together all the salsa ingredients. Taste it; it should be sweet, sour, and salty. Season with salt and pepper and leave to sit for at least 15 minutes for the flavors to evolve. (At this point, the salsa can be refrigerated for up to 24 hours, if necessary. Before serving, allow it to come to room temperature, refresh with extra chopped parsley, and adjust the seasoning.)
2   Preheat the broiler. Toss the mackerel fillets gently with the oil and some salt and pepper. Lay the fillets, skin side up, on a rimless baking sheet and place under the hot broiler for 3 to 4 minutes, until just cooked.
3   Serve the fish hot or at room temperature, with a spoonful of salsa on top.

serves 4

Salsa
4 oz / 125 g celery stalks, thinly sliced
scant ½ cup / 60 g good-quality pitted green olives, thinly sliced crosswise
3 tbsp capers, rinsed
scant ½ cup / 70 g mixed golden and dark raisins, plumped in hot water to cover
1½ tbsp sherry vinegar
4 tbsp olive oil
3 tbsp honey
½ oz / 15 g flat-leaf parsley, coarsely chopped
salt and freshly ground black pepper

8 mackerel fillets, pin bones removed
2 tbsp olive oil
coarse sea salt and freshly ground black pepper

This is definitely a weekend dish, as you will need to do a fair amount of preparation a day in advance. Lots of ingredients are involved and a bit of muscle work (even if the process isn't very complicated). Still, what you get is well worth it: first, a small jar of the most astounding spice paste, which you can use to marinate fish and meat (you need only a little of it for this recipe); second, a beautiful fish prepared in minutes on the day; and lastly, a round of applause from an impressed crowd.

Tamarind is a sour fruit originally from Asia that comes as a sticky, dark brown pulp. Often the seeds are left in and need to be removed. Also known as the Indian date, it is available in many Asian food shops and some supermarkets.

Thanks, once again, to Scully for this creation.

Broiled mackerel with sweet potato pickle and mint yogurt

serves 8 as a starter

day 1

1   To make the spice paste, place a heavy-bottomed frying pan over low heat and spread out all the spice paste ingredients, except the oil, in the pan. Cook gently for a few minutes, shaking the pan occasionally, until the spices start to release their aroma (do not let them brown or they will taste bitter). Tip everything into a mortar and pound to a uniform paste with a pestle. Continue working the spices while slowly adding the oil to get a smooth consistency. (You will only need 1 tablespoon of the spice paste for this recipe, but the rest can be stored in a clean jar in the fridge for a few months.)

2   To make the sweet potato pickle, take the limes and use a small, sharp knife to trim off their tops and tails. Now cut down the sides of the limes, following their natural curves, to remove the skin and all the white pith. Over a small bowl, remove the segments from each lime by slicing between the membranes. Squeeze out any remaining juice over the segments, then discard the membrane.

3   Add the sugar and 1 tablespoon of the spice paste to the lime segments. Stir well to dissolve the sugar, then add the chile and cilantro.

4   Put the sweet potato into a pan of boiling salted water and simmer for 3 to 5 minutes, until they are just cooked but still hold their shape. Drain thoroughly and transfer to a nonmetallic bowl. Dress with the lime mixture, leave to cool, and then cover with plastic wrap and chill overnight. Remove from the fridge an hour before using.

day 2

5   To make the mint yogurt, peel the cucumber, cut it in half lengthwise, and scoop out the seeds with a spoon. Cut the cucumber into 3/8-inch / 1-cm dice and place in a bowl. Add the yogurt, paprika, lemon juice, mint, and oil. Stir well, try a bit, and add salt and pepper to taste. Refrigerate until ready to serve.

6   To cook the fish, preheat the broiler. Brush the mackerel fillets with the oil and season with salt and pepper. Place the fillets skin side up on a baking sheet, and put under the broiler for 3 to 4 minutes, until they are cooked through.

7   To serve, place a large spoonful of the pickle on each plate and top with the hot fish. Finish with a little of the mint yogurt over the fish and serve the rest in a bowl on the side.

Spice paste
1½ tbsp cumin seeds
1½ tsp coriander seeds
1½ tsp caraway seeds
1½ tsp fennel seeds
½ cinnamon stick
1 star anise
1 tsp coarse sea salt
1 tsp black peppercorns
3 cloves garlic, crushed
½ red chile, seeded and coarsely chopped
2½ oz / 75 g fresh ginger, peeled and coarsely chopped
1¼ cups / 150 g tamarind paste
6½ tbsp / 100 ml vegetable oil

Sweet potato pickle
5 limes
4 tbsp / 50 g superfine sugar
½ red chile, seeded and finely diced
1 tsp chopped cilantro
1 lb / 500 g sweet potato, peeled and cut into 3/8-inch / 1-cm dice

Mint yogurt
1 mini cucumber
scant 1 cup / 225 g Greek yogurt
¾ tsp paprika
juice of ½ lemon
1½ tbsp chopped mint
1½ tbsp olive oil
salt and freshly ground black pepper

8 mackerel fillets, pin bones removed
2 tbsp olive oil
salt and freshly ground black pepper

You can prepare this simple dish in minutes if you make the salsa the day before and store it in the fridge; just remember to let it come back to room temperature before serving. Peeling the peppers is a chore you can choose to avoid if you are feeling lazy. The sauce will not be quite as smooth, but it will still taste fantastic.

Organic salmon with red pepper and hazelnut salsa

serves 4

Red pepper and hazelnut salsa
2 red bell peppers
6 tbsp / 90 ml olive oil
2 tbsp / 15 g hazelnuts
½ oz / 15 g chives, chopped
1 clove garlic, crushed
grated zest and juice of
    1 lemon
2 tbsp cider vinegar
salt and freshly ground black
    pepper

4 organic salmon fillets,
    7 oz / 200 g each
2 tbsp olive oil
salt and freshly ground black
    pepper

1 To make the salsa, preheat the oven to 400°F / 200°C. Quarter the peppers and remove the seeds. Put them on a baking sheet and toss with 2 tablespoons / 30 ml of the olive oil and a generous pinch of salt. Roast them in the oven for about 20 minutes, until they are cooked through and slightly charred. Transfer to a bowl, cover with plastic wrap, and leave to cool. Keep any of the roasting juices.

2 Roast the hazelnuts on a separate baking sheets for 10 minutes, until lightly colored (you can do this while the peppers are in the oven). Allow them to cool down and then rub with your hands to remove the skins. Chop them coarsely.

3 When the peppers are cool, peel them and cut into ¼-inch / 5-mm dice. Mix with the hazelnuts, the remaining 4 tablespoons / 60 ml olive oil, and all the rest of the salsa ingredients. Taste and add salt and pepper.

4 Put a ridged grill pan on the highest possible heat and leave for a few minutes. It needs to be very hot! Have a baking sheet lined with parchment paper ready. Brush the salmon fillets with the olive oil and sprinkle with salt and pepper. Put them, skin side up, on the hot grill pan and cook for about 3 minutes. Using a fish slicer, carefully but briskly remove the fillets from the pan and place them, skin side down, on the lined baking sheet. Be careful not to scrape off the nice char marks when you handle the fish. Bake in the oven for 5 to 8 minutes, until the fish are just done and very light pink inside. Serve warm, with a generous spoonful of salsa on top.

You can prepare both the tuna and the salsa a day in advance and keep them chilled. The salsa will actually improve as its flavors intensify. It will keep for up to 5 days in the fridge. Slice the tuna just before serving it. It is extremely important that the fruits for the salsa are ripe and sweet.

To get more flavor out of the pistachios, you could toast them in the oven at 325°F / 170°C for about 8 minutes. If it is the visual effect that you're after, leave them untoasted, as they lose some of their vibrant green color when toasted.

Seared tuna with pistachio crust and papaya salsa

serves 6

1 To make the salsa, peel the cucumber, halve it lengthwise, then scoop out and discard the seeds. Cut it into ⅜-inch / 1-cm dice and put it in a bowl. Add all the rest of the salsa ingredients, stir well, and season with salt and pepper. Taste and adjust the seasoning, then chill. It is advisable to allow it to rest for at least an hour for all the flavors to combine.

2 Now for the tuna. Preheat the oven to 500°F / 250°C, or as high as it will go. Chop the pistachios, preferably in a food processor, until you get fine crumbs. Scatter them on a baking sheet and mix with the lemon zest, then set aside.

3 Take the tuna loin and use a sharp knife to divide it along its length into 2 or 3 cylindrical pieces. They should be 2½ to 2¾ inches / 6 to 7 cm thick and show the layers of the loin at their ends. Brush the tuna with the olive oil and season with salt and pepper. Place a ridged grill pan or a heavy cast-iron pan over high heat and leave for a few minutes to heat up. Place the tuna pieces in the pan and sear lightly for 3 to 4 minutes total, turning them around as you go. Remove from the pan and leave to cool down a little.

4 Now brush the tuna generously with the mustard and then roll it in the chopped pistachio mixture, using your fingers to cover any bare patches. Place the tuna on a baking sheet, transfer to the oven, and roast for 5 to 6 minutes. Check carefully (stick a knife in; it should come out cold), as it might not take that long. What you want is a slightly raw center with a ⅜- to ¾-inch / 1- to 2-cm ring of cooked meat around it. Remove and allow to cool completely.

5 To serve, cut the tuna into slices ¾ inch / 2 cm thick. Serve with the salsa on the side or poured on top.

Papaya salsa
1 mini cucumber
1 large, ripe papaya, peeled, seeded, and cut into ⅜-inch / 1-cm cubes
1 large, ripe mango, peeled, pitted, and cut into ⅜-inch / 1-cm cubes
2 red chiles, seeded and finely chopped
⅓ oz / 10 g fresh ginger, peeled and grated
1 small red onion, finely chopped
grated zest and juice of 2 limes
2 tbsp lemon juice
2 tbsp Thai fish sauce
4 tbsp olive oil
2 tbsp superfine sugar
salt and freshly ground black pepper

scant 1¼ cups / 150 g shelled pistachio nuts
grated zest of 1 lemon
2¼ lb / 1 kg tuna loin
2 tbsp olive oil
5 tbsp Dijon mustard
coarse sea salt and freshly ground black pepper

Another incredible recipe from our former colleague Etti. It is so simple to make, yet the final result is very sophisticated, mixing contrasting textures, colors, and temperatures to a faultless harmony. This fresh dish is just right for a warm summer's night, and it doesn't need much more to go with it than a glass of chilled white wine.

Thick, full-fat yogurt, mixed with some olive oil, can be used instead of *labneh*. Reduce the amount of chile if you are not the spicy type.

Panfried sea bass on pita with labneh, tomato, and preserved lemon

serves 4 as a starter

1 To make the salsa, score a little shallow cross at the bottom of each tomato and then drop them into boiling water for about 30 seconds. Remove, refresh under plenty of cold water, and then peel. Grate them coarsely on a cheese grater and mix with the chile, red pepper flakes, herbs, and lemon juice. Add salt to taste, then set aside.

2 Remove and discard the flesh of the preserved lemon and slice the skin very finely. Set aside.

3 Now prepare the fish. First, heat the oven to 350°F / 180°C. Then season the fillets with plenty of salt and pepper. Heat the oil in a nonstick frying pan large enough to hold all the fillets at once. Add the sea bass, skin side down, and fry over medium heat for 3 minutes, until the skin is crisp. Turn the fish over and continue to fry for about 2 minutes, until it is cooked through.

4 While the fish are frying, place the pitas in the oven for 2 minutes, just to warm them slightly. Put 2 pita quarters on each serving plate and spread a rough, thick layer of labneh over them.

5 Place the hot fish on top of the pitas and spoon some of the salsa over and around the fish. Finish with a few slices of preserved lemon and the pomegranate seeds, if using.

Salsa
3 sweet and ripe tomatoes (about 12 oz / 350 g total)
1 mild red chile, seeded and finely chopped
½ tsp red pepper flakes
1 tbsp coarsely chopped flat-leaf parsley
2 tbsp coarsely chopped cilantro
3½ tbsp / 50 ml lemon juice
salt

2 wedges preserved lemon, store-bought or homemade ↗ page 273
4 sea bass fillets (about 1⅓ lb / 600 g total), pin bones removed and cut in half at an angle
3 tbsp olive oil
2 large pita breads, cut into quarters
4 oz / 120 g labneh, store-bought or homemade ↗ page 272
at room temperature
2 tbsp pomegranate seeds (optional)
coarse sea salt and freshly ground black pepper

This is a quick dish that can be assembled in a flash. The only hard work is getting the seeds out of the pomegranate. And even that isn't so bad (↗ Fennel and feta with pomegranate seeds and sumac, page 17). Have the tahini and seeds ready in advance (but not chilled) and the rest should be done in 10 minutes.

Keep all the pomegranate seeds that you don't use in this dish for the most delectable dessert: buy or make a polenta cake (↗ page 195) and serve warm with crème fraîche that has been lightly scented with rose water, then sprinkled with pomegranate seeds and broken pistachios.

Panfried sea bass with green tahini and pomegranate seeds

serves 4

1 Preheat the oven to 400°F / 200°C. Line a baking sheet with waxed paper. Season the fish with plenty of salt and pepper and lay it, skin side down, on the pan. Drizzle with the olive oil and then bake for 6 to 7 minutes. The fish should be firm and "bounce" back when you poke it with a finger.
2 Place the fish on serving plates and spoon the tahini sauce generously on top. Garnish with the chopped parsley, lemon zest, and pomegranate seeds. Place a lemon wedge next to the fish and serve at once.

4 sea bass fillets, pin bones removed
4 tbsp olive oil
½ recipe Green tahini sauce ↗ page 272 **at room temperature**
2 tbsp coarsely chopped flat-leaf parsley
grated zest of 1 lemon
⅔ cup / 100 g pomegranate seeds (about ½ pomegranate)
coarse sea salt and freshly ground black pepper
4 lemon wedges, for serving

We encourage you to be daring. Many people think they don't like sardines, associating them with cans, bones, and a mess in the kitchen. Make this sweet-and-sour delicacy, however, and we guarantee you will convert a few vehement sardinophobes.

Ask your fishmonger to scale, bone, and butterfly the sardines, leaving the tails on. It is practically impossible to do this at home. You could replace the sardines with mackerel fillets, cooking them for a couple of minutes longer.

Sardines stuffed with bulgur, currants, and pistachios

serves 4

1 Start with some preparations for the stuffing. Put the bulgur in a bowl, cover it with cold water, and leave to soak for 15 to 20 minutes, until soft. Drain in a fine sieve and squeeze to remove excess moisture. Return to the bowl.

2 In a separate bowl, cover the currants with a little warm water and leave to soak for 5 minutes, then drain.

3 Preheat the oven to 300°F / 150°C. Sprinkle the pistachios on a baking sheet and toast in the oven for 10 minutes, until lightly colored. Leave to cool and then chop coarsely.

4 Now add the drained currants and the pistachios to the bulgur, together with the lemon zest and juice and parsley (reserving a little parsley for garnish). Stir in the spices, mint, garlic, molasses, sugar, and 5 tablespoons of the olive oil, then season with salt and pepper to taste.

5 In a separate bowl, mix the prepared sardines with the remaining 1 tablespoon / 15 ml olive oil and season with a little salt and pepper.

6 Turn up the oven to 350°F / 180°C. To stuff the sardines, lay them, skin side down and with the tail facing away from you, on a cutting board. Spoon a little bit of the bulgur stuffing onto the middle of each fish and fold first the head end over the stuffing and then the tail to form a roll. Carefully push a wooden cocktail pick down through the fish, catching both sides of the fillets. The tail should stick up in the air slightly. Gently press back any mix that is escaping from the sides.

7 Arrange the sardines on a baking sheet lined with parchment paper, place in the oven, and roast for 5 to 6 minutes, until just cooked through. Serve hot or at room temperature, accompanied by the lemon wedges and garnished with a little chopped parsley.

scant 2/3 cup / 100 g medium
    bulgur wheat
scant 3½ tbsp / 30 g currants
4 tbsp / 30 g pistachio nuts
grated zest of 1 lemon
2½ tbsp / 40 ml lemon juice
2 tbsp chopped flat-leaf parsley
½ tsp ground cinnamon
1 tsp ground allspice
3 tbsp dried mint
2 cloves garlic, crushed
2 tbsp pomegranate molasses
    ↗ page xii

1 tsp superfine sugar
6 tbsp / 90 ml olive oil
8 fresh sardines, scaled, boned,
    and butterflied (see above)
salt and freshly ground black
    pepper
4 lemon wedges, for serving

148 Chapter 2   Meat and fish

Delicate yet exploding with flavor, this is a Scully classic that always seems to come back to our evening menu in Islington. The saffron potato and the aioli offer a mild, creamy base against which the scallops shine, while the asparagus and samphire bring freshness and an added taste of the sea.

Saffron is expensive but a little of it goes a long way, and it does impart the most incredible shade of red and a magnificent aroma. There is a lot of poor-quality saffron around, so look out for particular types, such as the Italian Aquila or the milder but still good Spanish La Mancha.

Choose diver-caught (day-boat) scallops if possible, and look for plump, creamy-colored ones.

Fried scallops with saffron potatoes, asparagus, and samphire

serves 4 as a starter

Aioli
7 cloves garlic, peeled
6½ tbsp / 100 ml olive oil, plus a little extra for roasting the garlic
3½ tbsp / 50 ml sunflower oil
1 free-range egg yolk
1½ tsp white wine vinegar
¼ tsp Dijon mustard
¼ tsp fine sea salt
freshly ground black pepper

14 oz / 400 g red-skinned boiling potatoes, peeled and cut into ³⁄₈-inch / 1-cm dice
large pinch of saffron threads
1 small tomato
1½ oz / 40 g samphire
8 medium asparagus spears
4 tbsp / 60 ml olive oil, plus more for drizzling
8 medium-large scallops, trimmed
4 scallop shells, washed (optional)
coarse sea salt and freshly ground black pepper

1 To make the aioli, preheat the oven to 300°F / 150°C. Place the garlic on a sheet of aluminium foil, drizzle with a little olive oil, and sprinkle with a pinch of salt. Wrap in the aluminum foil to seal and then roast in the oven for 25 to 35 minutes, until very tender. Remove from the oven and leave to cool, then mash with a fork.

2 Mix together the olive oil and sunflower oil. In a second mixing bowl, combine the egg yolk, vinegar, mustard, garlic, salt, and a good grind of black pepper. Whisk constantly by hand or in a food processor while slowly trickling in the oils. At the end, the aioli should be thick, like a mayonnaise (you might need a little more or a little less oil). Taste it and see if you want to add any more salt and pepper.

3 Put the potatoes in a medium saucepan, cover with cold water, then add the saffron and a generous pinch of salt. Bring to a boil, lower the heat, and simmer for 6 to 8 minutes; the potatoes should still be slightly firm. Drain and leave in a cool place.

4 While the potatoes are cooking, cut the tomato into 4 wedges and use a small, sharp knife to remove the seeds. Cut each quarter into ¼-inch / 5-mm dice and set aside.

5 Wash the samphire in plenty of water and then throw it into a pan of boiling water. Leave for just 1 minute, then use a slotted spoon to lift it from the pan and into a colander. Refresh under cold running water and set aside.

6 Trim the woody ends of the asparagus and cut each spear into 1¼-inch / 3-cm lengths. Drop into the pan of boiling water the samphire was cooked in, simmer for 2 to 3 minutes, then drain at once into a colander and run under plenty of cold water. Set aside to dry.

7 To serve, heat up 2 large frying pans with half the olive oil in each pan. When piping hot, add the potatoes to one of the pans. Toss them for a minute or two to get some color and then add the asparagus and samphire just to warm them up. Taste and season.

8 At the same time, season the scallops liberally with salt and pepper and put them into the other pan. Sear them for 30 to 50 seconds on each side, until just cooked (the timing will depend on their size).

9 Straightaway, divide the warm scallops and vegetables among small serving plates or the scallop shells, if using, and spoon about 1 teaspoon of the aioli on top of each portion (the leftover aioli will keep in the fridge for 2 days and can be used in sandwiches or for dressing fish). Garnish with the diced tomato and a drizzle of olive oil and serve at once.

This is another one of Etti's masterpieces. There is no other way to describe it. Two of our recipe testers for this book, Claudine Boulstridge and Philippa Shepherd, both said that it is now their favorite because it is dead easy and utterly delicious. The flavor of the arak, a Middle Eastern liquor made from aniseeds and distilled grapes, complements but also mellows the intensity of the tomato and olives, coating the prawns in a heavenly buttery sauce.

This dish needs to be served as soon as it is made, accompanied by pieces of wholesome bread to soak up the sauce.

Buttered prawns with tomato, olives, and arak

serves 4 as a starter

1 Start by preparing the tomatoes. Make a tiny shallow cross with a sharp knife at the bottom of each one and put them in boiling water for 30 seconds. Remove, refresh under plenty of cold water, then drain. Now peel the skin away and cut each tomato into 4 to 6 wedges. Set aside.
2 To prepare the prawns, peel the shells away from the bodies, keeping the tail segment of the shell on. Cut a shallow slit along the back of each prawn and use the tip of a small knife to remove the dark vein.
3 Place a frying pan over high heat. When very hot, add 1½ tablespoons / 20 g of the butter and sauté the prawns quickly for 2 minutes, shaking the pan as you go. Add the tomatoes, pepper flakes, and olives and cook for another 2 to 3 minutes, until the prawns are nearly cooked through. Add the arak carefully (it tends to catch fire!). Let the alcohol evaporate for a minute before quickly adding the remaining 2 tablespoons / 30 g butter along with the garlic, parsley, and some salt. Toss for a second for everything to come together in a runny sauce, then serve immediately.

4 plum tomatoes
12 tiger or king prawns
3½ tbsp / 50 g unsalted butter, softened
½ tsp red pepper flakes
⅓ cup / 50 g kalamata olives, pitted
4 tsp / 20 ml arak or Pernod
3 cloves garlic, very thinly sliced
2 tbsp chopped flat-leaf parsley
coarse sea salt

Baking and patisserie

Monday to *Thursday*
8am to 10.30pm
Sunday
9am to 7pm

take away

• small box £ 6.90

• large box £ 12.50

• main sold separately

Chapter 3   Baking and patisserie

We developed the obsession that led to this bread when we tried a heavenly loaf at Prune, our favorite restaurant in New York, down in the East Village. It had the crunchiest dark crust, one that almost cuts the top of your mouth, and a soft, waxy center, full of giant holes and a giant flavor. It came from the Sullivan Street Bakery.

When we got back to London, we rushed to Dan Lepard, our bread mastermind, and he came up with this recipe, which is (almost, we must admit) as good as Sullivan's. To achieve this creation takes two days and you need a good mixer, as the dough is very wet and sticky and takes a lot of kneading. Don't try to do it by hand or use an old, weak machine.

When making bread, follow our baking expert Jim Webb's vital points: accuracy when measuring the ingredients; tenderness when handling the dough; patience in giving the dough enough time to rise; warmth to keep the dough away from drafts and cold areas. Sounds like good advice for life in general.

Look for the malt powder online. It adds character and depth, but can be replaced by dark brown sugar, if necessary.

Crusty white Italian loaf

makes 1 loaf

Biga
2 cups / 200 g Italian flour
1¼ cups / 175 g bread flour
⅔ cup / 170 ml lukewarm water
1 tsp active dry yeast or 1½ tsp (tightly packed) fresh yeast

4 tbsp / 25 g Italian 00 flour, plus extra for dusting
2½ tsp polenta, plus extra for dusting
2 tsp dark spray malt powder
7½ tbsp / 110 ml lukewarm water
1 tsp salt
olive oil, for brushing

day 1

1   The day before you want to make your bread, you will need to make the biga starter. Using an electric mixer with the dough hook attached, knead together all the ingredients for the biga. Run the machine on low speed for about 7 minutes. This should create a very tight dough with no lumps. Place it in a bowl large enough to allow it to at least double in size, then cover the bowl with plastic wrap and leave at room temperature overnight—anything from 15 to 20 hours.

day 2

2   The starter should now have doubled in volume. Take it in your hands and cut it into small pieces with a pair of scissors. Put the pieces in the mixer bowl and add the flour, polenta, malt powder, and water. Run the mixer on a low speed for 5 minutes, then increase to a fast speed and knead for another 5 minutes. At this point the dough will look very wet and sticky. Add the salt and continue mixing on a fast speed for a further 5 minutes. The dough should now come together as a ball and appear shiny.

3   Take a large bowl and brush it with olive oil. Oil your hands and lift the dough from the mixer to the bowl. Cover with a damp cloth and leave in a warm place for 30 minutes.

4   Wet your hands with a little olive oil. While the dough is still in the bowl, pick it up from one edge and stretch it. Fold the stretched edge on top. Repeat this, stretching and folding the dough from all sides of the bowl. In the end you will get a few "flaps" gathered together on top of the dough. Now turn the dough over and place it back in the bowl, flaps on the bottom. Cover with the damp cloth and leave for another 30 minutes.

5   Repeat the same turning process once more and then leave to rest, covered, for about 10 minutes.

6 Now turn the dough out onto a floured work surface and gather the edges together on top of the dough to form a rustic ball shape. Lay out a clean kitchen towel on the work surface and dust it liberally with flour. Lift the ball gently and place it in the center of the towel, seam side down. Gently gather the edges of the towel and place them on top of the ball to cover it totally. Transfer the entire parcel to a bowl large enough to support its sides and leave to rise for about 30 minutes.

7 Place a small ovenproof dish with water in it in the bottom of your oven and preheat it to 450°F / 230°C. Make sure it reaches this temperature! Take a heavy baking sheet and dust it with a little polenta. Very gently turn the dough out onto the baking sheet and remove the cloth. Try not to lose much air.

8 Bake the loaf in the oven for about 25 minutes, until a good dark brown color forms. When you tap it on its bottom, the bread should sound hollow. Leave upside down on a wire rack to cool.

You can use the recipe above to make green olive bread, great with salty varieties of cheese, particularly goat and sheep's milk cheeses.

Green olive loaf

1 Make the dough as described above. Drain the olives and dry them well on a kitchen towel. Add them to the dough at the end of the final mixing stage and mix on medium speed for 2 minutes.

2 For a distinctive elongated shape, stretch the dough gently as you transfer it to the baking sheet to create a thick stick form. Bake as above.

makes 1 loaf

ingredients as for Crusty white Italian loaf
1⅓ cups / 200 g good-quality green olives, pitted

This bread is very easy to make and needs nothing more than some good cheese or cured meat to go with it. We like to use a white bread flour that includes rye flour, malted barley flour, and wheat flakes. The combination of the buckwheat flour and walnuts gives this loaf its unique earthy depth. Thanks again to Jim.

Sour cherry and walnut stick

scant ⅔ cup / 160 ml lukewarm water (not more than 86°F / 30°C)
1½ tsp active dry yeast or 2¼ tsp (tightly packed) fresh yeast
2½ tbsp / 40 ml orange juice
2 cups / 250 g bread flour, plus extra for dusting
½ cup / 65 g buckwheat flour
1 tsp salt
⅓ cup / 50 g dried sour cherries
½ cup / 50 g walnuts, coarsely broken into pieces

1 Put the water and yeast in the bowl of an electric mixer, stir together, and leave to stand for 10 minutes. Add the orange juice, mix again, and then add both types of flour. Set the machine on low speed and knead for 5 minutes with the dough hook until everything comes together in a rough ball.
2 Stop the machine and scrape the dough from the bottom of the bowl. Add the salt, turn up the speed to high, and work for 4 minutes, by which time the dough should be smoother and have a silky texture. Stop the mixer, add the cherries and walnuts, and mix on a medium speed for another minute.
3 Turn the dough out onto a lightly floured work surface and knead by hand, turning it as you do so, until all the cherries and walnuts have disappeared inside the dough and it appears smooth. Shape the dough into a ball and put it in a large bowl. Cover with a damp cloth and leave in a warm place for 1½ hours, until the dough has doubled in volume.
4 Turn the risen dough out onto a floured surface. Trying not to beat too much air out of it, pull the edges of the dough so that they all meet at the center top to form a puffed, round cushion shape. Use a long object such as the handle of a wooden spoon to divide the dough into 2 equal spheres. Press down a little and then fold one half over the other. Crimp the round edges together with your fingers to seal them as if you were making a Cornish pasty. Now roll this on the floured surface to create a torpedo-like baguette shape. Lay it gently on a floured kitchen towel, cover loosely with plastic wrap, and leave to rise in a warm place for another 45 minutes.
5 Preheat the oven to 425°F / 220°C and put a small, shallow pan of hot water in the bottom. Once the dough has risen by about 50 percent, roll it off the towel and onto a baking sheet. Be careful not to shake it too much or to press hard, so as not to lose air. Use a very sharp nonserrated knife to make 3 diagonal slashes, each ⅜ inch / 1 cm deep, on top of the bread (an old-fashioned razor blade is best for this job).
6 Place the pan in the oven and bake for 20 to 25 minutes. Check if the bread is ready by tapping on its base; it should sound hollow. Leave to cool on a wire rack.

Top to bottom: Green olive loaf (↗ page 163), Sour cherry and walnut stick (opposite), Crusty white Italian loaf (↗ page 162)

Soft, rich, and chewy, focaccia is our favorite when sipping a glass of wine before a meal. It is perfect with crumbly mature Parmesan. Jim Webb, who tried the book's sweet and baking recipes and played a huge part in their creation, always emphasizes the importance of not overdoing the topping. Focaccia isn't a fat pizza but a bread, enriched with oil and some flavoring. Just be sure to use the best olive oil and be generous with it.

The grape focaccia might seem unusual, but it goes wonderfully well with cheese. Try it with a mature Taleggio. Or, since the oil gives focaccia a prolonged life, have it the next day for breakfast, like a good Danish pastry.

Focaccia (plus three toppings)

1   To make the starter, put the yeast and water in a large mixing bowl and stir with a wooden spoon until the yeast dissolves. Add the flour and stir until you get a porridgelike consistency. Cover the bowl with a damp cloth and leave somewhere warm for about 2 hours, until doubled in size.
2   In a mixer fitted with a dough hook attachment, mix the starter with the flour, sugar, and olive oil. Knead on a low speed for 6 minutes, then add the salt and work on a fast speed for 2 minutes.
3   Brush a large bowl with oil, place the dough in it, and brush the surface of the dough with more oil. Cover the bowl with a damp cloth and leave in a warm place for 1 hour, until the dough has doubled in size.
4   Turn the dough out onto a floured work surface and stretch and flatten it into a rectangle. Try not to work it too much. Take one of the short edges of the rectangle and fold it into the center. Take the other end and fold it over the first one to form 3 layers of dough.
5   Take a heavy baking sheet, roughly 12 by 16 inches / 30 by 40 cm, and brush it with oil. Lift the dough onto the pan, placing it so the seam is at the bottom, and flatten it by pressing hard with your fingers. Cover with plastic wrap and leave to rise for another hour. During this time you will need to work on the dough 3 or 4 times. Press it down with your fingertips and stretch it out gently to the edges of the baking sheet each time. By the end of this process it should cover the whole pan in a layer about ¾ inch / 2 cm thick and have lots of bumps and little hills in it.
6   Preheat the oven to 425°F / 220°C. Follow one of the topping instructions opposite. Place the focaccia in the oven and bake for 10 minutes, then reduce the temperature to 375°F / 190°C and continue for 15 to 20 minutes. Check underneath the bread to make sure it is baked through. When it is out of the oven and still hot, brush with plenty of olive oil.

makes one 12 by 16-inch / 30 by 40-cm focaccia

Starter
1½ tsp active dry yeast or 2¼ tsp (tightly packed) fresh yeast
1¾ cups / 420 ml bottled springwater, lukewarm
2½ cups / 330 g bread flour

2½ cups / 330 g bread flour
1 tbsp light brown sugar
2 tbsp olive oil, plus extra for brushing
1 tbsp coarse sea salt

Parsley and olive topping

Stir together the olive oil, garlic, and parsley. Dot the mixture over the surface of the dough. Spread the pitted olives over the top, pressing them into the dough, and sprinkle with salt.

makes enough to top one 12 by 16-inch / 30 by 40-cm focaccia

2 tbsp olive oil
1 clove garlic, crushed
½ cup / 30 g flat-leaf parsley, chopped
⅓ cup / 50 g kalamata olives, pitted
coarse sea salt

Grape and fennel seed topping

Halve the grapes lengthwise. Mix the sugar and fennel seeds together. Stud the top of the dough with the grapes and sprinkle with the sugar and seeds.

makes enough to top one 12 by 16-inch / 30 by 40-cm focaccia

10½ oz / 300 g seedless red grapes
4 tbsp / 50 g superfine sugar
2 tsp fennel seeds

Red onion and goat cheese topping

Mix the onion with the olive oil and scatter it on top of the bread. Dot with pieces of the goat cheese and sprinkle with a little salt.

makes enough to top one 12 by 16-inch / 30 by 40-cm focaccia

1 small red onion, thinly sliced
2 tbsp olive oil
3½ oz / 100 g fresh goat cheese, crumbled
coarse sea salt

We don't miss an opportunity to sing the praises of Swiss chard—a very popular green where we come from (and in America) but not so easily found here in the UK. Its acidic aroma, with strong earthy notes, enhances the similar qualities of the Jerusalem artichoke. The added creamy texture here guarantees you'll want to make this tart again and again.

Jerusalem artichoke and Swiss chard tart

1 Lightly oil a 9-inch / 23-cm tart pan with a removable bottom. On a lightly floured surface, roll out the pastry to ¹⁄₁₆ to ⅛ inch / 2 to 3 mm thick. Use the pastry to line the pan, pressing it well into the corners and the sides and allowing it to spill over the edge by at least ¾ inch / 2 cm. This excess will be trimmed later. Prick the base with a fork in a few places, then leave the tart shell to rest in the fridge for at least half an hour.

2 Preheat the oven to 325°F / 170°C. Cut a circle of waxed paper greater in diameter than the base plus the sides of the tart pan. Tuck it in the pastry shell and fill with dried beans or rice. Blind bake the shell for 35 minutes, then remove the paper and the beans or rice (you can keep them and reuse indefinitely for baking blind). Return the pastry shell to the oven and bake for a further 5 to 10 minutes, until lightly golden and thoroughly cooked. Remove from the oven and leave to cool.

3 While your pastry is resting and baking, prepare the filling. Place the artichokes in a saucepan, cover with cold water, and bring to a boil with a little salt. Lower the heat and simmer for 15 minutes, until tender. Drain and leave to cool.

4 Cut the chard leaves off the stalks, then coarsely chop the leaves and stalks, keeping them separate. Heat the oil in a large frying pan, add the stalks, and fry for 2 minutes, then add the leaves and the rosemary. Sauté for 6 to 8 minutes, depending on how woody the chard is. It should wilt completely. Remove from the heat, stir in the lemon juice, garlic, and some salt and pepper and leave to cool.

5 Whisk together the heavy cream, crème fraîche, eggs, and a pinch of salt and pepper. Spread the artichokes, chard, and feta over the base of the pastry shell, arranging them so that all the ingredients are visible. Pour the custard mixture on top. Make sure that you don't fill the tart to the rim. You want bits of the filling to show above the custard. Carefully transfer the tart to the hot oven and bake for 15 minutes. Then cover with aluminum foil, keeping it away from the tart's surface, and bake for a further 45 minutes, until the filling is set. If the top is still pale at this point, remove the aluminum foil and leave the tart in the oven for a few extra minutes.

6 Remove from the oven and allow to cool slightly. Break off the excess pastry and take the tart out of the pan. Serve warm or at room temperature.

serves 4 to 6

vegetable oil, for brushing the pan
1 recipe Short-crust pastry ↗ page 281 **or 1 lb / 500 g store-bought pastry**

Filling
1⅓ lb / 600 g Jerusalem artichokes, peeled and cut into ¾-inch / 2-cm cubes
9 oz / 250 g Swiss chard (or spinach)
4 tbsp olive oil
½ tsp chopped rosemary
juice of ½ lemon
1 clove garlic, crushed
scant 1 cup / 220 ml heavy cream
3½ tbsp / 50 ml crème fraîche
2 free-range eggs
5 oz / 150 g feta cheese, broken into pieces
salt and freshly ground black pepper

Top to bottom: Sweet and spicy beef and pork pie (↗ page 174), Jerusalem artichoke and Swiss chard tart (↗ opposite)

This is not your usual meat pie. It is rich, sweet, and spicy, and looks impressive yet rustic when served whole at the table. Take it on a picnic or serve warm with a salad of mixed bitter leaves.

Sweet and spicy beef and pork pie

serves 6 to 8

1 Lightly oil a 9-inch / 23-cm tart pan with a removable bottom. On a lightly floured surface, roll out the pastry ¹⁄₁₆ to ⅛ inch / 2 to 3 mm thick. Use the pastry to line the pan, pressing it well into the corners and the sides and allowing it to spill over the edge by at least ¾ inch / 2 cm. This excess will be trimmed later. Prick the base with a fork in a few places, then leave the tart shell to rest in the fridge for at least half an hour.

2 Preheat the oven to 325°F / 170°C. Cut a circle of waxed paper greater in diameter than the base plus the sides of the tart pan. Tuck it in the pastry shell and fill with dried beans or rice. Blind bake the shell for 35 minutes, then remove the paper and the beans or rice (you can keep them and reuse indefinitely for baking blind). Return the pastry shell to the oven and bake for a further 5 to 10 minutes, until lightly golden and thoroughly cooked. Remove from the oven and leave to cool.

3 To make the filling, you can toast the pine nuts at the same time you bake the pastry shell. Scatter them on a baking sheet and leave in the oven for 8 minutes, until golden.

4 Heat 4 tablespoons / 60 ml of the olive oil in a large, heavy saucepan, add the beef, and break it down with a fork. Cook over high heat for a few minutes, until colored. Add the sausage meat, mix well with your fork, and keep on cooking over medium heat for 15 minutes, until golden. Stir in the tomato paste and sugar and cook for another 3 minutes. Then add the salt, pepper, mint, and all the spices and cook for 10 minutes over low heat.

5 In the meantime, fry the onions in the remaining 4 tablespoons / 60 ml olive oil in a separate pan for about 10 minutes, until golden brown. Drain off most of the oil and add the onions to the cooked meat. Add the pine nuts and taste for salt and pepper.

6 Increase the oven to 375°F / 190°C. To assemble the tart, spoon half the hot meat mixture into the pastry shell. Make 3 shallow holes in the mixture, then break 3 of the eggs, one by one, and pour them into the holes. Using a wooden spoon, stir the eggs gently into the meat—just enough to disperse them a little, while keeping areas with more egg and maintaining some distinction between white and yolk. Spoon the rest of the meat on top, create some holes in it, and break in the remaining 4 eggs, dispersing them as before.

7 Put the pie in the oven and bake for about 15 minutes, until the eggs are set. If the top begins to darken too much, cover it with aluminum foil for the remaining cooking period.

8 Remove from the oven and break off the excess pastry with your hands. Take the pie out of the pan and serve hot or warm, garnished with the parsley.

vegetable oil, for brushing the pan
1 quantity Short-crust pastry
↗ page 281 **or 1 lb / 500 g store-bought pastry**

Filling
6 tbsp / 50 g pine nuts
½ cup / 120 ml olive oil
14 oz / 400 g ground beef
14 oz / 400 g sausage meat
3 tbsp tomato paste
2 tsp sugar
2 tsp salt
1 tsp freshly ground black pepper
1 tbsp dried mint
2 tsp ground allspice
1 tsp ground cinnamon
½ tsp ground nutmeg
1 tsp sweet paprika
½ tsp cayenne pepper or red pepper flakes
2 onions, thinly sliced
7 free-range eggs
2 tbsp chopped flat-leaf parsley

These sweet and savory tarts are best served warm, or even at room temperature, but definitely not piping hot. The tart sweetness of the carrot relish and the savory taste of the goat cheese are a spectacular match (made in Scully's always creative mind).

Butternut, carrot, and goat cheese tartlets

makes 6

1 To make the pastry, sift the flour into a large bowl and add the salt and poppy seeds. Rub the butter into the flour with your fingertips, until the mixture resembles fine bread crumbs. Add the milk and stir until the mixture just starts to form a ball. Do not mix any more. Shape the dough into a fat disk, wrap in plastic wrap, and chill for a few hours.

2 Preheat the oven to 325°F / 170°C. Mix the diced squash with 1 table-spoon of the olive oil and some salt and pepper. Put the squash into a baking dish and cook in the oven for 15 minutes, until semisoft. Set aside to cool.

3 While the squash is cooking, heat the remaining 1 tablespoon oil in a large saucepan and add the mustard seeds. Cook until they start to pop, then add the grated carrots and cook, stirring frequently, for 10 minutes. Stir in the sugar, white wine vinegar, and orange juice, bring to a boil, and then decrease the heat to a low simmer. Cook for 20 to 25 minutes, stirring occasionally, until almost all the liquid has evaporated. Remove from the heat and leave to cool.

4 Take 6 tartlet pans, 4 inches / 10 cm in diameter and ¾ inch / 2 cm deep, and brush them lightly with the melted butter. On a lightly floured work surface, roll out the pastry to about ⅛ inch / 3 mm thick. Cut out circles big enough to line the pans and gently press them into each one, working with your fingers around the edges to line them evenly. Cut off any excess pastry, then chill the tartlet shells for at least 30 minutes. Line the base and sides of each one with a disk of waxed paper and fill it with baking beans or rice. Blind bake for 20 minutes, then remove the paper and beans or rice and return to the oven for 5 to 10 minutes, until golden brown. Leave to cool.

5 Turn the oven up to 350°F / 180°C. In a large bowl, combine the egg yolk with the cream, chives, Parmesan, a pinch of salt, and a good grind of black pepper. Whisk together until the cream firms up to form soft peaks and then refrigerate.

6 To assemble the tartlets, divide the carrot mixture equally among the pastry shells, spreading it over the bases. Top with the butternut squash and crumble the goat cheese over it. Place the tartlets on a baking sheet and spoon over the cream mixture, filling them almost to the top. Place in the oven and bake for 8 to 10 minutes, until the filling is golden and set. Once the tarts are cool enough to handle, remove them from their pans. Serve warm, with a peppery salad.

Pastry
2 cups minus 2 tbsp / 230 g all-purpose flour
½ tsp salt
3 tbsp / 25 g poppy seeds
7½ tbsp / 110 g cold butter, cut into small pieces
4 tbsp / 60 ml milk

1 lb / 450 g (net weight) peeled and seeded butternut squash, cut into ¾-inch / 2-cm dice
2 tbsp olive oil
1 tsp mustard seeds
6 oz / 180 g (net weight) peeled and coarsely grated carrots
2½ tbsp / 35 g superfine sugar
2 tbsp / 30 ml white wine vinegar
3½ tbsp / 50 ml orange juice
2 tbsp / 30 g unsalted butter, melted
1 free-range egg yolk
½ cup / 120 ml heavy cream
6½ tbsp / 20 g chopped chives
1½ oz / 40 g Parmesan cheese, freshly grated
5 oz / 150 g fresh goat cheese
salt and freshly ground black pepper

Of all the yeasted products, brioche is probably the easiest to make at home and extremely worth your while. It is deliciously buttery and has a smooth, light texture. When just out of the oven, it almost feels as if you are eating air.

You need to make the brioche dough a day in advance, as it requires a slow proofing process in the fridge. This will give it a deeper flavor and smoother texture. The method requires a stand mixer with a dough hook attachment. A beater attachment will also work. Don't attempt to use a whisk!

The quantity of brioche dough given below makes a small loaf, which you can serve for breakfast with (even) more butter and jam, or use to make a sinful French toast, accompanied by Mascarpone cream (↗ page 278) and maple syrup. Alternatively, use the dough as the base for some little "pizzas" (↗ page 178) or to make a sweet galotto (↗ page 264).

Brioche

makes one 1-lb / 500-g loaf

1 Place the lukewarm water and yeast in the bowl of an electric mixer. If using dry yeast, leave for 10 minutes for the yeast to activate. Gently stir with your finger until the yeast dissolves. Add all the rest of the ingredients except the butter and start working them together with a spatula until the flour is incorporated.

2 Attach the bowl to the machine and work on a low speed for about 3 minutes. The dough should become smooth but will still stick to the bowl. Once it has reached this stage, scrape it off the sides of the bowl, increase the speed of the machine to medium-high, and start adding the diced butter. Do this gradually, making sure that the butter is more or less incorporated into the dough before adding more. Once all the butter is in, keep the machine working until the dough is shiny, has no lumps of butter, and comes away naturally from the sides of the bowl. This will take about 9 minutes, depending on your machine (the dough will be lukewarm; make sure it doesn't get hot). Once or twice during the mixing process, you might need to stop the machine, scrape the sides of the bowl clean, and very(!) lightly dust with flour.

3 Remove the dough from the mixer and place in a lightly greased bowl or plastic container that is about twice as large as the dough. Cover with plastic wrap and leave at room temperature for 1 hour. Then transfer to the fridge and leave for 14 to 24 hours before using. During this time, the dough will not rise much or change significantly.

4 Have ready a 1-lb / 500-g loaf pan, lightly brushed with some melted butter. Take the dough out of the fridge, place it on a work surface, and dust very lightly with flour. Using your hands, knock the dough down and then shape it into a rectangle that is about the size of the pan base. Place it inside the pan, cover with plastic wrap, and leave somewhere warm for 2 to 3 hours, until almost doubled in height.

5 Preheat the oven to 325°F / 170°C. Brush the dough lightly with beaten egg. Put the pan on a baking sheet and place in the hot oven. After about 15 minutes, the loaf should be dark brown and baked through. Stick a skewer inside to make sure it is completely dry. Remove from the oven and leave until cool enough to handle, then take out of the pan and leave to cool completely.

2 tbsp lukewarm water (not more than 86°F / 30°C)

1 tsp active dry yeast or 1½ tsp (tightly packed) fresh yeast

1⅓ cups / 190 g bread flour, plus extra for dusting

½ tsp salt

5 tsp / 20 g superfine sugar

2 free-range eggs, at room temperature, plus 1 egg, beaten, to glaze the loaf

5 tbsp / 75 g cold unsalted butter, cut into ¾-inch / 2-cm dice, plus extra melted butter for brushing the pan

Hardly a pizza (but we couldn't think of a more suitable name), this is the ultimate comfort snack. The buttery, slightly sweet brioche makes a superior base for the salty feta and sweet and sour tomatoes.

"Pizza" with feta, tomato, and olives

1. Put the brioche dough on a lightly floured work surface and roll it out to a sheet about ¾ inch / 2 cm thick. Using a pastry cutter or the rim of a large cup, cut out 6 circles, 3½ to 4 inches / 9 to 10 cm in diameter. Place on a nonstick baking sheet and leave to rise for 1 to 2 hours, depending on how warm the kitchen is. The brioche disks should double in height.
2. While the brioche is rising, prepare the tomatoes. Cut the tomatoes into quarters lengthwise and then cut each quarter into 2 long pieces. Place the wedges, skin side down, on a baking sheet and drizzle over the oil and vinegar. Sprinkle the salt, pepper, and mint on top. Put in the oven for up to an hour, until the tomatoes have dried out but still retain some moisture. Leave to cool.
3. To make the caramelized onion, put the onion, oil, sugar, and salt in a large pan and cook for 7 minutes over high heat, stirring occasionally, until golden. Remove from the heat and stir in the crushed garlic. Leave to cool.
4. Preheat the oven to 325°F / 170°C. To assemble the brioche pizzas, brush the risen dough disks with a little beaten egg and place a generous amount of the caramelized onion in the center. Top with lots of tomatoes, feta, and olives. Remember, the size of the dough will increase substantially in the oven, so be generous! Drizzle with a little olive oil and season with salt and pepper. Bake for 15 to 20 minutes. Check the bottoms of the pastries to make sure they are thoroughly cooked.
5. Remove from the oven and leave to cool. Lightly brush with more olive oil and garnish with the parsley leaves.

makes 6 snack-size pizzas

1 recipe Brioche dough
↗ page 177

Oven-dried tomatoes
10½ oz / 300 g plum tomatoes
1 tsp olive oil
1 tsp balsamic vinegar
½ tsp coarse sea salt
¼ tsp freshly ground black pepper
½ tsp dried mint

Caramelized onion
1 onion, thinly sliced
1 tbsp olive oil
¼ tsp sugar
¼ tsp salt
1 clove garlic, crushed

1 free-range egg, lightly beaten
2½ oz / 75 g feta cheese, crumbled
scant ⅓ cup / 40 g kalamata olives, pitted
olive oil, for drizzling
6 flat-leaf parsley leaves, for garnish
coarse sea salt and freshly ground black pepper

Spicy, sweet, and punchy, baked fresh and served warm, this is the sort of starter that can precede almost anything. The generous sour cream base and the lightness of the puff pastry carry the sweet potato easily without the risk of a carb overdose. Serve with a plain green salad.

Sweet potato galettes

makes 4

1   Preheat the oven to 400°F / 200°C. Bake the sweet potatoes in their skins for 35 to 45 minutes, until they soften up but are still slightly raw in the center (check by inserting a small knife). Leave until cool enough to handle, then peel and cut into slices ⅛ inch / 3 mm thick.

2   While the sweet potatoes are in the oven, roll out the puff pastry to about ¹⁄₁₆ inch / 2 mm thick on a lightly floured work surface. Cut out four 2¾ by 5½-inch / 7 by 14-cm rectangles and prick them all over with a fork. Line a small baking sheet with parchment paper, place the pastry rectangles on it, well spaced apart, and leave to rest in the fridge for at least half an hour.

3   Remove the pastry from the fridge and brush lightly with the beaten egg. Using an icing spatula, spread a thin layer of sour cream on the pastries, leaving a ¼-inch / 5-mm border all round. Arrange the potato slices on the pastry, slightly overlapping, keeping the border clear. Season with salt and pepper, crumble the goat cheese on top, and sprinkle with the pumpkin seeds and chile. Bake for 20 to 25 minutes, until the pastry is cooked through. Check underneath; it should be golden brown.

4   While the galettes are cooking, stir together the olive oil, garlic, parsley, and a pinch of salt. As soon as the pastries come out of the oven, brush them with this mixture. Serve warm or at room temperature.

3 sweet potatoes, about
  12 oz / 350 g each
9 oz / 250 g puff pastry or
  ½ recipe Rough puff pastry
  ↗ page 280
1 free-range egg, lightly beaten
6½ tbsp / 100 ml sour cream
3½ tbsp / 100 g aged goat
  cheese
2 tbsp pumpkin seeds
1 medium-hot chile, finely
  chopped
1 tbsp olive oil
1 clove garlic, crushed
2 tsp chopped flat-leaf parsley
coarse sea salt and freshly
  ground black pepper

The roasted peppers come from Tamar Shany, a multitalented chef who is equally at ease in both the pastry and the savory sections. She is the one who set up our Kensington kitchen, her "baby."

Both the peppers and the cannellini bean paste are excellent fridge staples that keep well, so you can make this up quickly as a last-minute starter. The quantities below will give you enough bean spread for the toasts, plus extra for the fridge.

Roasted pepper and cannellini bruschetta

serves 4

1 Drain the beans and place in a large saucepan with enough cold water to cover them by twice their volume. Bring to a boil and simmer for 80 to 90 minutes, until they are very soft. You will need to skim the froth from the surface a few times during the cooking and might have to add some more boiling water. Drain the beans but keep the cooking liquid.

2 Preheat the oven to 400°F / 200°C. To prepare the peppers, cut them into quarters and shave off the white parts and the seeds. Put them on a baking sheet and toss with 2 tablespoons / 30 ml of the oil and a little salt. Roast in the oven for 35 minutes, until soft, then transfer the hot peppers to a bowl and cover it with plastic wrap; this will make them easier to peel. Once they are cool enough to handle, peel the peppers, place in a container with their cooking juices, and set aside. In a separate bowl, whisk 4 tablespoons / 60 ml of the olive oil with the balsamic vinegar, water, sugar, thyme, 2 sliced garlic cloves, and a pinch of salt. Pour this marinade over the peppers and leave for at least half an hour. If you are not using them on the day, keep the peppers refrigerated for up to a week, making sure they are well immersed in the marinade.

3 Put the warm beans in a food processor together with 1 crushed clove garlic, the lemon juice, the remaining 3 tablespoons / 45 ml oil, 1 teaspoon salt, a good grinding of black pepper, and 3½ tablespoons / 50 ml of the bean cooking liquid. Process to a smooth paste. Taste and see if you want to add any more salt, pepper, or lemon juice. Leave to cool and then taste again; you will probably need to add more salt.

4 Put the bread slices on a baking sheet, brush them with olive oil, and sprinkle with a little salt. Bake for 10 to 12 minutes, until golden brown. While they are still hot, rub the slices with 2 peeled cloves garlic, then leave them to cool on a wire rack.

5 Spread a good amount of the bean purée on each toast, top generously with the marinated peppers, then garnish with the green onions and a drizzle of olive oil.

¾ cup / 150 g dried cannellini beans, soaked overnight in plenty of cold water
2 red and 2 yellow bell peppers
½ cup plus 1 tbsp / 135 ml olive oil, plus extra for drizzling
2 tbsp balsamic vinegar
2 tbsp water
1 tsp muscovado sugar
4 sprigs thyme
5 cloves garlic, peeled
juice of 1 lemon
4 thick slices Crusty white Italian loaf ↗ page 162 **or other rustic loaf**
2 green onions, coarsely sliced
salt and freshly ground black pepper

Deliciously rich, this can be made even richer by using mascarpone instead of the cream cheese. Serve as a light, summery main course or cut smaller pieces of bread for party finger food.

Organic salmon and asparagus bruschetta

serves 4

1   Preheat the oven to 400°F / 200°C. Drizzle a baking dish with some olive oil and place the salmon fillet, skin side down, in the dish. Add the bay leaves, juniper, and wine, then sprinkle the fillet with a little salt. Squeeze over the lemon half and throw it in with the fish. Cover the dish with aluminum foil, and bake for 15 to 20 minutes. The fish should be just cooked and still lightly pink inside. Remove from the oven, take off the aluminum foil, and allow to cool.

2   To prepare the bread, lay out the slices on a baking sheet, brush with olive oil, and sprinkle with salt. Bake for 10 to 12 minutes, until golden brown. While they are still hot, rub the slices with the peeled cloves garlic, then leave on a wire rack to cool.

3   Trim off the woody ends of the asparagus. Add the asparagus to a large saucepan of boiling salted water and simmer for 2 minutes. Drain in a colander and refresh under cold water until completely cool. Drain again and leave to dry in a colander.

4   When the salmon has cooled sufficiently, flake it with your hands into big chunks, reserving the cooking liquor in a separate bowl.

5   Spread the toasts liberally with the cream cheese. Arrange the salmon and asparagus on top creatively. Spoon over some of the reserved cooking juices and finish with a good grind of black pepper and some salt. Garnish with a few sprigs of chervil and a wedge of lemon.

olive oil for drizzling and brushing the bread
12 oz / 350 g organic salmon fillet
4 bay leaves
4 juniper berries
½ cup / 120 ml Muscat or other sweet wine
½ lemon
4 thick slices Crusty white Italian loaf ↗ page 162 **or other rustic loaf**
2 cloves garlic, peeled
5 oz / 150 g asparagus spears
4 oz / 120 g cream cheese
coarse sea salt and freshly ground black pepper
a few sprigs chervil, for garnish
lemon wedges, for garnish

Olive oil crackers (↗ page 186) and Parmesan and poppy crackers (↗ page 187)

In our first year in Notting Hill, we used to cut these crackers into odd-shaped, long strips, then bake them and pile them up inside a large, black African bowl and place it in the window. It looked spectacular. Only one problem: they were so delicate they broke within an hour. So here we roll them into a more practical, though still beautifully elegant, shape. They are so easy to make that you'll never need to buy crackers again. They are perfect fresh from the oven, as crisp as can be, served with cheese or dips.

Olive oil crackers

makes about 25

1 In a large bowl, mix together all the ingredients except the sea salt to form a soft dough. You can do this by hand or in a mixer fitted with a dough hook. Work it until you get a firm consistency, then cover with plastic wrap and leave to rest in the fridge for 1 hour.

2 Preheat the oven to 425°F / 220°C. Turn the dough out onto a clean work surface. Have a bowl of flour for dusting ready at the side. Use a large, sharp knife to cut off walnut-size pieces (roughly ½ oz / 15 g each) from the dough. Roll out each piece as thinly as possible with a rolling pin, dusting with plenty of flour. They should end up looking like long, oval tongues, almost paper-thin.

3 Place the crackers on a baking sheet lined with parchment paper. Brush them with plenty of olive oil and sprinkle with sea salt. Bake for about 6 minutes, until crisp and golden.

2 cups / 250 g all-purpose flour, plus extra for dusting
1 tsp baking powder
scant ½ cup / 115 ml water
5 tsp / 25 ml olive oil, plus extra for brushing
½ tsp salt
1 tsp paprika
¼ tsp cayenne pepper
¼ tsp freshly ground black pepper
coarse sea salt for sprinkling

These are to have with drinks and they are more addictive than a fine Bordeaux. Beware! For the freshest of crackers, always keep a log of the dough in the freezer ready to defrost and bake.

The poppy seeds are not essential but they do make the crackers a bit more celebratory.

Parmesan and poppy crackers

makes about 35

1 Sift the flour, baking powder, paprika, and cayenne into a bowl and add the salt and pepper.

2 Mix the softened butter with the Parmesan until they are well blended. You can do this either by hand, using a spatula, or in a stand mixer fitted with the paddle attachment. Add the dry ingredients and continue mixing until a soft dough forms.

3 Turn the dough out onto a well-floured work surface and divide it in half. Use plenty of flour, both on your hands and on the work surface, to roll each piece into a long log, 1¼ to 1½ inches / 3 to 4 cm in diameter. Wrap each log in plastic wrap and place in the fridge for about 30 minutes to firm up.

4 Scatter the poppy seeds over a flat plate or tray. Brush the logs with the beaten egg and then roll them in the poppy seeds until covered. Refrigerate again for 1 hour (at this stage you can also wrap the logs and freeze them).

5 Preheat the oven to 325°F / 170°C. Line a baking sheet with parchment paper. Cut the logs into slices ¼ to ⅓ inch / 5 to 8 mm thick and arrange them on the pan, spaced 1¼ inches / 3 cm apart. Bake for 12 minutes. The crackers should be dark golden and smell amazing! Leave to cool completely before serving or storing in a tightly sealed container.

1⅔ cups / 210 g all-purpose flour, plus plenty extra for dusting
½ tsp baking powder
½ tsp paprika
pinch of cayenne pepper
pinch of salt
½ tsp freshly ground black pepper
⅔ cup / 165 g unsalted butter, at room temperature
6 oz / 165 g Parmesan cheese, freshly grated
½ cup plus 1 tbsp / 80 g poppy seeds
1 free-range egg, beaten

Utterly tasty, especially when just out of the oven. While they're baking, your kitchen will be filled with mouthwatering aromas. If the straws aren't devoured at once, heat them up slightly just before serving.

Claudine, who tried the recipe while in France where she couldn't get Cheddar, used mature Comté instead and said they were delectable.

One little piece of advice: when making the cheese straws, work fast and try to keep a flow of fresh, cool air in the kitchen. Otherwise, the pastry will heat up and turn sticky and difficult to manage.

Cheddar and caraway cheese straws

makes 10

all-purpose flour, for dusting
10½ oz / 300 g puff pastry,
  or ½ recipe Rough puff
  pastry ↗ page 280
1 free-range egg, lightly beaten
3½ oz / 100 g aged Cheddar
  cheese, finely grated
1 tsp caraway seeds

1   Dust a work surface lightly with flour and roll out the pastry into a rectangle ¹⁄₁₆ to ⅛ inch / 2 to 3 mm thick. Trim the edges with a sharp knife in order to get a perfect rectangle, about 12 by 8 inches / 30 by 20 cm. Place on a baking sheet dusted with flour and leave to rest in the fridge for 30 minutes.

2   Return the pastry sheet to the dusted work surface. Brush off any flour and then brush the top with the beaten egg and sprinkle over half the cheese. Press the cheese down lightly with your hands so it sticks to the pastry. Be brisk so that you don't warm up the butter in the pastry. Carefully turn the pastry over, brush off any excess flour, and repeat this process on the other side.

3   Now cut strips about 1¼ inches / 3 cm wide across the width of the pastry. Pick up a strip holding one end in each hand. Place one end on the work surface and hold still. Twist the other end on the work surface to make a tight spiral form. You will need to pull as you twist to get a long, hollow straw shape.

4   Carefully transfer the straws to a baking sheet lined with parchment paper. Space them at least 1¼ inches / 3 cm apart and sprinkle with the caraway seeds. Let them rest in the fridge for at least 30 minutes.

5   Preheat the oven to 350°F / 180°C. Place the pan of cheese straws in the oven and bake for 20 to 25 minutes. Make sure you do not open the oven door for the first 15 minutes. When ready, the straws should be a beautiful light brown. Let them cool slightly before serving.

NGHIOTTOLE

The olive oil gives this cake extra depth and intensity. The complex flavors mature over time, so consider wrapping the cake in plastic wrap and refrigerating it, ready to ice and serve, for up to 3 days. Somewhat less festive (and less calorie laden), this is still very satisfying without the maple icing. Just dust lightly with confectioners' sugar.

Apple and olive oil cake with maple icing

serves 6 to 8

1 Grease an 8-inch / 20-cm springform cake pan and line the bottom and sides with parchment paper. Place the raisins and water in a medium saucepan and simmer over low heat until all of the water has been absorbed. Leave to cool.

2 Preheat the oven to 325°F / 170°C. Sift together the flour, cinnamon, salt, baking powder, and baking soda and set aside.

3 Put the oil and superfine sugar in the bowl of a stand mixer fitted with a paddle attachment (or use a whisk if you don't have a mixer). Slit the vanilla bean lengthwise in half and, using a sharp knife, scrape the seeds out into the bowl. Beat the oil, sugar, and vanilla together, then gradually add the eggs. The mix should be smooth and thick at this stage. Mix in the diced apples, raisins, and lemon zest, then lightly fold in the sifted dry ingredients.

4 Whisk the egg whites in a clean bowl, either by hand or with a mixer, until they have a soft meringue consistency. Fold them into the batter in 2 additions, trying to maintain as much air as possible.

5 Pour the batter into the lined pan, level it with an icing spatula, and place in the oven. Bake for 1½ hours, until a skewer inserted into the center comes out clean. Remove from the oven and leave to cool in the pan.

6 Once the cake is completely cold, you can assemble it. Remove from the pan and use a large serrated knife to cut it in half horizontally. You should end up with 2 similar disks. If the cake is very domed, you might need to shave a bit off the top half to level it.

7 To make the icing, beat together the butter, muscovado sugar, and maple syrup until light and airy. You can do this by hand, or, preferably, in a mixer, fitted with the paddle attachment. Add the cream cheese and beat until the icing is totally smooth.

8 Using the icing spatula, spread a layer of icing 3/8 inch / 1 cm thick over the bottom half of the cake. Carefully place the top half on it. Spoon the rest of the icing on top and use the icing spatula to create a wavelike or any other pattern. Dust it with confectioners' sugar, if you like.

heaping ½ cup / 80 g golden raisins
4 tbsp water
2¼ cups / 280 g all-purpose flour
½ tsp ground cinnamon
¼ tsp salt
½ tsp baking powder
1¼ tsp baking soda
½ cup / 120 ml olive oil
¾ cup / 160 g superfine sugar
½ vanilla bean
2 free-range eggs, lightly beaten
3 large Granny Smith apples, peeled, cored, and cut into 3/8-inch / 1-cm dice
grated zest of 1 lemon
2 free-range egg whites
confectioners' sugar for dusting (optional)

Maple icing
7 tbsp / 100 g unsalted butter, at room temperature
scant ½ cup / 100 g light muscovado sugar
scant 6 tbsp / 85 ml maple syrup
8 oz / 220 g cream cheese, at room temperature

A beautiful-looking and even better-tasting cake. Use blood oranges when in season (January to April) for a spectacular effect.

Quick-cooking polenta works better in cakes than standard polenta; it doesn't leave a gritty texture. One warning: Alison Quinn, who tried many recipes for us, used a springform pan to make this cake but forgot to line the corners and sides of the pan with parchment paper. The caramel and the juices from the oranges leaked all over her oven . . . a nasty cleaning job!

Orange polenta cake

serves 6 to 8

1   Lightly grease an 8-inch / 20-cm round cake pan and line the bottom and sides with parchment paper. If using a springform pan, make sure the paper circle you cut for the base is large enough to go some of the way up the sides as well, to prevent leaking.
2   To make the caramel, have ready by the stove a small pastry brush and a cup of water. Put the sugar for the caramel topping in a heavy-bottomed saucepan and add the 2 tablespoons water. Stir gently to dampen the sugar evenly and then place over medium-low heat. Slowly bring the sugar to a boil. While it bubbles away, brush the sides of the pan occasionally with a little of the water in the cup to get rid of any crystals that form close to the bubbling sugar. After a few minutes, the water should evaporate and the sugar will start to darken. Keep your eyes on the sugar at all times as it can easily burn. As soon as it reaches a nice golden color, remove the pan from the heat. With your face at a safe distance, add the butter. Stir with a wooden spoon and pour the caramel over the lined base of the cake pan. Carefully but quickly (so it doesn't set) tilt it to spread evenly.
3   Grate the zest of the 2 oranges, making sure you don't reach the white part of the skin. Set the grated zest aside. Using a small, sharp knife, slice off ⅜ inch / 1 cm from the top and bottom of each orange. Standing each orange up on a board, carefully follow the natural curves of the orange with the knife to peel off the remaining skin and all the white pith. Cut each orange horizontally into 6 slices. Remove the seeds and lay the slices tightly over the caramel. (You might need to peel and slice another orange to cover the whole space.)
4   Now move on to the cake batter. Preheat the oven to 325°F / 170°C. Sift together the flour, baking powder, and salt and set aside.
5   In an electric mixer fitted with the paddle attachment, cream the butter and sugar together lightly. Make sure they are well combined but do not incorporate much air into the mixture. With the mixer on low speed, gradually add the eggs. Next add the reserved orange zest and the orange blossom water, followed by the almonds, polenta, and sifted dry ingredients. As soon as they are all mixed in, stop the machine.
6   Transfer the batter to the prepared cake pan, making sure the oranges underneath stay in a single neat layer. Level the mixture carefully with an icing spatula. Place the cake in the oven and bake for 40 to 45 minutes, until a skewer inserted into the center comes out dry. Remove from the oven and leave to cool for about 5 minutes.
7   While the cake is still hot (warm it up a little if you forgot, otherwise the caramel will stick to the paper), place a cardboard disk or a flat plate on top. Briskly turn over and then remove the pan and the lining paper. Leave the cake to cool completely.
8   To make the glaze, bring the marmalade and water to a boil in a small saucepan and then pass through a sieve. While the glaze is still hot, lightly brush the top of the cake with it.

Caramel topping
scant ½ cup / 90 g superfine sugar
2 tbsp water
4 tsp / 20 g unsalted butter, diced
2 oranges, plus a possible extra one

6½ tbsp / 50 g all-purpose flour
1 tsp baking powder
½ tsp salt
¾ cup plus 2 tbsp / 200 g unsalted butter
1 cup / 200 g superfine sugar
3 free-range eggs, lightly beaten
2 tsp orange blossom water
  (↗ page xii)
2½ cups / 240 g ground almonds
¾ cup / 120 g quick-cooking polenta

Glaze (optional)
4 tbsp orange marmalade
1 tbsp water

This is a simple cake to prepare and a most delectable one, made a bit more complicated by baking in two stages. The result is two chocolate layers with slightly different consistencies: one a bit firmer and cakey, the other more mousselike. Chocolate connoisseurs will appreciate that. For a less discerning audience, or if you want to hasten the process or are feeling lazy, cook the whole cake at once. The result will still be highly satisfying.

Chocolate fudge cake

serves 6 to 8

1 Preheat the oven to 325°F / 170°C. Grease an 8-inch / 20-cm springform pan and line the bottom and sides with parchment paper.
2 Place the butter and both types of chocolate in a very large heatproof bowl. It should be big enough to accommodate the entire mix. Put the muscovado sugar and water in a small saucepan, stir to mix, then bring to a boil over medium heat. Pour the boiling syrup over the butter and chocolate and stir well until they have melted and you are left with a runny chocolate sauce. Stir in the egg yolks, one at a time. Set aside until the mixture cools to room temperature.
3 Put the egg whites and salt in a large bowl and whisk to a firm, but not too dry, meringue. Using a rubber spatula or a large metal spoon, gently fold the meringue into the cooled chocolate mixture one-third at a time. The whites should be fully incorporated but there is no harm if you can see small bits of meringue in the mix.
4 Pour 1¾ pounds / 800 g (about two-thirds) of the mixture into the prepared cake pan and level gently with an icing spatula. Leave the rest of the batter for later. Place the cake in the oven and bake for about 40 minutes, until a skewer inserted into the center comes out almost clean. Remove from the oven and leave to cool completely.
5 Flatten the top of the cake with the icing spatula. Don't worry about breaking the crust. Pour the rest of the batter on top and level the surface again. Return to the oven and bake for 20 to 25 minutes. The cake should still have moist crumbs when checked with a skewer. Leave to cool completely before removing from the pan. Dust with cocoa powder and serve. The cake will keep, covered, at room temperature for 4 days.

1 cup / 240 g unsalted butter,
   cut into small cubes
9½ oz / 265 g dark chocolate
   (52 percent cacao solids),
   cut into small pieces
3½ oz / 95 g dark chocolate
   (70 percent cacao solids),
   cut into small pieces
1¼ cups / 290 g light muscovado
   sugar
4 tbsp water
5 large free-range eggs, separated
pinch of salt
cocoa powder for dusting

Once you've baked this cake, you'll be able to take your A-levels on the subject of caramel. You make it twice here, using different methods, but don't be scared. It is one of those things that seems intimidating from a distance but is actually not that hard to do. A note of advice: to get the caramel off your pans, fill them with water and boil on the stove. Remove the water and wash normally.

Caramel and macadamia cheesecake

1 Preheat the oven to 275°F / 140°C. Lightly grease an 8-inch / 20-cm springform pan and line the bottom and sides with parchment paper.

2 To make the base, whiz the cookies into crumbs in a food processor (or put them in a plastic bag and bash with a mallet or rolling pin). Mix with the melted butter to a wet, sandy consistency. Transfer to the lined pan and flatten with the back of a tablespoon to create a level base.

3 To make the cake batter, put the cream cheese and sugar in a mixing bowl. Slit the vanilla bean in half lengthwise and, using a sharp knife, scrape the seeds out into the bowl. Whisk by hand or, more easily, with an electric mixer, until smooth. Gradually add the eggs and sour cream, whisking until smooth. Pour the mixture over the cookie base and place in the oven. Bake for 60 to 70 minutes, until set; a skewer inserted into the center should come out with a slightly wet crumb attached. Leave to cool to room temperature, then turn out of the pan. Removing the cake from the pan bottom can be a little tricky. You can leave it there and serve from the bottom, if you prefer. Otherwise, get a flat 8-inch / 20-cm cake board and gently squeeze it between the base of the cake and the parchment. As a last resort, get a couple of fish slicers and someone to help you lift the whole thing onto a flat serving plate. Now chill the cake for at least a couple of hours.

4 To prepare the nut topping, preheat the oven to 275°F / 140°C, scatter the nuts over a baking sheet, and roast for about 15 minutes, until golden. Remove from the oven and set aside. Line the baking sheet with parchment paper. Place the sugar in a saucepan with a very thick bottom (it is important that the layer of sugar not be more than 1/8 inch / 3 mm high in the pan, so choose a large one). Heat the sugar gently until it turns into a golden brown caramel. Do not stir it at any stage. Don't worry if some small bits of sugar don't totally dissolve. Carefully add the toasted nuts and mix gently with a wooden spoon. When most of the nuts are coated with caramel, pour them into the lined pan and leave to set. Break bits off and chop them very coarsely with a large knife. It's nice to leave some of the nuts just halved or even left whole.

5 To make the sauce, put the butter and sugar in a heavy-bottomed saucepan and stir constantly over medium heat with a wooden spoon until it becomes a smooth, dark caramel. The butter and sugar will look as if they have split. Don't worry; just keep on stirring. Once the desired color is reached, carefully add the cream while stirring vigorously. Remove from the heat and leave to cool.

6 To finish the cake, dust the edges and sides with plenty of confectioners' sugar. Spoon the sauce onto the center, allowing it to spill over a little. Scatter lots of caramelized nuts on top. The cheesecake will keep in the fridge for 3 days.

serves 8

Base
160 g plain oatmeal cookies
2½ tbsp / 40 g unsalted butter, melted

Cake batter
1⅓ lb / 600 g good-quality cream cheese, at room temperature
½ cup plus 4 tsp / 120 g superfine sugar
½ vanilla bean
4 free-range eggs, lightly beaten
4 tbsp / 60 ml sour cream
confectioners' sugar for dusting

Nut topping
heaping 1 cup / 150 g macadamia nuts
scant ½ cup / 90 g superfine sugar

Caramel sauce
scant 4½ tbsp / 65 g unsalted butter
¾ cup plus 1 tbsp / 160 g superfine sugar
7 tbsp / 100 ml heavy cream

There are two warring camps at Ottolenghi over the vital issue of . . . carrot cake. Helen Goh and Sarit Packer, who are always on the lookout for new ideas and some earth-shattering recipes, like their carrot cakes dense and fruity. We prefer them light and fluffy, like this one. So far the issue hasn't been resolved—there's just a tense ceasefire. Watch out for the next Ottolenghi cookbook: if the balance of power shifts, you might find a totally different carrot cake.

Carrot and walnut cake

serves 6 to 8

1 Preheat the oven to 325°F / 170°C. Grease an 8-inch / 20-cm springform pan and line the bottom and sides with parchment paper.
2 Sift together the flour, baking powder, baking soda, and spices. Lightly whisk the whole egg with the egg yolk.
3 Put the sunflower oil and superfine sugar in the bowl of an electric mixer fitted with the paddle attachment and beat for about 1 minute on medium speed. On low speed, slowly add the beaten egg. Mix in the walnuts, coconut, and carrot and then the sifted dry ingredients. Don't overmix.
4 Transfer the mixture to a large bowl. Wash and dry the mixer bowl, making sure it is totally clean, then put the egg whites and salt in it and whisk on high speed until firm peaks form. Gently fold the egg whites into the carrot mixture in 3 additions, being careful not to overmix. Streaks of white in the mixture are okay.
5 Pour the cake mixture into the prepared pan and bake for about 1 hour; it could take longer. A skewer inserted into the center should come out dry. If the cake starts getting dark before the center is cooked through, cover it with aluminum foil. Let the cake cool completely and then remove from the pan.
6 To make the icing, beat the cream cheese in a mixer until light and smooth. Remove from the mixer. Beat the butter, confectioners' sugar, and honey in the mixer until light and airy. Fold together the cheese and butter mixes. Spread waves of icing on top of the cake and sprinkle with the nuts.

1¼ cups plus 1½ tsp / 160 g all-purpose flour
½ tsp baking powder
½ tsp baking soda
1 tsp ground cinnamon
¼ tsp ground cloves
1 extra-large free-range egg
1 large free-range egg yolk
¾ cup plus 1 tbsp / 200 g sunflower oil
1⅓ cups / 270 g superfine sugar
½ cup / 50 g walnuts, chopped
⅔ cup / 50 g flaked coconut
4½ oz / 135 g carrots, coarsely grated
2 large free-range egg whites
pinch of salt

Icing
6¼ oz / 175 g cream cheese, at room temperature
4½ tbsp / 70 g unsalted butter
4½ tbsp / 35 g confectioners' sugar
4 tsp / 25 g honey
⅓ cup / 30 g walnuts, chopped and lightly toasted

Teacakes

We are not sure how we came to call these teacakes. They are definitely not related to the British fruited bun bearing the name. In any case, these distinctively shaped individual cakes have become one of Ottolenghi's trademarks and are now made by many other patisseries.

In America, the Bundt pans that we use for making these cakes come in many different sizes, from giant family size to tiny petits fours. Ours are medium-small, taking 5 to 7 ounces / 150 to 200 g of cake batter, enough for one generous serving. Bundt pans are not so easy to find in the United Kingdom, but a close alternative you can use for making these teacakes is a mini kugelhopf pan 4 inches / 10 cm in diameter.

The volcano-like shape of a Bundt or kugelhopf pan allows you to play creatively with different icings and glazes. Still, you could do the same with other pans or molds of similar capacity. These cakes can even be made like muffins in paper liners, in which case you would probably get more than six.

It is important to grease Bundt pans well before filling them. We chill the pans first and then brush them generously with melted butter.

Peach and raspberry

1 Preheat the oven to 325°F / 170°C. Leave 6 small Bundt or kugelhopf pans in the fridge for a few minutes, then remove and brush with plenty of melted butter. Return them to the fridge.

2 Start by sifting together the flour, baking powder, baking soda, and salt, then set aside. Cream the butter and superfine sugar together until light and fluffy, preferably using an electric mixer. Mix the eggs with the vanilla, then gradually add to the creamed mixture, beating well until each little addition has been fully incorporated. Gently fold in one-third of the flour mixture, followed by one-third of the sour cream. Continue like this until both are mixed in and the batter is smooth. Fold in the diced peach.

3 Either pipe or spoon the mixture into the pans, filling them to within about ¾ inch / 2 cm from the top. Press 4 raspberries into each cake, sinking them with your finger to just below the surface of the batter (keep the remaining raspberries to scatter over the finished cakes). Place the cakes in the oven and bake for 25 to 30 minutes. Poke with a skewer to make sure they are completely dry inside; it should come out clean. Remove them from the oven and leave in their pans for 10 minutes to cool slightly, then turn out onto a wire rack and leave to cool completely.

4 To make the glaze, place all the ingredients in a small saucepan and bring to a boil. Stir and leave to simmer for 4 minutes. Pass the hot glaze through a fine sieve, rubbing the raspberry seeds with a wooden spoon to release as much of the juice as you can. Brush or drizzle the hot glaze over the cakes and leave to set (if the glaze is too thin to coat the cakes, simmer it over medium heat until reduced; if it is too thick, add a little water and heat gently). Pile the remaining raspberries on top of the cakes and dust with confectioners' sugar.

makes 6

¾ cup / 180 g unsalted butter,
 plus melted butter
 for greasing the pans
2 cups plus 2 tsp / 260 g
 all-purpose flour
1 tsp baking powder
½ tsp baking soda
¼ tsp salt
¾ cup plus 2 tsp / 160 g
 superfine sugar
2 free-range eggs
1 tsp vanilla extract
⅔ cup / 170 ml sour cream
1 peach, halved, pitted,
 and cut into ⅜-inch / 1-cm dice
2 cups / 250 g raspberries
confectioners' sugar for dusting

Glaze
1⅔ cups / 200 g raspberries
½ cup / 170 g apricot jam
7 tbsp / 100 ml water

Lemon and blueberry

1 Preheat the oven to 325°F / 170°C. Leave 6 small Bundt or kugelhopf pans in the fridge for a few minutes, then remove and brush with plenty of melted butter. Return them to the fridge.

2 Mix together the flour and ground almonds and set aside. Using an electric mixer, or by hand, cream the butter and superfine sugar together until pale and fluffy. Break the eggs into a cup and mix lightly with a fork. Gradually add the eggs to the butter mix, beating well until each little addition has been fully incorporated. If the mixture looks as if it has split, add a little of the almond-and-flour mixture and it should come back together. Once all the egg is incorporated, gently fold in the almonds and flour, followed by the lemon zest, juice, and blueberries. Be gentle, so the blueberries don't break.

3 Take the molds from the fridge. Either pipe or spoon the mixture into the pans, filling all the way up to the rim. Level the mixture and clean the edges of the pans if necessary. Bake in the oven for 30 to 35 minutes, until a skewer inserted into the center of a cake comes out clean. Remove them from the oven and leave them in their pans for 10 minutes, then turn out onto a wire rack and leave to cool completely.

4 To make the glaze, whisk the lemon juice and confectioners' sugar together in a small bowl, adding more lemon juice or sugar if necessary to make an icing with a drizzling consistency. Spoon it liberally over the cakes or brush with a pastry brush, letting the icing drip down the sides.

1 cup plus 2½ tbsp / 280 g unsalted butter, plus melted butter for greasing the pans
½ cup / 65 g all-purpose flour
scant 3 cups / 280 g ground almonds
1 cup plus 6½ tbsp / 280 g superfine sugar
5 free-range eggs
grated zest of 2 lemons
6½ tbsp / 100 ml lemon juice
¾ cup / 120 g blueberries

Glaze
3½ tbsp / 50 ml lemon juice
1¼ cups / 150 g confectioners' sugar

Lavender and honey

1 Preheat the oven to 325°F / 170°C. Leave 6 small Bundt or kugelhopf pans in the fridge for a few minutes, then remove and brush with plenty of melted butter. Return them to the fridge.

2 Cream the butter, superfine sugar, and honey together until pale and fluffy, preferably using an electric mixer. Break the eggs into a cup, beat them lightly with a fork, and gradually add to the creamed mixture, beating well until each addition has been fully incorporated. Sift together the flour, baking powder, baking soda, salt, and cinnamon, then stir in the lavender. Gently fold the flour mixture into the creamed mix in 3 additions, alternating with the sour cream.

3 Either pipe or spoon the mixture into the pans, filling them to within about ⅔ inch / 1.5 cm of the top. Level out the mix and clean the edges of the pans if necessary. Place in the oven and bake for 25 to 30 minutes, until a skewer inserted into the center of a cake comes out clean. Remove them from the oven and leave in their pans for 10 minutes, then turn out onto a wire rack and leave to cool completely.

4 To make the glaze, mix the lemon juice and honey together in a small bowl, then whisk in enough confectioners' sugar to make a thick, pourable glaze. Use a pastry brush or a spoon to coat the top of the cakes, allowing the icing to drip down the sides. Sprinkle with a little dried lavender.

1 cup minus 1 tbsp / 225 g unsalted butter, plus melted butter for greasing the pans
½ cup plus 1 tbsp / 115 g superfine sugar
⅓ cup / 115 g lavender honey (or plain honey if you can't get it)
3 free-range eggs
2 cups / 245 g all-purpose flour
1 tsp baking powder
½ tsp baking soda
½ tsp salt
½ tsp ground cinnamon
½ tsp chopped dried lavender, plus extra for garnish
scant ½ cup / 110 ml sour cream

Glaze
4 tsp / 20 ml lemon juice
2 tsp honey
heaping ¾ cup / 100 g confectioners' sugar

Muffins

What makes muffins so attractive to home bakers is that they are quick, dead easy to make, require very little preparation, and can be done with the most basic kitchen equipment (no need for a mixer or blender).

Unlike other cakes, it's best not to incorporate much air into a muffin batter, or to work the flour to develop the protein in it. For this reason, it is essential that at the last stage, when mixing the dry and wet ingredients together, you keep the stirring to a minimum. The key is to stop while there are still plenty of unmixed lumps. This will give the muffins their typical light and short texture.

The plum muffin below has a celebration look. To turn it into a casual breakfast, skip the compote topping and serve plain (it will still be delicious).

Use dark red, ripe plums for the best visual effect. As for the marzipan, try to avoid the luminous yellow stuff, artificial in substance and flavor. Look for good-tasting marzipan, preferably organic, in health food stores and some supermarkets.

Plum, marzipan, and cinnamon

makes 10 to 12

Plum compote
**1½ lb / 700 g ripe red plums,
    pitted and quartered**
4½ tbsp / 60 g superfine sugar
1 cinnamon stick

**4 cups minus 2½ tbsp /
    480 g all-purpose flour**
1 tsp baking powder
½ tsp baking soda
1 tsp ground cinnamon
pinch of salt
1 cup / 200 g superfine sugar
2 free-range eggs
1 cup plus 2½ tbsp / 280 ml milk
**7½ tbsp / 110 g unsalted butter,
    melted**
4 oz / 120 g marzipan
grated zest of 2 oranges
confectioners' sugar for dusting

1 To make the plum compote, preheat the oven to 325°F / 170°C. Place the plums in a shallow baking dish, add the sugar and cinnamon stick, and mix together. Place in the oven and bake for 10 to 20 minutes, until the plums are soft and their skin starts to separate from the flesh (the cooking time will vary significantly, depending on the ripeness of the fruit). Remove from the oven and set aside to cool. Discard the cinnamon stick.

2 Sift the flour, baking powder, baking soda, cinnamon, and salt into a bowl. Put the superfine sugar and eggs in a large mixing bowl and whisk together. Add the milk and butter (make sure it is not too hot) and whisk to combine.

3 Grate the marzipan on the coarse side of a grater and add this to the batter, together with the orange zest. Now add 3 oz / 80 g of the plum compote (pulp and juices) and stir together. Set the rest of the compote aside for later.

4 Using a rubber spatula, gently fold the flour mixture into the wet mix just until combined (there may still be a few lumps and bits of flour; that is what you want).

5 Line a muffin pan with paper liners and spoon in the mixture, filling them to the top. Bake for 25 to 30 minutes, until a skewer inserted into the center of a muffin comes out clean. When cool enough to handle, take the muffins out of the pans and leave on a wire rack until cold.

6 Just before serving, dust the tops with a little confectioners' sugar and top with the reserved cooked plums.

Chapter 3 Baking and patisserie

Blueberries are the all-time favorite muffin flavor. The reason is their unique ability to keep their shape and most of their wonderful characteristics throughout the baking process.

Blueberry crumble

makes 10 to 12

1 Preheat the oven to 325°F / 170°C. Line a muffin pan with paper liners.
2 Sift together the flour, baking powder, and salt and set aside. In a large mixing bowl, lightly whisk together the eggs, sugar, and melted butter (make sure it is not too hot). Whisk in the milk and lemon zest, then gently fold in the fruits.
3 Add the sifted dry Ingredients and fold together very gently. Make sure you stir the mix just enough to combine, it should remain lumpy and rough.
4 Spoon the mixture into the muffin liners, filling them to the top. Generously cover with the crumble topping to form small domes over the batter, then dot with a few extra blueberries. Bake for 30 to 35 minutes, until a skewer inserted into the center of a muffin comes out clean. Remove the muffins from the pan while they are still warm.

4⅓ cups / 540 g all-purpose flour
5 tsp baking powder
½ tsp salt
2 free-range eggs
1¾ cups / 340 g superfine sugar
½ cup plus 1½ tbsp / 140 g unsalted butter, melted
1½ cups plus 4 tsp / 380 ml milk
grated zest of 1 lemon
1 Granny Smith apple (unpeeled), cut into ⅜-inch / 1-cm dice
1⅓ cups / 200 g fresh blueberries, plus a few extra for the topping
½ recipe Crumble ↗ page 279

A wholesome option but extremely tasty, with lots of spice and tons of flavor. Beware, you will end up eating much more than you intended to. Thanks to Tamar Shany for developing this recipe during one of her sleepless nights in Notting Hill.

Carrot, apple, and pecan

makes 10 to 12

1 To make the topping, in a bowl, stir together the butter, flour, and muscovado sugar. Rub with your fingertips until the butter is incorporated and you have a crumbly texture. Mix in the oats and seeds and then the water, oil, and honey. Stir everything together, resulting in a wet, sandy texture. Set aside.

2 Preheat the oven to 325°F / 170°C. Line a muffin pan with paper liners.

3 Sift together the flour, baking powder, cinnamon, and salt. In a large mixing bowl, whisk together the eggs, oil, superfine sugar, vanilla, and grated carrot and apple. Gently fold in the pecans, raisins, and coconut, and then the sifted flour mixture. Do not overmix, and don't worry if the batter is lumpy and irregular. Spoon into the muffin liners and scatter the topping generously over the top. Bake for about 25 minutes, until a skewer inserted into the center of a muffin comes out clean. Remove the muffins from the pan when they are just warm and allow them to cool before serving. Their flavor will actually improve after a couple of hours.

Topping
3 tbsp plus 1 tsp / 50 g unsalted butter, cut into small pieces
½ cup plus 1½ tbsp / 75 g all-purpose flour
5 tsp / 25 g light muscovado sugar
½ cup / 50 g rolled oats
1½ tbsp / 15 g sunflower seeds
3 tbsp / 25 g pumpkin seeds
1½ tbsp / 15 g black sesame seeds
1 tsp water
1 tsp sunflower oil
1½ tbsp honey

2 cups plus 6 tbsp / 300 g all-purpose flour
2 tsp baking powder
2 tsp ground cinnamon
pinch of salt
4 free-range eggs
⅔ cup / 160 ml sunflower oil
1 cup / 280 g superfine sugar
2 tsp vanilla extract
8 oz / 220 g peeled carrots, grated
7 oz / 200 g Granny Smith apples, coarsely grated
1 cup / 100 g pecans, coarsely chopped
⅔ cup / 100 g golden raisins
⅔ cup / 50 g flaked coconut

Cupcakes

The secret of a good cupcake is in the icing. Ours are a bit serious, with no food coloring and frilly decorations but still madly rich and luscious. We also love the over-the-top American cupcakes, like the ones at the Magnolia Bakery in New York. Whichever version you choose, don't torment yourself—you only live once!

Hazelnut

1   Preheat the oven to 300°F / 150°C. Place the hazelnuts on a baking sheet and toast for 15 minutes, until lightly colored. Remove from the oven. Once they have thoroughly cooled, rub them in a kitchen towel and shake it in your hands to get rid of most of the skins. Blitz them in a food processor with half the superfine sugar until finely chopped.
2   Now make the cupcakes. Increase the oven temperature to 325°F / 170°C. Line a muffin pan with 8 to 12 paper liners. Sift together the flour, baking powder, and salt. Cream together the butter, remaining sugar, hazelnut oil, and finely chopped hazelnuts until light and airy. Mix in the beaten eggs, a little at a time, waiting until each addition is fully incorporated before adding the next bit. Use a spatula or large metal spoon to fold in half the sifted dry ingredients, then half the sour cream, followed by the rest of the dry ingredients and then the remaining sour cream. Spoon the mixture into the cupcake liners, filling them to within ¼ inch / 5 mm of the rim. Bake for 20 to 25 minutes, until a skewer inserted into the center comes out clean. Remove from the oven and leave to cool.
3   Make the icing only once the cupcakes are cold. Beat the cream cheese and mascarpone together until they are smooth and light. In a separate bowl, beat the butter and confectioners' sugar together, either with an electric mixer or by hand, for at least 5 minutes (if the mixer attachment doesn't reach the bottom of the bowl you might need to do this by hand). The mixture should turn almost white and become fluffy and light. Fold in the cream cheese mixture and then use a spatula to sculpt a wavy topping on each cupcake.

makes 8 to 12

⅓ cup / 45 g unskinned
   hazelnuts
¾ cup / 150 g superfine sugar
1½ cups minus 1 tbsp / 180 g
   all-purpose flour
1¼ tsp baking powder
scant ½ tsp salt
⅔ cup / 150 g unsalted butter
1 tbsp hazelnut oil
2 small free-range eggs,
   lightly beaten
⅔ cup / 150 ml sour cream

Icing
5¼ oz / 150 g cream cheese,
   at room temperature
5¼ oz / 150 g mascarpone
   cheese, at room temperature
5½ tbsp / 80 g unsalted butter,
   at room temperature
¾ cup plus 1 tbsp / 100 g
   confectioners' sugar

Chocolate

1   Preheat the oven to 325°F / 170°C. Line a muffin pan with 12 paper liners.

2   Whisk together the eggs, sour cream, oil, molasses, butter, and both sugars in a large mixing bowl until they are just combined. Don't overmix. Sift together the flour, cocoa, baking powder, and baking soda. Add them to the wet mix, along with the salt and almonds, and fold together gently. Fold in the chocolate pieces.

3   Spoon the batter into the cupcake liners, filling them to the top. Bake for 20 to 25 minutes; if you insert a skewer into the center of a cupcake, it should come out with quite a bit of crumb attached. Remove from the oven and leave to cool, then take the cupcakes out of the pan.

4   While the cupcakes are in the oven, start making the icing. It will take time to set and become spreadable. Place the chocolate in a heatproof bowl. Put the cream in a small saucepan and heat almost to the boiling point, then pour it over the chocolate. Use a rubber spatula to stir until all the chocolate has melted. Add the butter and Amaretto and beat until smooth.

5   Transfer the icing to a clean bowl and cover the surface with plastic wrap. Leave at room temperature until the cupcakes have fully cooled and the icing has started to set. You want to catch it at the point when it spreads easily but isn't hard. Do not rush it by refrigerating!

6   Spoon a generous amount of icing on top of each cupcake and shape with an icing spatula.

2 free-range eggs
½ cup / 115 ml sour cream
5½ tbsp / 80 ml sunflower oil
4 tsp / 20 ml molasses
4 tsp / 20 g unsalted butter, melted
5 tbsp / 60 g superfine sugar
4 tbsp / 60 g light muscovado sugar
scant 1 cup / 120 g all-purpose flour
6½ tbsp / 35 g cocoa powder
1 tsp baking powder
½ tsp baking soda
¼ tsp salt
6 tbsp / 40 g ground almonds
7 oz / 200 g dark chocolate, cut into small pieces

Icing
6 oz / 165 g dark chocolate, cut into small pieces
½ cup plus 1 tbsp / 135 ml heavy cream
2 tbsp plus 1 tsp / 35 g unsalted butter, diced
1 tbsp Amaretto liqueur

CHOCOLATE and
HAZELNUT BROWNIE
£2.10

For us, this is the cake God had in mind when inventing tea. It is the ideal counterpart—pure warmth, comfort, and reassurance. Or serve it warm with melting ice cream at the end of a good meal.

Instead of two small pans, you can also use one large one, in which case increase the baking time by 5 to 10 minutes.

Pear and Amaretto crumble cake

makes 2 small loaves (serves 4 to 6)

1 Preheat the oven to 325°F / 170°C. Grease 2 small (1-pound / 500-g) loaf pans with melted butter and line the bottom and sides with parchment paper.
2 Mix the chopped apple and pear with the walnuts, lemon zest, and Amaretto. In a separate bowl, sift together the flour, baking powder, cinnamon, and cloves. Add the ground almonds.
3 Separate 2 of the eggs, keeping the whites separate while mixing the yolks with the third egg. Using an electric mixer, beat together the oil and sugar for about 1 minute (this can also be done by hand, mixing briskly with a whisk). On low speed, slowly add the yolk and egg mix. Quickly add the sifted dry ingredients, followed by the fruit mix. Stop the machine as soon as everything is incorporated.
4 Whisk the egg whites with the salt until they form firm peaks, then gently fold them into the cake mix, using a spatula or metal spoon. Again, be careful not to overmix. Streaks of white in the mixture are okay.
5 Divide the cake mix between the pans and scatter the crumble on top. Bake for 40 to 45 minutes, until a skewer inserted into the center comes out clean (it might take a bit longer, depending on the moisture content of the fruit). If the cakes start going dark before the center is cooked, cover them with aluminum foil. Remove from the oven and leave to cool, then remove the cakes from the pans.

melted butter for greasing the pans
3½ oz / 100 g (peeled weight) Granny Smith apple, peeled and cut into ⅔-inch / 1.5-cm dice (about ½ apple)
5¼ oz / 150 g (peeled weight) pear, peeled and cut into ⅔-inch / 1.5-cm dice (about 1 pear)
5 tbsp / 30 g toasted walnuts, coarsely chopped
grated zest of 1 lemon
2 tbsp Amaretto liqueur
1⅔ cups / 210 g all-purpose flour
¾ tsp baking powder
¾ tsp ground cinnamon
scant ½ tsp ground cloves
6½ tbsp / 45 g ground almonds
3 free-range eggs
¾ cup / 180 ml sunflower oil
1 cup plus 2½ tbsp / 230 g superfine sugar
scant ½ tsp salt
4 oz / 120 g Crumble ↗ page 279

This is a rich cake—deliciously moist, with a depth of flavor formed by a mix of "grown-up" ingredients. But don't let this fool you; it is as irresistible as any chocolate cake gets.

The recipe also works as one large loaf. You just need to bake the cake 5 to 10 minutes longer.

Sticky chocolate loaf

1 Preheat the oven to 325°F / 170°C. Butter 2 small (1-pound / 500-g) loaf pans and line the bottom and sides with parchment paper.
2 Place half the prunes in a small saucepan and add the Armagnac. Warm very slightly, then set aside.
3 Put the remaining prunes in a blender or food processor and blend together with the buttermilk and oil until you get a light, shiny paste, a bit like mayonnaise. Transfer to a large mixing bowl and, using a hand whisk, mix in the egg, both types of sugar, and the molasses.
4 Sift together the flour, baking powder, baking soda, salt, and cocoa powder. Fold them gently into the prune mix with a rubber spatula. Fold in the chopped chocolate and divide the mixture equally between the prepared pans. Level the surface with a rubber spatula. Cut each soaked prune in half with scissors and use your fingers to press them below the surface of the cakes. Place in the oven and bake for 45 to 50 minutes, until a skewer inserted into the center comes out clean.
5 While the cakes are in the oven, make the syrup. Mix the water and sugar in a small saucepan and place over medium heat. As soon as the water begins to simmer and the sugar is completely dissolved, remove from the heat and set aside for 10 minutes to cool slightly. Finally, stir in the Armagnac (you can also add any liquid left from soaking the prunes).
6 As soon as the cakes are out of the oven, pierce them through in a few places with a skewer and use a pastry brush to soak them with the warm syrup. Let them cool completely before removing from the pans.

makes 2 small loaves (serves 4 to 6)

7½ oz / 220 g Agen prunes, pitted
6½ tbsp / 100 ml Armagnac or Cognac
4 tbsp / 60 ml buttermilk or yogurt
4 tbsp / 60 ml sunflower oil
1 free-range egg
2 tbsp plus 1 tsp / 30 g superfine sugar
4 tbsp / 60 g light brown sugar
2½ tbsp / 40 ml molasses
1 cup minus 2 tsp / 115 g all-purpose flour
½ tsp baking powder
½ tsp baking soda
pinch of salt
2½ tbsp / 15 g cocoa powder
5¼ oz / 150 g dark chocolate, chopped

Syrup
5½ tbsp / 80 ml water
6½ tbsp / 80 g superfine sugar
2 tbsp Armagnac or Cognac

To make these shortbreads, you shape the uncooked mixture into long logs and roll them in pistachios. Have a couple of those wrapped in plastic wrap in the freezer, ready to thaw, slice, and bake. There is nothing like a warm cookie!

Pistachio shortbreads

makes about 20

1 Use a mortar and pestle to crush the cardamom pods, then remove the skins and work the seeds into a fine powder.
2 Using an electric mixer fitted with the paddle attachment, mix together the butter, ground rice, flour, salt, ground cardamom, and confectioners' sugar. Run the machine until a paste forms, then stop the mixer at once. You don't need to incorporate much air (you could also do this by hand using a large plastic scraper; a strong wrist is required!).
3 Turn out the dough and, dusting with a little flour, roll it with your hands into a log 1¼ to 1½ inches / 3 to 4 cm in diameter. Wrap in plastic wrap and leave in the fridge for at least an hour.
4 While the dough is chilling, chop the pistachios finely with a sharp knife, but not as fine as ground almonds. Or, if using a food processor, pulse them a few times until ground with some chunkier bits remaining. Scatter the pistachios on a flat tray.
5 Brush the log with the beaten egg and roll it in the ground pistachios. Rewrap in plastic wrap and leave in the fridge to set for at least 30 minutes.
6 Preheat the oven to 300°F / 150°C. Unwrap the log and cut into slices ¼ to ⅜ inch / 5 mm to 1 cm thick. Lay them out on a baking sheet lined with parchment paper, spacing them at least ¾ inch / 2 cm apart. Dust with the vanilla sugar.
7 Bake the shortbreads for roughly 20 minutes. They must not take on too much color but should remain golden. Remove from the oven and allow to cool completely before storing in a sealed jar. They will keep for up to a week.

8 cardamom pods
¾ cup plus 1 tbsp / 200 g unsalted butter
4 tbsp / 25 g ground rice
2 cups / 240 g all-purpose flour
½ tsp salt
4½ tbsp / 35 g confectioners' sugar
½ cup / 60 g shelled pistachio nuts
1 free-range egg, lightly beaten
2 tbsp vanilla sugar

Pistachio and ginger biscotti (↗ page 224)

Cranberry and white choc'
Disa

White chocolate and cranberry cookies (↗ page 225)

These are not the traditional tooth-breaking Italian biscotti but a softer, friendlier version. Still, they count as biscotti because they are baked twice: once as a log and then after they are cut into thin slices. Thank you to Helen for this marvelous recipe.

Pistachio and ginger biscotti

makes 25

1. Line a baking sheet with parchment paper.
2. Using an electric mixer (or a good spatula and both your hands), cream the butter and sugar together until they lighten in color and texture. Gradually add the eggs, beating well after each addition. Stir in the brandy and orange zest, followed by the flour, ground ginger, and salt. Lastly, fold in the pistachios and stem ginger.
3. Lightly dust the lined baking sheet with flour and spoon the mixture onto the tray. Leave to rest in the fridge for about 30 minutes so it firms up a little. Preheat the oven to 325°F / 170°C.
4. Take the dough out of the fridge and, using your hands and a bit of extra flour, form a log shape about 10 inches / 25 cm long. It does not need to be perfect, as the mix will spread during baking. Bake for 20 minutes, then remove from the oven and leave to cool. At this point the log will be partially baked and still quite soft. Lower the oven temperature to 265°F / 130°C.
5. Once the log has cooled down, use a serated knife to cut it across into slices 3/8 inch / 1 cm thick. Lay them flat on the baking sheet and return to the oven for about 40 minutes, turning them over halfway through, until crisp. Remove and leave to cool. Store in a sealed container.

5½ tbsp / 80 g unsalted butter
½ cup plus 2 tsp / 110 g superfine sugar
2 free-range eggs, lightly beaten
1 tbsp brandy
grated zest of 1½ oranges
1 cup plus 3 tbsp / 150 g all-purpose flour, plus extra for dusting
½ tsp ground ginger
¼ tsp salt
⅔ cup / 80 g shelled pistachio nuts
2 oz / 60 g stem ginger in syrup, drained and coarsely chopped

This is a traditional recipe for chocolate chip cookies of the crunchy variety, only using white chocolate instead of dark, and adding dried cranberries for a little fruity freshness. The brown sugar gives them depth and a crisp texture. They are very popular with kids and adults alike. Have a container of shaped cookies in the freezer, ready to bake when you need them.

Dried blueberries make a good alternative to cranberries, making the cookies more "grown-up."

White chocolate and cranberry cookies

makes 25 to 30

1 Preheat the oven to 325°F / 170°C. Line 2 baking sheets with parchment paper.
2 Sift together the flour, salt, baking powder, and baking soda and set aside.
3 Put the butter, vanilla, and sugars in a large mixing bowl and beat with a wooden spoon until the mixture is lighter in color and texture. Gradually add the egg, making sure each addition is fully incorporated before adding more. Add the flour mixture and the oats, then the chocolate and cranberries. Do not continue mixing once the dry ingredients are blended in.
4 Chill the mixture slightly to help you shape the cookies. Scoop out a bit of the mix with a spoon and use your hands to roll it into a ball, somewhere between the size of an olive and a walnut. Press the balls lightly onto the baking sheets. Make sure you space them a good 2½ to 2¾ inches / 6 to 7 cm apart (they will spread more than you expect!). Place in the oven and bake for about 10 minutes, until they are a good brown color. Remove from the oven and allow to cool on the pans before serving.

¾ cup / 90 g all-purpose flour
¼ tsp salt
½ tsp baking powder
½ tsp baking soda
6½ tbsp / 100 g unsalted butter, at room temperature
1 tsp vanilla extract
½ cup / 110 g light brown sugar
2 tbsp / 25 g superfine sugar
1 egg, lightly beaten
¾ cup / 80 g rolled oats
2 oz / 60 g white chocolate, chopped into chocolate-chip-size pieces
⅔ cup / 75 g dried cranberries

Not a traditional Florentine, this lacelike biscuit is the kind you just can't leave alone. Although its crisp lightness is quite extraordinary, you could brush one side with melted dark chocolate if you like, to justify the name and give it a more substantial texture.

They will keep for 4 to 5 days in an airtight container; just make sure you don't leave them out very long or they will lose their crispness.

Thanks to Jim for this recipe.

Almond and orange Florentines

makes about 20

vegetable oil for brushing
2 free-range egg whites
**¾ cup plus 1 tbsp / 100 g
    confectioners' sugar**
2¾ cups / 260 g sliced almonds
grated zest of 1 orange

1 Preheat the oven to 300°F / 150°C. Line a heavy baking sheet with parchment paper and brush lightly with vegetable oil. Next to you have a small bowl of cold water.
2 Put the egg whites, confectioners' sugar, sliced almonds, and orange zest in a bowl and gently mix them together. Dip your hand in the bowl of water and pick up portions of the mix to make little mounds on the lined pan, well spaced apart. Dip a fork in the water and flatten each mound very thinly. Try to make them as thin as possible without creating too many gaps between the almond slices. They should be about 3¼ inches / 8 cm in diameter.
3 Place the baking sheet in the oven and bake for about 12 minutes, until the cookies are golden brown. Check underneath one cookie to make sure they are cooked through.
4 Allow to cool, then gently, using an icing spatula, remove the cookies from the baking sheet. Store in a sealed jar.

Choose the best dark chocolate you can find to make these marvelous truffles (well, not quite truffles, since they are squarish, but that's just a formality). We recommend one of Valrhona's Grand Cru or Amedei's Porcelana.

Champagne chocolates

makes about 40

2 oz / 60 g milk chocolate
7 oz / 200 g dark chocolate
⅔ cup / 150 g unsalted butter
5½ tbsp / 80 ml champagne
2 tbsp plus 2 tsp / 40 ml good-quality brandy
6¼ oz / 180 g dark chocolate for coating
½ cup plus 1 tbsp / 50 g cocoa powder for dusting

1 Take a cake pan roughly 5½ inches / 14 cm square and line it with plastic wrap. Using a sharp knife, chop both kinds of chocolate into small pieces and place them in a heatproof bowl large enough to accommodate all the ingredients. Warm the chocolate for a couple of minutes in a microwave or over a pan of simmering water until it is semi-melted; be careful not to heat it much. Cut the butter into small pieces and keep it separate.
2 Pour the champagne and brandy into a small saucepan and place on the stove until they warm up to around 175°F / 80°C; they should be hot to the touch but not boiling. Pour the alcohol over the chocolate and stir gently with a rubber spatula until it melts completely. Stir in the butter in a few additions, then continue stirring until the mixture is smooth. Pour it into the lined pan and place in the fridge for at least 3 hours, until it has set firm.
3 Place the chocolate for coating in a mixing bowl and put it over a pan of simmering water. Stir occasionally and, as soon as the chocolate has melted, remove the bowl from the steam bath. Spread the cocoa powder on a flat plate.
4 Turn the chilled chocolate block out of the pan onto a sheet of parchment paper and remove the plastic wrap. Use a very sharp, long knife to cut it into roughly ¾-inch / 2-cm squares. Clean the knife in hot water and wipe dry after each cut.
5 Using 2 skewers or forks, dip the squares into the melted chocolate, wiping off any excess on the side of the bowl. Quickly roll the squares in the cocoa powder and place on a clean tray. Allow the chocolates to set in the fridge, but make sure you leave them out at room temperature for at least half an hour before serving.

Sour cherry amaretti (↗ page 232)

Prune and brandy truffles (↗ page 233)

This is our version of the popular little Italian cookie. Serve them with coffee or, even better, break them over chocolate ice cream.

If you don't mind the effort, make your own ground almonds (blanch, peel, and very lightly toast the almonds, then blitz them in a food processor until fine). This will give a much deeper almond flavor. In any case, don't get carried away with the almond extract. Too much of it will give a terrible artificial aroma.

You can omit the sour cherries if you wish, or use dried apricots or dried blueberries instead.

Sour cherry amaretti

makes about 20

1 Preheat the oven to 325°F / 170°C. Put the ground almonds, superfine sugar, lemon zest, almond extract, and salt in a large bowl and rub with your fingertips to disperse the zest and extract evenly. Add the cherries and set aside.

2 Using an electric mixer fitted with the whisk attachment, or by hand with a whisk, beat the egg whites and honey until they reach a soft meringue consistency. Gently fold the meringue into the almond mixture. At this stage you should have a soft, malleable paste.

3 With your hands, form the mixture into 20 irregular shapes. Roll them in plenty of confectioners' sugar, then arrange them on a baking sheet lined with parchment paper. Place in the oven and bake for about 12 minutes. The cookies should have taken on some color but remain relatively pale and chewy in the center. Leave to cool completely before indulging or storing them in a sealed jar.

1⅔ cups / 180 g ground almonds
½ cup plus 1½ tbsp / 120 g superfine sugar
grated zest of 1 lemon
3 drops natural almond extract
pinch of salt
scant ½ cup / 60 g dried sour cherries, coarsely chopped
2 free-range egg whites
2 tsp honey
plenty of confectioners' sugar for rolling

We normally don't like mixing fruit and chocolate. There are exceptions, though. When the fruit isn't very acidic or juicy, it can easily carry the intensity of chocolate and its buttery texture. Agen prunes are perfect for this. The slow drying process gives them a mature, sweet aroma that lends itself dramatically well to the combination of chocolate and alcohol. Khalid Assyb invented this recipe for a special Christmas menu, a perfect time for this hefty indulgence.

Glucose syrup, available in some supermarkets and online, gives the chocolate ganache an extra-smooth texture. To get it out of the tub, wet your hand with water and lift a bit with your fingers. If you don't do this it will stick terribly.

Prune and brandy truffles

makoo 24

1 To make the ganache filling, chop up the chocolate and butter into very small pieces and place in a heatproof bowl. Put the cream and glucose into a small saucepan and bring to a boil, watching carefully. As soon as they boil, pour them over the chocolate and butter. Stir gently with a rubber spatula until you get a smooth, shiny mix (if the chocolate doesn't melt fully, you can "help" it by placing the bowl over a saucepan of simmering water for a few seconds). Stir in the brandy until well blended. Place a sheet of plastic wrap over the surface of the ganache and leave to set overnight at room temperature. Alternatively, you can set it in the fridge, but you will need to take it out in advance and let it come to room temperature before using.

2 Once the ganache has set, split each prune down one side with a knife and carefully remove the stone. Spoon some ganache into each prune, filling it. Close to form a little parcel and then chill for at least half an hour.

3 To coat the prunes, coarsely chop the dark chocolate and place in a bowl set over a saucepan of simmering water, making sure the bowl does not touch the water. Stir gently until melted, then remove from the pan. Spread the cocoa powder on a flat plate.

4 Using 2 forks, dip the prunes into the melted chocolate, wiping off any excess chocolate on the side of the bowl. Roll them in the cocoa powder straightaway and place on a clean plate. Allow to set, preferably in a cool place, or otherwise in the fridge. Don't serve straight from the fridge.

Ganache filling
5¼ oz / 150 g dark chocolate
4 tsp / 20 g unsalted butter
6½ tbsp / 100 ml heavy cream
4 tsp glucose syrup
4 tsp brandy

24 Agen prunes
7 oz / 200 g dark chocolate for coating
4 tbsp cocoa powder for dusting

More than a snack but less than a proper cake, these bars are nutty and fruity. Wonderful with a strong after-dinner coffee.

Raspberry and oat bars

1 Preheat the oven to 325°F / 170°C. Lightly grease an 8-inch / 20-cm square pan and line it with parchment paper.
2 To make the base, sift together the flour and baking powder. Add the butter, sugar, and salt and rub everything together with your fingertips to form crumbs. Stir in the oats. Spread this mixture over the bottom of the prepared pan; don't press down too much, so the base remains light. Bake for 20 minutes, until light brown. Remove from the oven and allow to cool a little, then spread with the jam.
3 To make the topping, place all the nuts in a large bowl. In a small saucepan, heat the butter, sugar, milk, and vanilla. Stir until the sugar has dissolved, then pour the mixture over the chopped nuts and stir together. Pack the nut mix evenly over the jam and return the pan to the oven for 30 minutes, until the nuts have turned a nice golden brown.
4 Leave to cool, then remove from the pan and slice into bars or squares.

makes 6 to 8

Base
1 cup / 120 g all-purpose flour
scant ½ tsp baking powder
6½ tbsp / 100 g unsalted butter, diced
scant 5 tbsp / 60 g superfine sugar
pinch of salt
¾ cup / 80 g rolled oats
¾ cup / 220 g raspberry jam, store-bought or homemade
↗ page 276

Topping
¾ cup / 70 g sliced almonds
¾ cup / 70 g pecans, coarsely chopped
½ cup / 70 g hazelnuts, coarsely chopped
½ cup / 70 g Brazil nuts, coarsely chopped
6½ tbsp / 100 g unsalted butter
6 tbsp / 75 g superfine sugar
2 tbsp plus 2 tsp / 40 ml milk
1 tsp vanilla extract

Forget their healthy image. Our granola bars are as tasty as any rich, sticky snack bar. Children love them and some of our grown-up customers can't go through the whole day without one.

Granola bars

makes 6 to 8

1 Preheat the oven to 275°F / 140°C. Lightly grease an 8-inch / 20-cm square pan and line it with parchment paper.
2 Scatter the pecans on a baking sheet and toast for 8 minutes. Remove from the oven and increase the temperature to 325°F / 160°C.
3 Half fill a small bowl with hot water and add the apricots and cherries. Leave to soak for about 10 minutes and then drain in a colander.
4 In a large mixing bowl, stir together the toasted pecans, plumped apricots and cherries, both seeds, almonds, oats, cinnamon, and salt. Place the butter, honey, and sugar in a small saucepan and bring to a light simmer over medium heat. Leave to cook to a light brown color, watching the whole time so the caramel doesn't spill over or go too dark. Once light brown, pour it over the dry ingredients and stir to mix everything together. Spoon the mixture into the lined pan and pack it down lightly with an offset spatula or spoon.
5 Bake for about 22 minutes, until lightly colored on top. The bar will still be soft when removed from the oven but will firm up as it cools. Take out of the pan and cut into individual bars. Eat straightaway or store in a sealed container.

scant ½ cup / 45 g pecans
⅓ cup / 45 g dried apricots, very coarsely chopped
⅓ cup / 45 g dried sour cherries
5½ tbsp / 45 g pumpkin seeds
3 tbsp / 30 g sesame seeds
1½ tbsp / 30 g ground almonds
scant 2 cups / 190 g rolled oats
1¼ tsp ground cinnamon
pinch of salt
6 tbsp plus 1 tsp / 95 g unsalted butter
4 tbsp / 85 g honey
6 tbsp / 95 g Demerara sugar

Brownies

The basic principle for a heavenly brownie is getting the baking time right. There is nothing worse than a brownie that turns into a cake. It is worse even than overdone meat. Actually, it is a similar kind of expertise; being able to tell how far to cook a brownie or a sirloin steak is knowledge that comes with time.

When you stick a skewer inside your cooked brownie it must come out covered with lots of gooey crumb, not with dry crumbs, but it mustn't be the type of wet mix you started off with. It should be thicker and sticky to the touch, with a tendency to set once it has cooled a bit. The brownie should also have risen slightly (10 to 20 percent) in the oven and its surface should be totally dry.

The time it takes to reach this stage will vary depending on your oven, where the brownie is placed in it, the size and dimensions of your pan, and other small variables. So we strongly recommend that you check the brownie well before the indicated baking time has elapsed. If it turns out to be underbaked, chilling it will make it set hard and you will still be able to slice it and enjoy it.

The recipes that follow are for an 8½-inch / 22-cm square pan, but you could easily swap that for another pan or dish with a similar surface area or a round cake pan 10 inches / 25 cm in diameter.

Macadamia and white chocolate brownies (↗ page 240)

Khalid's chocolate and chestnut bars (↗ page 241), Toffee brownies (↗ page 240)

Toffee

1 To make the butter toffee, lightly brush a baking pan (not the one you will use to bake the brownies in) with melted butter. Put the butter and sugar in a heavy saucepan and place over medium heat. Stir constantly with a wooden spoon until the mixture turns a dark caramel color (at one point it might seem the mixture has split; it will come back together when you stir vigorously). Carefully pour the toffee into the buttered pan and leave aside until it sets.

2 When you are ready to make the brownies, brush an 8½-inch / 22-cm square baking pan with melted butter and line with parchment paper. Preheat the oven to 325°F / 170°C. Sift together the flour and salt.

3 Put the butter and chocolate in a heatproof bowl and place over a saucepan of simmering water, making sure the water does not touch the base of the bowl. Leave to melt, stirring from time to time. As soon as the butter and chocolate have melted, remove the bowl from above the water. This is important! You need to avoid getting the mix very hot.

4 In a large bowl, lightly whisk together the eggs, sugar, and vanilla. Work them just until combined, a few seconds only, as there is no need to incorporate any air into the eggs. Fold in the melted chocolate mixture and then the sifted flour. Break the toffee into small pieces and fold them in as well.

5 Pour the mix into the lined pan. Drop the jam in spoonfuls into the mixture and swirl it around with a knife.

6 Place on the center rack of the oven and bake for roughly 25 minutes. Make sure you check the instructions on page 236 before deciding to remove the brownie from the oven. Once out, allow it to cool completely before removing from the pan (you might even need to chill it first). Cut into any shape you like and keep in an airtight container for up to 5 days.

makes 8 to 10

Butter toffee
5 tsp / 25 g unsalted butter, plus melted butter for greasing
6 tbsp / 75 g superfine sugar

¾ cup plus 1 tbsp / 200 g unsalted butter, plus melted butter for greasing
2¼ cups / 280 g all-purpose flour
½ tsp salt
11 oz / 300 g dark chocolate, broken into pieces
2 free-range eggs
1 cup plus 1½ tbsp / 220 g superfine sugar
1 tsp vanilla extract
scant ½ cup / 140 g apricot, banana, or raspberry jam

↗ page 276

Macadamia and white chocolate

1 Preheat the oven to 325°F / 170°C. Spread the nuts on a baking sheet and toast for 5 minutes, then remove from the oven.

2 Using the ingredients listed here, follow the brownie instructions in the above recipe up to the stage at which you fold in the toffee, adding the instant coffee to the eggs, sugar, and vanilla. Instead of the toffee, fold in the white chocolate and half the nuts. Pour the mix into the lined pan and top with the remaining nuts.

3 Continue as in the above brownie recipe.

makes 8 to 10

1½ cups / 200 g macadamia nuts
¾ cup plus 1 tbsp / 200 g unsalted butter, plus melted butter for greasing
2¼ cups / 280 g all-purpose flour
½ tsp salt
10½ oz / 300 g dark chocolate, broken into pieces
2 free-range eggs
1 cup plus 2½ tbsp / 230 g superfine sugar
1 tsp vanilla extract
2 tsp instant coffee
7 oz / 200 g white chocolate, broken into pieces (or use chocolate chips)

Decadent is probably the most truthful description of this delicacy. It is both rich and luxurious, with its remarkable mixture of chestnut, fig, and chocolate. Soaking the figs in rum or brandy will add an extra dimension. Consider cutting the bars into tiny squares to serve with good coffee at the end of a meal.

You can buy cooked peeled chestnuts, usually canned or vacuum packed. Avoid the ones cooked in syrup, as they are too sweet for this recipe. If you feel like collecting them, sweet chestnuts fall from the trees in abundance around October (but don't get them confused with horse chestnut, or conkers). To prepare them, score each one down one side and place in a saucepan. Cover with boiling water, bring back to a boil, and simmer for 15 minutes. Drain and leave until cool enough to handle, then peel away the skins, both outer and inner.

Khalid's chocolate and chestnut bars

makes 8 to 10

1   Preheat the oven to 300°F / 150°C. Lightly grease an 8-inch / 20-cm square pan and line it with aluminum foil or parchment paper.
2   To make the base, place the biscuits in a large bowl and crush with your hands or a rolling pin. Add the melted butter and mix together to make a sandy paste. Scatter this mixture in the pan and press hard onto the bottom until level. Leave in the fridge to set.
3   Meanwhile, put the dark chocolate and butter in a heatproof bowl set over a saucepan of simmering water and leave to melt. Stir occasionally with a wooden spoon and remove from the pan as soon as they melt so that they don't get too hot.
4   Use an electric mixer to whisk together the eggs, yolk, and sugar until thick and pale (you could also do it with a hand whisk). Gently fold the chocolate mixture into the eggs, followed by the chopped chestnuts, figs, and white chocolate. Spread evenly over the biscuit base and bake on the middle rack of the oven for 15 to 20 minutes. A skewer inserted into the bar should come out with lots of gooey crumb attached, the same as when you make brownies (↗ page 236 for a full description). Make sure you don't go beyond this point. Remove from the oven, leave to cool, then refrigerate for a few hours until set.
5   Take the bar out of the pan and peel off the aluminum foil or paper. Cut into bars or squares and dust lightly with cocoa powder. Let them come to room temperature before serving.

Base
6¾ oz / 190 g digestive biscuits (such as McVitie's brand) or graham crackers
6 tbsp / 90 g unsalted butter, melted

8 oz / 225 g dark chocolate
⅔ cup / 150 g unsalted butter, diced
2 free-range eggs
1 free-range egg yolk
4 tbsp / 45 g superfine sugar
¾ cup / 120 g cooked peeled chestnuts, coarsely chopped
¾ cup / 120 g dried figs (the soft, ready-to-eat type), stalks removed, coarsely chopped
4 oz / 120 g white chocolate, coarsely chopped
cocoa powder for dusting

Macarons

The popularity of these traditional French delicacies has soared over the last few years and they are now seen everywhere. The best ones, admittedly, are made by the Parisian confectioner, Ladurée, which now has a branch at Harrods. We highly recommend going there to sample their classic French patisserie-style macarons. Our macarons are more "homely," as we prefer to keep them as natural as possible. As such, they don't have the same dazzling effect, but they are still wonderfully tasty—soft, with a slight crunch, richly flavored, and stunning to look at. Some of the flavor combinations, like Lime and basil (↗ page 247), are quirky yet scrumptious.

On the following page we give the general method for making macarons, followed by three variations. Shaping the macarons does take a bit of skill, but even odd-shaped ones will taste great. If you accidentally overbake your macarons and they go hard, try freezing them, uncovered, for a while before sandwiching them together with the filling. They will absorb moisture and soften a little.

Salty peanut and caramel, Chocolate, and Lime and basil macarons (↗ page 247)

General method
See the individual macaron recipes for ingredients.

1   Preheat the oven to 325°F / 170°C. Using a fine sieve, sift the confectioners' sugar and ground almonds into a clean, dry bowl.

2   Place the egg whites and superfine sugar in the bowl of a stand mixer and start whisking on full speed until the whites have formed a thick, aerated meringue, firm but not too dry. Remove the bowl from the machine; take one-third of the meringue and fold it gently into the sifted almond and sugar mix. Once incorporated, add half of the remaining meringue and continue similarly until all the meringue has been added and the mix appears smooth and glossy.

3   Take a sheet of parchment paper and "glue" it onto a baking sheet by dotting the pan in a few places with a tiny amount of the macaron mix.

4   Now you need to use the mix to create uniform shallow disks a generous 1 inch / 2.5 cm in diameter and about 1/8 inch / 3 mm thick. In our kitchens, we pipe the macaron mix onto the lined pan using a piping bag fitted with a small nozzle. This requires a bit of experience, but you can try it. To assist you, draw little circles on the paper, spaced well apart. This will guide you in achieving uniform macarons. Then either pipe or spoon little blobs of the macaron mix onto the lined pan. Alternatively, take a bowl of confectioners' sugar, dip your fingers in it, and shape the macarons with your fingers. Now hold the pan firmly and tap its underside vigorously. This should help spread and smooth out the disks. Leave the macarons out and uncovered for 15 minutes before baking.

5   To bake, place the macarons in the preheated oven and leave for about 12 minutes. They might take longer, depending on your oven. The macarons are ready when they come freely off the paper when lifted with an icing spatula. Remove from the oven as soon as they reach this stage, so that you don't overbake them, and leave aside to cool completely.

6   To assemble the macarons, use a small spoon or a piping bag to deposit a pea-size (or slightly larger) amount of the filling on the flat side of half the cookies. Sandwich them with the other half, squeezing them together gently. Leave at room temperature to set within a couple of hours, or chill them to hasten the process. Just remember not to serve your macarons cold from the fridge.

This combination was thought up by Carol Brough.

Salty peanut and caramel

1   To make the macarons, follow the instructions on page 246, using all the ingredients listed except the chopped peanuts. These you add after you have laid out (or piped) the macarons onto the baking sheet and before the 15-minute rest. Just dot each disk with a few pieces of chopped peanut, leave them to rest, then bake.
2   To make the filling, mix the peanuts with the dulce de leche, stir in the salt, then taste. You want to get a sweetness that is balanced by a fair amount of saltiness, a bit like peanut butter.

makes about 20

1 cup minus 4 tsp / 110 g confectioners' sugar
½ cup plus 1 tbsp / 60 g ground almonds
2 free-range egg whites
3½ tbsp / 40 g superfine sugar
2 tbsp / 20 g natural roasted peanuts, coarsely chopped

Caramel filling
3 tbsp / 30 g natural roasted peanuts, finely chopped
5 tbsp / 100 g dulce de leche
small pinch of salt

Lime and basil

1   To make the macarons, follow the instructions on page 246, using all the ingredients listed. Fold the basil and lime zest into the mix at the final stage, after the almonds and confectioners' sugar are fully incorporated into the meringue.
2   To make the buttercream filling, place the butter and confectioners' sugar in a mixing bowl and beat them together with a rubber spatula until pale in color and light in texture. Add the lime zest and juice and the basil and beat until fully incorporated. Cover the buttercream with plastic wrap and leave in a cool place (not the fridge) until ready to use.

makes about 20

1 cup minus 4 tsp / 110 g confectioners' sugar
½ cup plus 1 tbsp / 60 g ground almonds
2 free-range egg whites
scant 4 tbsp / 40 g superfine sugar
5 large basil leaves, finely chopped
finely grated zest of 1 lime

Buttercream filling
6½ tbsp / 100 g unsalted butter, at room temperature
6 tbsp / 45 g confectioners' sugar
finely grated zest and juice of 1 lime
5 large basil leaves, finely chopped

Chocolate

1   Start by making the ganache filling. Chop the chocolate into tiny pieces and the butter into small dice. Place them in a heatproof bowl. Pour the cream into a small saucepan and bring to a boil, watching it carefully. As soon as it boils, pour it over the chocolate and butter. Stir gently with a rubber spatula until you get a smooth mix (if the chocolate doesn't melt easily, help it by placing the bowl over a pot of simmering water and stirring). Stir in the rum until well blended.
2   Place a sheet of plastic wrap over the surface of the ganache and leave to set somewhere cool (not the fridge) for a couple of hours.
3   To make the macarons, follow the instructions on page 246, using the ingredients listed and adding the cocoa powder to the confectioners' sugar and ground almonds when sifting them.

makes about 20

1 cup minus 4 tsp / 110 g confectioners' sugar
½ cup / 50 g ground almonds
2 tbsp / 12 g cocoa powder
2 free-range egg whites
3½ tbsp / 40 g superfine sugar

Ganache filling
2¼ oz / 65 g dark chocolate
1 tbsp / 15 g unsalted butter
3½ tbsp / 50 ml heavy cream
2 tsp dark rum

Meringues

If you ask someone if they've heard of Ottolenghi, the answer is often, "Yes, I know, it's the place with the meringues." Although we learned how to make the giant meringues at Baker and Spice, it was our multiflavored, multicolored ones (proudly filling our windows) that became synonymous with Ottolenghi and earned us lots of imitators, both good and bad. And now, whether we like it or not, we are identified with those giant balls of sweetness.

To make meringues you need a good stand mixer. Making them by hand is out of the question and using a handheld electric mixer is also not very practical, as the mixture needs a long whisking time and turns too hard for most weak machines.

Pistachio and rose water

1 Preheat the oven to 400°F / 200°C. Spread the sugar evenly over a large baking sheet lined with parchment paper. Place the pan in the oven for about 8 minutes, until the sugar is hot (over 212°F / 100°C). You should be able to see it beginning to dissolve at the edges.

2 While the sugar is in the oven, place the egg whites in the bowl of a stand mixer fitted with the whisk attachment. When the sugar is almost ready, start the machine on high speed and let it work for a minute or so, until the whites just begin to froth up.

3 Carefully pour the sugar slowly onto the whisking whites. Once it has all been added, add the rose water and continue whisking on high speed for 10 minutes, until the meringue is cold. At this point, it should keep its shape when you lift a bit from the bowl and look homogenously silky (you can now taste the mixture and fold in some more rose water if you want a more distinctive rose flavor).

4 Turn down the oven temperature to 225°F / 110°C. To shape the meringues, line a baking sheet (or 2, depending on their size) with parchment paper, sticking it firmly to the pan with a bit of meringue. Spread the pistachios on a flat plate.

5 Have ready 2 large kitchen spoons. Use one of them to scoop up a big dollop of meringue, the size of a medium apple, then use the other spoon to scrape it off onto the plate of pistachios. Roll the meringue so it is covered with nuts on one side and then gently place it on the lined baking tray. Repeat to make more meringues, spacing them well apart on the tray. Remember, the meringues will almost double in size in the oven.

6 Place in the oven and leave there for about 2 hours. Check if they are done by lifting them from the pan and gently prodding to make sure the outside is completely firm and the center is still a little soft. Remove from the oven and leave to cool. The meringues will keep in a dry place, at room temperature, for quite a few days.

makes 12 large meringues

3 cups / 600 g superfine sugar
10½ oz / 300 g free-range egg whites (about 10)
2 tsp rose water ↗ page xii
½ cup / 60 g pistachio nuts, finely chopped

We use the Swiss meringue method here. It involves dissolving the sugars in the egg whites before whipping them up. This enables the brown sugar to mix properly with the whites, creating a uniform mix. Thanks to Carol for making this work, after many trials and tribulations.

Cinnamon and hazelnut

makes 10 large meringues

7 oz / 200 g free-range egg whites (about 7)
2½ cups / 260 g superfine sugar
⅔ cup / 140 g dark brown muscovado sugar
½ tsp ground cinnamon
3½ tbsp / 30 g unskinned hazelnuts, coarsely chopped

1 Preheat the oven to 225°F / 110°C.
2 Fill a medium saucepan with water and bring it to a light simmer. Place the egg whites and both sugars in a heatproof bowl large enough to sit on top of the pan. Put it over the simmering water, making sure it doesn't actually touch the water, and leave it there for about 10 minutes, stirring occasionally, until the mixture is quite hot (105°F / 40°C) and the sugars have dissolved into the whites.
3 Pour the whites into the bowl of a stand mixer fitted with the whisk attachment and whip on high speed. Work the meringue for about 8 minutes, until the mix has cooled completely. When ready, it should be firm and glossy and keep its shape when you lift a bit with a spoon.
4 Sprinkle the cinnamon over the meringue mix and use a rubber spatula to fold it in gently.
5 Line a flat baking sheet (or 2, depending on their size) with parchment paper. You can stick the edges to the pan with a few blobs of the meringue mix. This will hold the paper in place while you shape the meringues.
6 Have ready 2 large kitchen spoons. Use one of them to scoop up a generous spoonful of the meringue and the other to scrape this out onto the lined pan (leave plenty of room between the meringues for them to expand in the oven; they can almost double in size). Using the spoons, shape the meringues into spiky dollops, the size of medium apples, and sprinkle with the chopped hazelnuts. Place in the oven and bake for 1¼ to 2 hours, depending on the oven and the size of your meringues. To check, poke them gently inside and look underneath. The meringues should be nice and dry underneath and still a little soft in the center.
7 Remove from the oven and leave to cool. Stored in a dry place, but not the fridge, the meringues will keep for a few days.

Tartlets

For all the tartlet recipes you will need 6 tartlet pans, 2 to 2¾ inches / 5 to 7 cm in diameter and about 1¼ inches / 3 cm deep. You can use small muffin pans instead or any other pan of similar proportions. Whatever you choose, just make sure you cut out pastry disks that are suitable for the size of your pans. A disk should cover the bottom and sides of the pan, plus ¹⁄₁₆ to ⅛ inch / 2 to 3 mm excess to give the tarts extra height.

We recommend making a whole batch of Sweet pastry (↗ page 281) and using as much of it as you need. This will vary according to how large your pans are and how thinly you roll out the pastry. Freeze what is left and keep it for a rainy day.

Prebaked shells

makes 6

3 tbsp / 40 g unsalted butter, melted, for brushing
¼ to ⅓ recipe Sweet pastry
↗ page 281
all-purpose flour for dusting

1   Start by brushing your tartlet pans with a thin layer of melted butter, then leave to set in the fridge.
2   Meanwhile, prepare a wide, clean working surface and have ready a rolling pin and a small amount of flour. Lightly dust the work surface, place the pastry in the middle, and roll out the pastry thinly, turning it around as you go. Work quickly so it doesn't get warm. Once the pastry is no more than ¹⁄₁₆ to ⅛ inch / 2 to 3 mm thick, cut out 6 circles using a pastry cutter or the rim of a bowl. Line the buttered pans by placing the circles inside and gently pressing them into the corners and sides. Leave to rest in the fridge for at least 30 minutes.
3   Preheat the oven to 300°F / 150°C. Line each pastry shell with a circle of scrunched-up waxed paper or a piece of foil. It should come ⅜ inch / 1 cm above the edge of the pastry (paper muffin liners are another great solution). Fill them with rice or dried beans, then place in the oven and blind bake for about 25 minutes. By then they should have taken on a golden brown color. If they are not quite there yet, remove the beans and lining paper and continue baking for 5 to 10 minutes. Remove from the oven.
4   Keep the beans or rice and the paper holding them for future use. Remove the tart shells from the pans while they are still slightly warm and leave them to cool down completely.

Fresh berries, Dark chocolate, White chocolate and raspberry tartlets (↗ page 258), Lemon meringue, Banana and hazelnut tartlets (↗ page 259)

Fresh berries

Use a piping bag or a spoon to fill the tart shells three-quarters full with the mascarpone cream. Be creative when topping generously with the berries. You can throw them on in a beautiful mess or arrange them meticulously—a matter of personality. Dust with confectioners' sugar, if you like, then chill. Serve within 6 hours, but preferably at once.

makes 6

6 prebaked tartlet shells
↗ page 255

1 recipe Mascarpone cream
↗ page 278

about ⅓ cup / 50 g strawberries, halved or quartered

about ⅓ cup / 50 g raspberries

about ⅓ cup / 50 g blueberries

confectioners' sugar for dusting (optional)

Dark chocolate

1 Preheat the oven to 325°F / 170°C. Put the chocolate and butter in a bowl, set it over a pan of simmering water, and leave to melt. Whisk the egg and yolk with the sugar until thick and pale yellow, then fold the mixture into the melted chocolate.
2 If using the jam, put a spoonful in the base of each tartlet shell. Fill them up with the chocolate mix; it should reach right up to the rim. Place in the oven and bake for 5 minutes. Cool a little, then remove the tartlets from their pans and allow them to cool completely.
3 Lightly dust with cocoa powder and serve at room temperature.

makes 6

5¼ oz / 150 g dark chocolate, broken up

6½ tbsp / 100 g unsalted butter, diced

1 free-range egg

1 free-range egg yolk

2½ tbsp / 30 g superfine sugar

3 tbsp / 60 g raspberry jam (optional) ↗ page 276

6 prebaked tartlet shells
↗ page 255 — baked 5 minutes less than suggested and left in their pans

cocoa powder for dusting

White chocolate and raspberry

1 Crush the fresh raspberries with a fork and then pass them through a fine sieve to remove the seeds. Set the smooth coulis aside.
2 Put the white chocolate and the butter in a heatproof bowl. Heat the cream in a small saucepan and bring to a boil, watching it constantly. As soon as it comes to a boil, pour it over the chocolate and butter and stir gently with a rubber spatula. Continue until all the chocolate has melted and you are left with a smooth, shiny ganache.
3 Immediately, before the ganache begins to set, spoon 1 teaspoon jam into each shell. Carefully pour in the ganache; it should almost reach to the rim (if the ganache does begin to set, heat it gently over a pan of hot water before pouring). Be very gentle now and don't shake the shells.
4 Spoon a tiny amount of the raspberry coulis—not more than ½ teaspoon—into the center of each tartlet. Use the tip of a knife or a skewer to swirl the coulis around. Carefully transfer the tartlets to the fridge and leave them there to set. Remove at least 30 minutes before serving.

makes 6

scant ⅓ cup / 40 g raspberries

6½ oz / 180 g white chocolate, chopped into tiny pieces

4 tsp / 20 g unsalted butter, cut into ¼-inch / 5-mm dice

6 tbsp / 90 ml heavy cream

6 tsp raspberry jam, store-bought or homemade ↗ page 276

6 prebaked tartlet shells
↗ page 255

Lemon meringue

makes 6

1 Preheat the oven to 400°F / 200°C. Spoon the cold lemon curd into the tart shells, filling them three-quarters full. Leave aside, preferably in the fridge.
2 To make the meringue, spread the sugar on a baking sheet lined with parchment paper. Place in the hot oven for 5 to 6 minutes. The sugar should become very hot but mustn't begin to dissolve. Remove from the oven and lower the temperature to 300°F / 150°C.
3 At the last minute of heating up the sugar, place the egg whites in the bowl of a stand mixer fitted with the whisk attachment. Whip on high speed for a few seconds, until they begin to froth up. Now carefully pour the hot sugar onto the whisking whites in a slow stream. Once finished, continue whisking for a good 15 minutes, until the meringue is firm, shiny, and cold.
4 Use 2 spoons or a piping bag to dispense the meringue on top of the curd and create a pattern. At this point, you can either leave the meringue totally white or you can place it in the oven for 1 to 3 minutes to brown the top very lightly. Serve at once or chill for up to 12 hours.

½ **recipe Lemon curd** ↗ page 277 **chilled for at least 6 hours**
6 **prebaked tartlet shells** ↗ page 255
½ **cup plus 1½ tbsp / 120 g superfine sugar**
2 **free-range egg whites**

Banana and hazelnut

makes 6

1 Preheat the oven to 300°F / 150°C. Scatter the hazelnuts on a baking sheet and toast for 12 minutes. Remove and allow to cool.
2 Put the butter in a medium pan and cook over medium heat. After a few minutes, it should start to darken and smell nutty. Take off the heat and leave to cool slightly.
3 Set aside about 1 tablespoon / 10 g of the nuts. The rest (plus their skins) put in a food processor, together with ½ cup plus 1 tablespoon / 70 g of the confectioners' sugar. Work to a fine powder and then add the flour. Pulse together to mix. Add the egg whites and work the machine very briefly, just to mix them in. Repeat with the vanilla and the butter. It is important to stop the machine as soon as the ingredients are incorporated.
4 Mix the mashed banana with the lemon juice and the remaining ¼ cup / 30 g confectioners' sugar. Spoon about 2 teaspoons of this mixture into each prebaked tart shell (still in its pan). Top with the hazelnut batter. It should come to within 1/16 to 1/8 inch / 2 to 3 mm of the top. Place in the oven and bake for 20 to 22 minutes, until the hazelnut filling is completely set. You can check this with a skewer. Remove the tartlets from the oven and cool slightly, then carefully remove them from their pans.
5 Put the apricot jam in a small saucepan, stir in the water, and bring to a boil. Remove from the heat and brush lightly over the tartlet tops. Coarsely chop the reserved nuts and scatter them on the jam.
6 If using the chocolate, put it in a heatproof bowl and place over a pan of simmering water. Stir gently just until the chocolate melts. Use a spoon to drizzle the tartlets gently with the chocolate, trying to create thin, delicate lines.

⅓ **cup / 45 g unskinned hazelnuts**
6 **tbsp / 90 g unsalted butter**
¾ **cup plus 1 tbsp / 100 g confectioners' sugar**
5 **tbsp / 40 g all-purpose flour**
2 **free-range egg whites**
½ **tsp vanilla extract**
3½ **tbsp / 50 g mashed banana**
2 **tsp lemon juice**
6 **prebaked tartlet shells** ↗ page 255 **baked 5 minutes less than suggested and left in their pans**
2½ **tbsp / 50 g smooth apricot jam**
1 **tbsp water**
1¾ **oz / 50 g dark chocolate, broken into pieces (optional)**

This tart is the pinnacle of comfort. The porridgelike vanilla and semolina filling makes the creamiest, most soothing base, on which the raspberry flavor shines.

Khalid Assyb, who was with us for many years and made a big contribution to our pastry repertoire, came up with the idea. He used to ascribe it, along with many other recipes, to a made-up grandmother. We were all fully aware that this particular grandma had never existed. We loved her anyhow.

Semolina and raspberry tart

serves 4 to 6

1 Lightly brush a 7-inch / 18-cm springform pan with a tiny amount of oil, then set aside.

2 Make sure you have a clean work surface and a bit of flour to dust it with. Using a rolling pin, roll out the pastry into a rough disk, 1/16 to 1/8 inch / 2 to 3 mm thick. Work quickly, turning the pastry around as you go. Once you have reached the right thickness, cut the pastry into a circle large enough to cover the pan and most of the sides comfortably. Carefully line the pan, patching up any holes with excess pastry if necessary. When the pastry is in place, use a sharp little knife to trim it so you have a neat edge, about 1¼ inches / 3 cm high. Place in the fridge to rest for 30 minutes.

3 Preheat the oven to 325°F / 170°C. Cut out a circle of parchment paper large enough to cover the base and sides of the cake pan. Place it inside the pastry shell and fill with dried beans or rice so the sides of the pastry are totally supported by the beans and won't collapse during baking. Blind bake the shell for 25 to 35 minutes, until it is very light brown. Remove from the oven and take out the beans or rice (you can keep them for future tarts).

4 To make the filling, put the butter, cream, milk, and sugar in a saucepan. Slit the vanilla bean open lengthwise with a sharp knife and scrape out all the flavorful seeds. Drop the seeds and the scraped pod into the pan. Place the pan on the stove and bring to a boil. Let it simmer while you whisk in the semolina in a slow stream. Continue whisking until the mix comes back to a boil and thickens up like porridge. Remove from the heat and whisk in the egg. Remove the vanilla pod.

5 Pour the semolina mixture into the pastry shell and level it with a wet icing spatula. Push half the raspberries inside, allowing them to show on the surface. Bake for 20 to 25 minutes, until the filling is slightly golden. Remove from the oven and let cool slightly before removing the tart from the pan.

6 Put the apricot jam in a small pan with the water and bring to a boil. Strain it through a sieve and brush it over the tart. Finish with the remaining raspberries piled over and a dusting of confectioners' sugar.

vegetable oil for brushing the pan
all-purpose flour for dusting
9 oz / 250 g Sweet pastry
   ↗ page 281 **or store-bought pastry**
⅓ cup / 80 g unsalted butter
¾ cup / 180 ml heavy cream
1½ cups / 345 ml milk
5 tbsp / 60 g superfine sugar
½ vanilla bean
⅓ cup / 60 g semolina
1 free-range egg
1⅔ cups / 200 g raspberries
2½ tbsp / 50 g apricot jam
   (optional)
1 tbsp water
confectioners' sugar, for dusting

We break away from tradition here. The French clafoutis batter is normally poured over unpitted fresh cherries in a large ovenproof dish, then baked to make a rustic, soufflélike dessert. Instead, we make stand-alone individual cakes.

You can easily revert back to tradition and use an 8-inch / 20-cm round or oval baking dish to create a communal plate from which everybody helps themselves to the warm pudding.

Our individual clafoutis can be served warm with ice cream or at room temperature with coffee.

Individual plum clafoutis

makes 6

1 Preheat the oven to 325°F / 170°C. Take 6 small baking dishes or pans, roughly 4 inches / 10 cm in diameter and ¾ inch / 2 cm deep (ceramic ramekins are a good solution here), and brush them lightly with vegetable oil. Line with parchment paper disks that come ⅔ inch / 1.5 cm above the rim of each dish.
2 Halve the plums, remove the pits, and cut each half into 3 or 4 wedges. Arrange half the fruit over the bottom of the lined dishes and set the rest aside.
3 To make the batter, whisk the egg yolks with half the sugar until thick and pale. You can do this by hand or with an electric mixer. Use a rubber spatula to fold in first the flour and then the vanilla extract, cream, and salt. Slit the vanilla bean open along its length with a sharp knife and scrape out all the seeds, then add them to the batter.
4 Whisk the egg whites with the remaining sugar until they form stiff, but not dry, peaks. Fold them gently into the batter. Pour the batter over the plums to reach about three-quarters of the way up the paper liners. Place in the oven for 15 to 20 minutes. Take out and quickly arrange the remaining plums on top, slightly overlapping. Continue to bake for about 5 minutes, until a skewer inserted into the center comes out dry. Allow to cool slightly before removing from the pans. Dust with a little confectioners' sugar, if you like, and serve.

vegetable oil for brushing the
  pans
4 ripe red plums
3 free-range eggs, separated
5½ tbsp / 70 g superfine sugar
½ cup plus 1 tbsp / 70 g
  all-purpose flour
1 tsp vanilla extract
⅔ cup / 150 ml heavy cream
pinch of salt
½ vanilla bean
confectioners' sugar, for dusting
  (optional)

This makes a substantial treat for an afternoon tea or, served with lightly sweetened crème fraîche, a show-offy dessert after a light meal.

You need to make the dough a day in advance (to make your life easier, prepare the mascarpone cream and crumble then, too), then roll it and leave to proof. Assemble and bake close to when you want to serve it. It is best warm.

Brioche galette

serves 4 to 6

1 After the brioche dough has been in the fridge for 14 to 24 hours, transfer it to a lightly floured work surface and use a rolling pin to roll it into an oval about ¾ inch / 2 cm thick (it doesn't need to be perfect). Transfer to a heavy-duty baking sheet lightly dusted with flour. Using a pastry brush, lightly brush the rim of the brioche with a small amount of water. Fold in the edge to form a border ⅜ inch / 1 cm thick. Prick the center of the dough all over with a fork. Cover loosely with plastic wrap and leave somewhere warm until it has risen by about half its volume.

2 Preheat the oven to 325°F / 170°C. When the brioche has risen sufficiently, brush the edges with a little milk. Spread the center with the mascarpone cream, being careful not to press down too hard. Scatter the plum slices over the cream and then arrange the berries on top. Brush the berries with the melted butter. Mix the crumble with the almonds and cinnamon and sprinkle on top.

3 Bake for 25 to 30 minutes. Check the bottom by lifting with an icing spatula to make sure it is evenly colored. Transfer to a wire rack and leave to cool slightly.

4 Just before serving, scoop out the inside of the passion fruit and drizzle it over the fruits.

1 recipe Brioche dough
↗ page 177
all-purpose flour for dusting
milk for brushing
⅓ recipe Mascarpone cream
↗ page 278
1 red plum, halved, pitted, and cut into slices about ¹⁄₁₆ inch / 2 mm thick
1¼ cups / 150 g mixed berries (such as raspberries, black currants, blueberries)
2 tbsp / 30 g lightly salted butter, melted
¼ recipe Crumble ↗ page 279
2½ tbsp / 15 g sliced almonds
1 tsp ground cinnamon
1 ripe passion fruit

Larder

Tahini works in total harmony with roasted or fresh vegetables, with grilled fish or with grilled meat. When making it into a sauce, be sure to adjust the amount of liquid according to the brand you use. The sauce should be thick but runny, almost like honey. Once chilled it will thicken, so you will need to whisk it again and possibly add more water.

Green tahini sauce

1 In a bowl, thoroughly whisk together the tahini, water, lemon juice, garlic, and salt. The mixture should be creamy and smooth. If it is too thick, add more water. Stir in the chopped parsley, then taste and add more salt if needed.
2 If using a food processor or a blender, process together all the ingredients except the parsley until smooth. Add more water if needed. Add the parsley and turn the machine on again for a second or two. Taste for seasoning.

makes about 1½ cups / 400 g

⅔ cup / 150 ml tahini paste
↗ page xii
⅔ cup / 150 ml water
5 tbsp / 80 ml lemon juice
2 cloves garlic, crushed
½ tsp salt
½ cup / 30 g flat-leaf parsley leaves, finely chopped if making by hand

Labneh is an Arab cheese made by draining yogurt so it loses most of its liquid. Use natural goat's milk yogurt or, if unavailable, natural full-fat cow's milk yogurt, but not the Greek varieties.

This recipe takes at least 48 hours to make. If this is all too much, you can buy *labneh* from Middle Eastern grocery stores. Store the *labneh* in the fridge to use as a spread, like any cream cheese. A more labor-intensive option is to roll it into balls and then preserve them in a jar of oil. The jar will look beautiful, the cheese keeps for weeks at room temperature, and the balls will create a special visual effect when used, as they are, in salads and legume dishes (↗ Couscous and mograbiah with oven-dried tomatoes on page 77).

Labneh

1 Line a large bowl with a piece of cheesecloth or other fine cloth. In another bowl, mix the yogurt and salt well. Transfer the yogurt to the cheesecloth, pick up the edges of the cloth, and tie them together well to form a bundle. Hang this over your sink or over a large bowl and leave for 48 hours. By this time the yogurt will have lost most of its liquid and be ready to use as a spread.
2 To go the whole hog, leave it hanging for a day longer. Remove the cheese from the cloth and place in a sealed container in the fridge. Once it is thoroughly chilled, preferably after 24 hours, roll the cheese into balls, somewhere between the size of an olive and a walnut.
3 Take a sterilized jar about 2½ cups / 600 ml in capacity (see Preserved lemons, opposite, for how to sterilize jars). Pour some of the oil inside and gently lay the balls in the oil. Add some more oil and continue with the balls until all the cheese is in the jar and immersed in oil. Seal the jar and keep until needed.
4 Before serving, scatter the mint and pepper on a flat plate and roll the balls in it.

makes 1 pint / 600 ml

4½ cups / 1 liter natural goat's milk yogurt (or full-fat cow's milk yogurt)
¾ tsp salt
1 to 1¼ cups / 200 to 300 ml olive oil
⅓ to ½ cup / 10 to 15 g dried mint
good grind of black pepper

The preserving process will take a few weeks, starting with just the lemon and salt and later adding the rest. The same method can be used with limes.

Preserved lemons

makes 6

1 Before starting, get a jar just large enough to accommodate all the lemons tightly. To sterilize it, fill it with boiling water, leave for a minute, and then empty it. Allow it to dry out naturally without wiping it so it remains sterilized.
2 Wash the lemons and cut a deep cross all the way from the top to within ¾ inch / 2 cm from the base, so you are left with 4 quarters attached. Stuff each lemon with a spoonful of salt and place in the jar. Push the lemons in tightly so they are all squeezed together well. Seal the jar and leave for at least a week.
3 After this initial period, remove the lid and press the lemons as hard as you can to squeeze as much of the juice out of them as possible. Add the rosemary, chile, and lemon juice and cover with a thin layer of olive oil. Seal the jar and leave in a cool place for at least 4 weeks. The longer you leave them, the better the flavor.

6 unwaxed lemons
6 tbsp coarse sea salt
2 sprigs rosemary
1 large red chile
juice of 6 lemons
olive oil

This recipe has almost reached the sphere of mythology, due to the anticipation involved every time Yotam goes to Israel, before he comes back with a bag full of jars containing his mother's famous mayonnaise. Well here it is, the legendary recipe, and it makes the best addition to a grilled chicken and tomato sandwich.

Ruth's mayonnaise

makes about 3 cups / 650 g

1 The best way to make this mayonnaise is by using an immersion blender. You could also use a food processor or stand blender, or make it by hand, using a whisk. If doing it by hand, you need to crush the garlic and chop the cilantro finely before you start.
2 If using an immersion blender, put the egg, mustard, sugar, salt, garlic, and vinegar in a large mixing bowl. Process a little and then start adding the oil in a slow trickle. Keep the machine working as you pour in the oil in a very light stream. Once the mayonnaise starts to thicken, you can increase the stream until all the oil is fully incorporated. Now add the cilantro and continue processing until all of it is chopped and properly mixed in. Transfer to a clean jar and chill. The mayonnaise will keep in the fridge for up to 2 weeks.

1 free-range egg
2½ tsp Dijon mustard
2 tsp superfine sugar
½ tsp salt
3 cloves garlic, peeled
2 tbsp cider vinegar
2 cups / 500 ml sunflower oil
½ oz / 15 g fresh cilantro,
   leaves and stems

This is extremely useful for pouring over cakes, fruit salads, Pavlovas—anything sweet, really. Only use passion fruits that are nice and ripe—that is, when their skin turns dark brown and starts to shrivel.

Passion fruit jam

makes about 1½ cups / 400 g

10½ oz / 300 g passion fruit pulp (roughly 10 passion fruit)
¾ cup / 150 g superfine sugar

1 Halve the passion fruit and use a spoon to scoop out the pulp straight into a small saucepan. Add the sugar, stir well with a wooden spoon, and put over low heat. Bring to a slow simmer and cook for about 5 minutes, stirring frequently and taking great care that it doesn't stick to the bottom of the pan. When ready, it should be as thick as honey. To make sure, chill a little bit of the jam in a bowl in the fridge and check its consistency.

2 Once ready, pour into a clean jar, leave to cool completely, then seal and store in the fridge. The jam will keep for at least 2 weeks.

Not quite a jam but somewhere in between a jam and a coulis, this is extremely handy in many cakes and sweets. The tartness of the raspberry cuts the sweetness and balances it. The raspberry seeds add fruitiness and freshness.

You can flavor the jam with vanilla or star anise. Just add ½ vanilla bean or 2 star anise while cooking, then strain out.

Raspberry jam

makes about 1⅓ cups / 350 g

2½ cups / 300 g raspberries
½ cup / 100 g superfine sugar

Put the raspberries and sugar in a small, heavy-bottomed saucepan and stir them together. Put over low heat, bring to a light simmer, and cook for 7 to 8 minutes. Remove from the heat, transfer to a bowl, cover the surface with plastic wrap, leave to cool, and then refrigerate.

Lemon curd

1 Put all the ingredients in a large, heavy-bottomed saucepan, leaving out about half the butter. Place over medium heat and, using a hand whisk, whisk constantly while you cook the curd. Lower the heat if it starts sticking to the bottom of the pan. Once the curd reaches the boiling point, you will notice large bubbles coming to the surface. Continue whisking vigorously for another minute and then remove from the heat.
2 Off the heat, add the remaining butter and whisk until it has melted. Pass the curd through a sieve and into a plastic container. Cover the surface with plastic wrap, allow it to come to room temperature, and then chill for at least 6 hours, preferably overnight, for it to firm up well. It will keep in the fridge for up to 4 days.

½ cup plus 1 tbsp / 200 ml lemon juice (4 to 6 lemons)
grated zest of 4 lemons
1 cup / 200 g superfine sugar
4 free-range eggs
4 free-range egg yolks
¾ cup / 180 g unsalted butter, cut into cubes

Vanilla extract

Use a small, sharp knife to slit the vanilla beans open along their length, then scrape the seeds out with the tip of the knife. Place the seeds and pods in a medium saucepan, cover with the water and sugar, and bring to a boil. Boil rapidly for about 15 minutes, until the mixture has reduced to one-third of its original volume. Pour into a jar and leave to cool, then seal with a tight-fitting lid. Keep refrigerated for up to 1 month.

4 vanilla beans
2 cups / 500 ml water
½ cup plus 1½ tbsp / 120 g superfine sugar

This cream makes a very versatile condiment. It is heavenly with fresh berries or roasted fruits and goes incredibly well with a cake just out of the oven (try it with Peach and raspberry teacakes, ↗ page 206). If you have a spice grinder, consider substituting ¼ teaspoon ground star anise for the vanilla.

Mascarpone cream

makes 1⅓ cups / 250 g

Put the mascarpone in a mixing bowl and loosen it up with a whisk. Add the rest of the ingredients and continue whisking until the cream thickens up again. It should hold its shape when lifted with a spoon. Chill until ready to use.

4 oz / 110 g mascarpone cheese
scant ½ cup / 110 ml crème fraîche
¼ tsp vanilla extract ↗ page 277
2 tbsp / 25 g confectioners' sugar

Crumble

makes about 1 pound 5 ounces / 600 g

1 Put the flour, sugar, and butter in a bowl and mix with your hands or an electric mixer fitted with the paddle attachment to work it to a uniform bread crumb consistency. Make sure there are no lumps of butter left. If using a mixer, watch it carefully. Within a few seconds, a crumble can turn into a cookie dough. (If this unpleasant scenario happens, roll it out thinly, cut out cookies, bake them, and dip half of each cookie in melted chocolate.)
2 Transfer the crumble to a plastic container. It will keep in the fridge for up to 5 days or for ages in the freezer.

2⅓ cups / 300 g all-purpose flour
½ cup / 100 g superfine sugar
¾ cup plus 1 tbsp / 200 g cold unsalted butter, cut into small cubes

There is nothing more satisfying than making your own granola. We give you poetic license to add any of your favorite nuts, fruits, or seeds.

Granola

makes about 7 cups / 750 g

1 Preheat the oven to 275°F / 140°C. Coarsely chop all the nuts and put them in a large mixing bowl. Add the oats and seeds and set aside.
2 To make the syrup, mix together all the syrup ingredients in a small saucepan. Place over low heat and stir while you warm the syrup gently. Once it is warm, pour it over the seeds, nuts, and oats and stir well with a wooden spoon.
3 Line a large baking sheet with parchment paper and spread the granola over it evenly. It should form a layer no more than ⅜ inch / 1 cm thick. If it is too thick, consider using 2 pans. Bake for 40 minutes, turning and mixing the granola 2 or 3 times. When ready, it will have taken on a dark, honeylike color. Don't worry if it is soft; once it is cool it will turn crunchy. Remove from the oven. While the granola is still warm, but not hot, stir in the fruit. Leave to cool in the pan and then transfer to a sealed container. It will keep for up to 2 weeks.

6½ tbsp / 60 g whole unskinned almonds
5 tbsp / 40 g Brazil nuts
5 tbsp / 40 g cashew nuts
3 cups / 300 g rolled oats
scant ½ cup / 60 g pumpkin seeds
scant ½ cup / 60 g sunflower seeds
scant 1 cup / 100 g dried apricots, coarsely chopped
½ cup / 60 g dried cranberries
½ cup / 60 g dried blueberries

Syrup
¼ tsp salt
3 tbsp water
2 tbsp canola oil
2 tbsp sunflower oil
½ cup / 120 ml maple syrup
½ cup / 120 ml honey

Making your own puff pastry is definitely a challenge. This recipe isn't so difficult, but we won't hold it against you if you choose to buy your puff. To upgrade a commercial variety, brush it with plenty of melted butter before baking.

Rough puff pastry

makes about 1 pound 6 ounces / 620 g

2⅓ cups / 300 g all-purpose flour
1 tsp salt
¾ cup / 180 g unsalted butter, frozen
½ cup plus 1 tbsp / 140 ml ice-cold water

1 Sift the flour and salt into a large mixing bowl. Use a coarse cheese grater to grate 6 tablespoons / 80 g of the frozen butter into the flour. Lightly mix together. Add the cold water and, using a knife, stir the flour and water together until a dough starts to form. Now use your hands to bring it together into a ball. You may need to add a little more water if some dry bits remain in the bowl. Press the dough into a neat square, wrap it in plastic wrap, and chill for 30 minutes.

2 Using a rolling pin, roll out the pastry on a lightly floured work surface into a rectangle with a long edge that is 3 times its width. Grate the remaining 12 tablespoons / 100 g butter and spread it evenly over two-thirds of the rectangle. Take the third that is not scattered with butter and fold it over onto the middle of the buttered part. Then fold the 2 layers over the remaining single layer. You will be left with 3 layers of pastry and 2 layers of butter separating them.

3 Turn the pastry by 90 degrees. Dust your work surface lightly with flour and roll out the pastry again into a long rectangle with the same proportions as before. The 2 short edges will reveal the 3 layers of pastry and 2 layers of butter.

4 Take one of the short sides and fold it over to reach the middle of the remaining part of the pastry. Fold the remaining third on top of the first one to get 3 layers on top of one another. Wrap the pastry in plastic wrap and let rest in the fridge for 30 minutes.

5 Roll the pastry again into a rectangle with the short edges displaying the seams. Fold into 3 layers as before. Let rest in the fridge again for 30 minutes.

6 Repeat the process one last time and then wrap and chill for at least an hour.

7 The pastry will keep in the fridge for up to 4 days and in the freezer for 1 month. Thaw in the fridge overnight.

Short-crust pastry

makes about 1 pound 3 ounces / 530 g

1 Put the flour and salt into a bowl and add the butter. Rub it in by hand, or using a mixer fitted with the paddle attachment, until you reach a fine bread crumb texture. A third easy option is to use a food processor.
2 Add the water and continue working just until the dough comes together. Stop at once. Shape the pastry into a disk roughly 1½ inches / 4 cm thick, wrap it in plastic wrap, and chill for at least 2 hours.
3 The pastry will keep in the fridge for 5 days and for at least a month in the freezer. Thaw in the fridge overnight.

2⅓ cups / 300 g all-purpose flour
½ tsp salt
⅔ cup / 160 g cold unsalted butter, cut into ⅜-inch / 1-cm dice
4½ tbsp / 70 ml ice-cold water

Sweet pastry

makes 1 pound 8 ounces / 680 g

1 Put the flour, confectioners' sugar, lemon zest, and salt in a bowl and add the butter. Rub it in with your hands or, more easily, using a mixer fitted with the paddle attachment. Or, you can do the job in a food processor. In all cases, you need to mix the ingredients until you get a coarse bread crumb consistency, making sure there aren't any large lumps of butter left.
2 Add the egg yolk and water and mix just until the dough comes together, being careful not to mix any longer than necessary. You might need to add a tiny amount of additional water.
3 Remove the dough from the mixing bowl and knead very lightly for a few seconds only, just to shape it into a smooth disk, 2 to 2½ inches / 5 to 6 cm thick. Wrap in plastic wrap and chill until ready to use. The pastry will keep in the fridge for a week and for at least a month in the freezer. Thaw in the fridge overnight.

2⅔ cups / 330 g all-purpose flour
scant ½ cup / 100 g confectioners' sugar
grated zest of ½ lemon
¼ teaspoon salt
¾ cup / 80 g cold unsalted butter, cut into small cubes
1 free-range egg yolk
2 tbsp cold water

Index

The Ottolenghi people

Trying to tell the Ottolenghi story always ends up being the story of the individuals who have participated in forming it. We can only mention here a few of the many who contributed over the years. We are deeply thankful to all the others.

First, Noam Bar, who is a senior partner in the company and has the exceptional combination of an acute business understanding and the ability to grasp the vision and drive us all forward with it.

Second, Cornelia Staeubli, a partner and general manager, the people's person, and the one who, incredibly, holds it all together, physically and spiritually.

Then (in rough order of appearance at Ottolenghi): Jim Webb—creative force, manager of all projects, a man of infinite talents; Khalid Assyb—chef de patisserie; Lingchee Ang—master of the pastries and the pastry counter; Mariusz Uszakiewicz—head baker, ex-footballer, and original thinker; Tamar Shany—gifted chef and star of all musicals; Nicole Steel—service provider of the year and the one with the most leaving dos; Francis Pereira—the real manager of Notting Hill; Daniela Geatti—manager, and mother of the first Ottolenghi baby; Alejandra Chavero—the one who brought Ottolenghi standards to Mexico with a big smile; Diana Daniel-Thomas—the one who miraculously manages to put our accounts in order; Reka Fabian—person of details and great devotion; Dan Lepard—the magician who always sorts out our bread; Etti Mordo—passionately original chef with rare execution; Colleen Murphy—head pastry chef, head chef, and our token East Ender; Tricia Jadoonanan—gifted, good humored, and a commander of many manly chefs; Marketa Kratochvilova—the brilliantly artistic arranger of the display; Emma Christian—efficient catering princess; Danielle Postma—creative culinary star with many admirers; Ramael Scully—the calmest and one of the most consistently inspired chefs; Jason Chuck—a sportsman and a chef who never gets dirty; Erica Rossi—Italian energy bomb and Camden town beloved; Maria Oskarsson—the only person in the world who managed to get into Cornelia's shoes; Helene Sauvage—assistant manager and a Notting Hill star with French elegance; Nguyo Milcinovic—our evening star and Scully's right-hand man; Tal Kimchi—great kitchen organizer and a multitalent; Karl Allen—the customers' favorite manager; Carol Brough—patient cake maker and inventor; Helen Goh—creator, perfectionist, and analyst of a rare kind; Nir Feller—fiery foodie and bohemian; Marina Dos Santos—the one who brought us Continental chic and restaurant zeal; Gerard Viccars—meticulous and conscientious chef, plus a few tattoos; Sara Lee—the quality guard and promoter of wonderful packed products; Arek Karas—ultimate problem solver and computer wiz; Sara Fereidooni—a serious manager with an infectious charm; Basia Murphy—living proof that you can be an effective manager and smile; Itamar Strulovich—a rising talent of food and wit; and Sarit Packer—merry mistress of the pastry department.

Thank-yous

Big thanks to Alex Meitlis and Tirza Florentin, not-so-silent partners, whom, in two opposite departments, had a huge part in molding Ottolenghi.

We would like to thank Amos Oppenheim for his limitless trust and generosity. His constant smile is deeply missed. And thank you to the others who had early faith: Tamara Meitlis, Ariela Oppenheim, David Oppenheim, Itzik and Ilana Lederfeind, Danny Florentin, Keren Margalit, and Yoram Ever-Hadani.

For making this book happen, infinite thanks to Felicity Rubinstein and Sarah Lavelle; for making it so breathtakingly beautiful, thanks to Axel Feldmann, Sam Wolfson, Richard Learoyd, and Adam Laycock; and for taking care of the details, thanks to Jane Middleton.

For the spectacular dishes and plates used in the photography, we are indebted to Lindy Wiffen from Ceramica Blue. And thanks to Gerry Ure for smiling through the hassle.

For precious assistance in making the recipes work: Jim Webb, Alison Quinn, Claudine Boulstridge, Marianne Lumb, and Philippa Shepherd.

And more warm thanks, for many different reasons, to Charley Bradley, Leigh Genis, Dino Cura, Paul and Ossi Burger, Adrien von Ferscht, Tamasin Day-Lewis, Patricia Michelson, Sarah Bilney, Binnie Dansby, Patrick Houser, Caroline Waldegrave, Jenny Stringer, Viv Pidgeon, Max Clark, Sue Spaull, Gail Mejia, Dariusz Przystasz, Przemek Suszek, Karen Handler-Kremmerman, Dorit Mintzer, Sigal Baranowitz, Pete and Greta Allen, and Jenny and Tony Taylor.

Thank you to all our devoted suppliers, without whom the wheels of the machine would not be turning.

And most humble thanks to all the Ottolenghi customers, the ultimate source of our pleasure and livelihood.